FARM POLICY: NEW DIRECTIONS

FARM POLICY: NEW DIRECTIONS

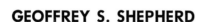

GEOFFREY S. SHEPHERD

Professor of Economics, Iowa State University

Iowa State University Press, *Ames,* **Iowa, U.S.A.**

About the Author

GEOFFREY S. SHEPHERD is professor of economics in agricultural marketing and price policy in the Department of Economics and Sociology at Iowa State University.

His deep-seated interest in solving problems has influenced his progress through a broad range of research. Not content to stop with analyzing data and appraising existing theories, he forges ahead with practical recommendations designed to lead to the solution of major farm problems.

Geoff Shepherd is no "book theorist"—his early years were spent on a ranch in western Canada, so he knows and understands farmers as well as farm problems.

In addition to his undergraduate work at the University of Saskatchewan he holds the master's degree from Iowa State University and a doctorate from Harvard University. He has been a vice president of the Farm Economics Association and has served in a number of advisory positions in Washington, D.C., West Germany, Japan, Burma, and Venezuela.

Dr. Shepherd is author of three other books, *Marketing Farm Products, Agricultural Price Analysis,* and *Agricultural Price and Income Policy,* numerous bulletins and technical papers, and articles in professional journals and in the *Encyclopedia Britannica.* A specialized periodical, *Farm Policy Forum,* was developed under his chairmanship.

© 1964 The Iowa State University Press

First edition, 1964
Second printing, 1965

Library of Congress Catalog Card Number: 64–13367

PREFACE

The farm problem in the United States apparently is a hardy perennial. Partly because the problem has been inaccurately defined, and partly because some of the programs to deal with the problem have been inappropriate for the job, the farm problem remains unsolved after more than 30 years of programs that now cost several billions of dollars a year.

It is not so much the magnitude of these expenditures that calls for a reconstruction of agricultural policy, as the fact that the expenditures have not solved the problem. The chief purpose and effect of the programs in recent years, indeed, has been merely to undo some of the harm (reduce the storage stocks) created by the earlier price-support programs. Other harmful effects will be still more difficult to undo. Meanwhile, the basic problem remains about as it was before any programs were undertaken, and farm incomes remain low.

This 30-year laboratory experiment in mass education has been expensive, but the United States can learn highly valuable economic lessons from it. Given the state of the art, perhaps the lesson could be learned in no other way, at least not in so short a time. We need to study the lesson so that we get value received for the tuition fee, and get enough grasp of the subject matter so that we will not flunk the course again.

For that purpose, we need analysis and appraisal of the agricultural policies and programs that have been tried in the past, and of others that might work better in the future. Research of this kind has been scarce. George Brandow, in the December, 1959, issue of *Journal of Farm Economics*, expresses it: ". . . agricultural economists have not done enough research on the means of carrying out alternative approaches to farm policy or on probable results of particular programs. Much research in such areas as price analysis, farm management, and marketing has important application to policy, and this is one justification for doing the work. But policy research itself deals principally with applying knowledge of facts and relationships, drawn from all of economics, to the study of ways of dealing with problems involving group decisions and interests. Policy research as thus defined currently accounts for only a very small part of agricultural economists' research efforts."

This point was well illustrated a few years ago. The Interregional Committee on Agricultural Policy Research (IRM-1) which was set up to help fill this research gap, had enough funds to establish a specific research project in agricultural policy. This offer went to nearly a dozen of the most likely land-grant colleges in the United States; all but two turned it down, either because they considered the subject too hot to handle, or not important, or did not have adequate staff.

A good deal has been written—good stuff, too—on the specialized aspects and bits and pieces of the farm policy problem. But what is most urgently needed now is an over-all analysis and appraisal by someone who will try to see the problem steadily and see it whole. This book is an attempt to meet this need.

The book first reviews the early concepts of the farm problem in the United States, and traces briefly the development of the farm programs over the past three decades. It then appraises the programs, and in the light of their revealed inadequacy to deal with the problem, outlines programs of a different kind to take their place.

The book does not just talk about farm programs, nor conclude that the farm problem is insoluble; it develops specific recommendations for programs required to implement the "new directions" that farm policy needs to take if it is to be effective. It outlines programs that would solve the farm problem and keep it solved in the years ahead.

This is a big undertaking. The author has the temerity, if not the competence, to undertake it, chiefly because he has spent most of his professional life teaching graduate students and doing research at Iowa State University in this field, and has served on the staffs of the CCC, USDA, OPA, and OPS in this country, and as advisor to similar agencies in West Germany, Japan, Burma, and Venezuela. He has tackled the job, however, more because he believes that the job needs to be done than because he feels competent to do it.

I should like to express my feeling of indebtedness to a number of colleagues for the quotations from their work which appear in this book. No one can be top man in all parts of the field of farm policy, and whenever I can buttress one of my conclusions by a quotation from a specialist who is more competent than I am in that part of the field, I have done so.

This may also help to reassure the general reader that I am not off on some tangent here and there all by myself. I must admit that if I were, so far as I am concerned I would be prepared to defend my position among my colleagues; but in this case I would quote from an opposing view, thus giving the reader the benefit of both views as well as the defense of my own.

GEOFFREY S. SHEPHERD

■
CONTENTS

The Farm Problem
in the United States

Part ■ *1*

The setting of the agricultural problem in the United States has been well summarized in a few whimsical but pertinent paragraphs.

"Washington Crossing the Delaware is a striking painting for two reasons. It concerns the struggle in which our Nation was born; the floating ice and the raggedness of the soldiers vividly portray the hardships of the war and the patriots' endurance of them; the magnificence of Washington towering in the prow of the tiny boat elevates him above mortal men; and, as every school boy knows, and some adults, the venture was capped by victory over the Hessians at Trenton.

"On a more prosaic and literal plane, the picture is also arresting. Was Washington so supernatural that he could defy the law of gravity? Was he so inexperienced that he had no idea of what happens to a man standing up in a boat when it strikes an ice floe? Does the Delaware River drain Greenland's glaciers as the size of the floes suggests? One wonders what the crossing actually was like.

"The painting of Washington's crossing is pertinent to the contrast between an idealistic description of how farm economic policy should be made and how it actually develops. In the idealistic view, the group fixes upon a distant objective and steadfastly and with common purpose works toward it, undeterred by perils that often threaten but never strike. In actual practice, the boatmen often have only the vaguest notion of where they wish to go and disagree on that; ultimate destinations are superseded by the pressing necessity of avoiding dangers immediately at hand; some men may be backing upon their oars while others are pulling ahead; and even the top brass can fall over the side. Very important, also, are the currents of the stream and the force of prevailing winds. Despite tremendous shouting and splashing of oars, a disorganized crew can end up just about where the wind and current would naturally deposit them, and even the best crew will need to take the wind and current into account in deciding what they will try to do and how to do it.

"The analogy to a river is also useful for emphasizing the dynamic nature of farm policy. The setting in which policy is made is not a pond with a fixed, familiar shoreline along which one can anchor in a chosen position as long as he likes. It is a flowing stream in which technological and social change constitute the current. At times the river rushes along so powerfully that even the most skillful crew must adapt itself to its force. Occasionally, the waters widen and flow quietly; here there is opportunity for maneuver." (George Brandow, "Recent Developments in Agricultural Policy," Proceedings of the Western Farm Economics Association, Aug. 1958, pp. 13–15.)

1

Is the Farm Problem a Price Problem?

Opinion is divided concerning what to do about the farm problem. This is confusing enough; but the situation is doubly confusing—opinion is even divided about what the farm problem is in the first place.

Furthermore, the farm programs designed to solve the farm problem have been expensive. The "realized cost" of "programs primarily for stabilization of farm prices and income" in fiscal 1962 was $3 billion. Other agricultural programs brought the total appropriation for agriculture in 1962 up to about $6 billion.[1] This is a lot of money. Chief objection to this expenditure, however, is not that it is large but that it has been ineffective. "The farm problem," judging by USDA statistics, reports in the newspapers and magazines, and actions of Congress, remains unsolved. Evidently, more basic programs are needed than those that have been in effect for the past 30 years.

WHAT IS THE FARM PROBLEM?

Just what is this farm problem that seems so insoluble?

"The farm problem" is really several farm problems. There is the instability of farm prices and incomes, which may put a farmer in the black one year and in the red the next. There is the problem of rural poverty; many farms are too small to provide a decent living. There are any number of special commodity problems: those of the wheat farmers, cotton farmers, dairy farmers, and so on—some related to others, and some unrelated.

---

[1] USDA, "Food and Agriculture, A Program for the 1960's." Bul., 1962, p. 52.

Each problem is different from the rest, yet each one is related to the others, and the solution for each one is likely to affect the others. One of the problems of wheat farmers, for example, has been over-production in relation to the demand at supported prices. A solution for this problem—reduction in wheat acreage—was tried in 1954 and 1955. It was partially successful in reducing wheat production; but many of the acres taken out of wheat production were put into feed grains production, thus accentuating the problems of feed grains producers. And a solution of *their* problems by reducing the level of loan rates—which at first temporarily eased the problems of livestock producers by providing them with cheaper feed—soon led to an increase in livestock production, and this led to lower livestock prices and incomes, thus making livestock producers' problems worse.

Similarly, the 1961 feed grains program reduced feed grains acreage about 20 million acres, but the loan rate for soybeans was raised from $1.85 to $2.30 per bushel, and soybean acreage increased 3.5 million.

The different commodity problems, then, are interrelated. Some observers believe that they all arise from an over-all farm problem—a low level of agricultural prices and incomes relative to nonagricultural prices and incomes. They consider that the agricultural problem is a low-price problem, and that the remedy is simple: get the prices up. The fact that prices remain low, in the face of massive and expensive government programs designed to raise them, means to them that the efforts need to be further increased. Some advocate compulsory reduction controls to this end.[2]

Others believe that the farm problem is not one of prices but of incomes, and point to the low farm incomes in recent years. Among these observers, however, there is disagreement whether the problem is low United States average per capita farm income—the objective then being to raise all farm incomes; or whether the problem is only a low per capita income at the low end of the farm income scale—the objective then being only to raise those low incomes, leaving the incomes of the rest of the farmers unaffected. The decision between these two identifications of the problem is important; the two different problems require entirely different programs for their solution.

---

[2] Willard W. Cochrane, "Some Further Reflections on Supply Control." *Jour. Farm Econ.*, pp. 697–98, Nov. 1959.

Still other observers believe that the low levels of farm income are largely illusory, that the low levels are chiefly a statistical phenomenon arising from the way the average farm income is computed each year—by dividing total United States agricultural income by the total number of farmers in the United States. This denominator, based on the Census definition of a farm, includes more than a million part-time and residential "farmers" who are not really farmers at all. These "not really farmers" number about a third of the total number of "farmers," but they produce less than 4 per cent of total farm production. The use of this unduly large denominator reduces the apparent level of "farm" income below the actual level that exists when only the real farmers are included.

Still others believe that farm income levels, whatever they may be, are only symptoms of problems, not problems themselves. The real problem, they say, is maladjustment—overcapacity in agriculture resulting from rapid and widespread adoption of new technology in agricultural production—and that measures to support agricultural prices and incomes do not relieve this problem, but instead make it worse. The remedy they propose is not more price raising effort, but less, or none at all; some of them propose abolishing farm programs and returning agriculture to the open market.[3]

Which of these diagnoses are correct?

It is essential to answer this question clearly. It is necessary to distinguish just what the agricultural price and income problem is—whether there really is a problem, or only appears to be; whether it is a price problem, or an income problem, or an adjustment problem; whether it is a problem of income stability, or level, or production overcapacity; whether it affects all farmers, or only small farmers, or large commercial family farms, or livestock or crop farmers, or some other group—and then to determine the causes, so as to be in the best position to appraise remedial action.

IS THE AGRICULTURAL PROBLEM A PRICE PROBLEM?

Those who consider the agricultural problem to be a price problem use as evidence the record of prices received by farmers and the prices paid by farmers, and the ratios between these two series. These are shown in Table 1.1 and Figure 1.1.

---

[3] "An Adaptive Program for Agriculture." Committee for Economic Development, 711 Fifth Avenue, New York 22, July 1962.

TABLE 1.1

INDEXES OF PRICES RECEIVED BY FARMERS FOR COMMODITIES, AND PRICES PAID FOR
COMMODITIES, INTEREST, TAXES, AND WAGE RATES, AND PARITY RATIOS,
UNITED STATES, 1910–58*

(Index base, 1910–14 = 100)

Year	Index of Prices Received	Index of Prices Paid	Parity Ratio
1910	104	97	107
1920	211	214	99
1930	125	151	83
1940	100	124	81
1941	124	133	93
1942	159	152	105
1943	193	171	113
1944	197	182	108
1945	207	190	109
1946	236	208	113
1947	276	240	115
1948	287	260	110
1949	250	251	100
1950	258	256	101
1951	302	282	107
1952	288	287	100
1953	255	277	92
1954	246	277	89
1955	232	276	84
1956	230	278	83
1957	235	286	82
1958	250	293	85
1959	240	297	81
1960	238	299	80
1961	240	301	80
1962	243	306	80

* Source: Agricultural Statistics, USDA.

This table and figure show that in recent years the index of prices received by farmers has been running substantially lower than the index of prices paid by farmers. The "parity ratio"— the ratio between the two indexes—was only 80 in 1962. This situation is frequently referred to as "the cost-price squeeze."

These price relations in themselves, however, are not conclusive evidence of the existence of a farm problem, nor do they measure the severity of the problem accurately.

The term "price-cost squeeze" is itself erroneous. The situation that is referred to by that name is not a price-cost squeeze,

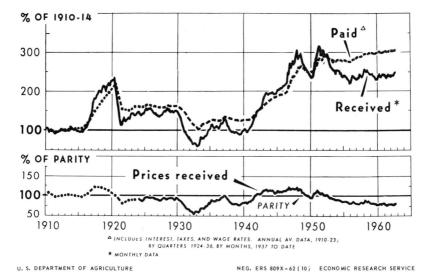

% OF 1910-14

300

200

100

Paid△

Received*

% OF PARITY
150
100
50

Prices received

PARITY

1910   1920   1930   1940   1950   1960

△ INCLUDES INTEREST, TAXES, AND WAGE RATES. ANNUAL AV. DATA, 1910-23;
BY QUARTERS 1924-36, BY MONTHS, 1937 TO DATE
* MONTHLY DATA

U. S. DEPARTMENT OF AGRICULTURE   NEG. ERS 809X-62(10)   ECONOMIC RESEARCH SERVICE

Fig. 1.1. Farmers' prices received and paid, and parity ratio, 1910–1963.

but only a "prices-received–prices-paid squeeze." Prices and costs are not comparable terms. Cost is computed by multiplying the prices of goods and services purchased by the quantities purchased. If the prices of goods and services per unit had risen 20 per cent, relative to the prices of farm products per unit sold, but the quantities purchased had declined 25 per cent, the farmer's position would have improved 5 per cent, not worsened 20 per cent. There would have been no "price-cost squeeze." Conversely, if the quantities purchased had increased 25 per cent, the farmer's position would have worsened more than 45 per cent—much worse than the price relations alone would have shown.

Price relations like these ignore the effects of the rapid changes in technology which have been proceeding at a spectacular rate in recent years. These changes affect the quantities sold and purchased; they therefore affect income—the thing that really counts—as much as prices do. The price relations shown in Figure 1.1 and Table 1.1, therefore, do not measure the farm problem at all accurately.

Suppose, for example, that the indexes of prices received and prices paid had remained unchanged over the past several years. Would that mean that there would have been no farm problem?

TABLE 1.2

INDEX NUMBERS OF FARM OUTPUT AND POPULATION,
UNITED STATES, 1950–60 AND PROJECTED 1965*

Year	Population 1950 = 100	Farm Output 1950 = 100
1950.......	100	100
1951.......	102	103
1952.......	103	107
1953.......	105	108
1954.......	107	108
1955.......	109	112
1956.......	111	113
1957.......	113	110
1958.......	115	119
1959.......	117	120
1960.......	119	123
1961[a].....	121	124
1962[b].....	123	123
1965.......	129[b]	133–138[c]

* Source: USDA, *Agricultural Outlook Chartbook*,
1963, ERS, FAS, ARS, SRS, Nov. 1962, p. 15.
[a] Preliminary
[b] Estimated
[c] Farm output based on data from USDA,
"Changes in Farm Production and Efficiency,"
Stat. Bul. 233, Sept. 1962.

It would not have meant this, because if fertility and production had been declining, and demand also had been declining, so that only 80 or 90 per cent as much had been produced and consumed as previously, there would have been a severe farm problem, because gross farm incomes and net farm incomes both would have declined substantially. Conversely, if fertility and production had been increasing greatly, and consumption had also been increasing similarly, there would have been no farm problem; farm incomes, in fact, would have been rising substantially, and farmers would have been prospering more and more. Yet in both cases, the price indexes would have shown no change.

The actual production situation since the late 1940's has been more like the second than the first situation outlined above; farm production has been increasing substantially, from an index of 100 in 1947–49, to an index of 129 in 1960. Thus production has risen 29 per cent since 1947–49, while the parity price ratio has fallen only 24 per cent. Price ratios tell only half of the story; their effect upon incomes can be more than offset by what happens to production.

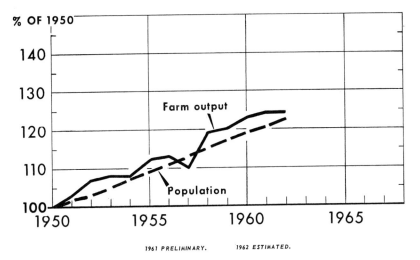

Fig. 1.2. Farm output in closer balance with population. (Source: USDA. 1961 preliminary, 1962 estimated.)

AGRICULTURAL PRODUCTION HAS BEEN INCREASING RAPIDLY

Let us see what has in fact been happening to agricultural production.

Table 1.2 and Figure 1.2 show that farm output in the United States since 1950 has been increasing more rapidly than has population. By 1962 the emergency feed grains and wheat programs temporarily slowed down the rate of increase in farm output, but still left it higher than population. This rapid increase in farm output, at a faster rate than population growth until 1962, was the main thing that depressed agricultural prices relative to other prices.

Figure 1.3 shows that the increase in farm output resulted entirely from an increase in crop yields per acre. In fact, the total acreage in crops in the United States declined from 336 million in 1950 to 321 million in 1960.[4] The emergency feed grains and wheat programs reduced total acreage further, to about 300 million acres in 1962. Meanwhile, yields per acre rose 34 per cent.

It is generally believed that yields increased because of the application of new production technology. New implements were manufactured, new insecticides and herbicides were developed, and the use of fertilizer was increased greatly.

---

[4] USDA, *Agricultural Statistics 1961*, p. 450. These figures show the acreage in the 59 principal crops harvested.

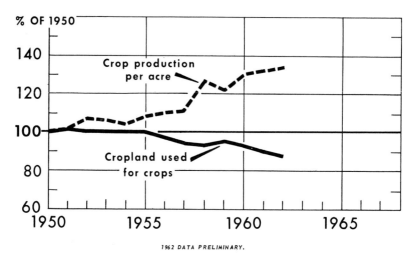

U. S. DEPARTMENT OF AGRICULTURE   NEG. ERS 1355-62 (8) ECONOMIC RESEARCH SERVICE

Fig. 1.3. Index of crop production, acreage harvested, and yield per acre.

Steele and Langren say: [5]

The impact of technological innovations on land-use requirements is not necessarily confined to innovations directly affecting the productivity of land. For example, a development in animal nutrition that improves the feeding efficiency of livestock permits a given output of product from less feed. Since less feed is required, less land is required to produce it. Hence, such a development indirectly increases the productivity of land. Excepting broilers and turkeys, no spectacular breakthroughs in feeding efficiency have occurred during the past 40 years. But some progress has been made and the technical possibilities for major advances are known.

Thus the technological developments which have increased agricultural productivity are many and varied. They are biological as well as mechanical, and include fertilizers, power machinery, mechanical equipment, pesticides, herbicides, and insecticides, to name only a few. Although necessarily limited in the number of resources shown, Figure 1.4 illustrates the nature of the revolution in the adoption of technology which has produced a large increase in output per acre and an even greater increase in output per man hour.

USDA BUDGETS HAVE GROWN

Large programs were put into effect by the USDA to deal with the depressing effect on prices of the rapid increase in ag-

[5] Harry A. Steele and Norman E. Langren, "Demands for Land for Agriculture—Past, Present, and Future." USDA, Land and Water Economics Branch, Homestead Centennial Symposium, Lincoln, Nebr., June 12, 1962, *Proceedings*, p. 12.

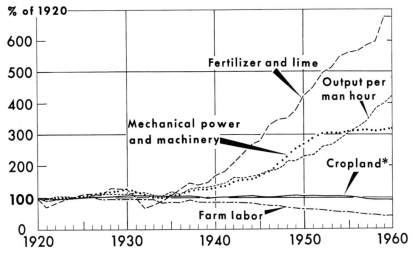

% of 1920

*CROPLAND USED IS THE SUM OF THE ACREAGE OF LAND FROM WHICH ONE OR MORE CROPS WERE HARVESTED PLUS ACREAGES OF CROP FAILURE AND SUMMER FALLOW.

U.S. DEPARTMENT OF AGRICULTURE   NEG. ERS 1135-62(5)   ECONOMIC RESEARCH SERVICE

Fig. 1.4. Selected farm inputs used and labor productivity.

ricultural production that resulted from the application of new technology. These programs included price-support storage programs, acreage reduction programs, domestic food distribution programs, and export subsidy programs. These plus the regular research and regulatory USDA programs added up to several billion dollars each year. The proposed USDA budget for the fiscal year July 1, 1964 to June 30, 1965, is shown in Table 1.3.

The size of this budget alarms a good many people. If you divide the $6.5 billion total by 3.5 million—that is about the number of farmers projected for 1964 (the 1959 Census figure was 3.7 million)—you get nearly $2,000 per farm. If you eliminate the 1.6 million noncommercial farms (those with total sales less than $2,500) that leaves only about 2 million real farms; dividing this into the $6.5 billion gives $3,500 per farm.

This makes a good horror story; but a little closer examination of Table 1.3 suggests some second thoughts.[6]

---

[6] The next few paragraphs and Table 1.3 are quoted from Lauren Soth, "Farm Subsidies—Fact and Fiction." *Des Moines Sunday Register*, March 24, 1963, p. 2–F.

TABLE 1.3

PROPOSED USDA BUDGET, 1964–65*

Programs Which Benefit General Public

(Millions)

Food Distribution Programs:
Purchase of surplus agricultural commodities ....$ 164
Pilot food stamp plan 51
School lunch program 182
Special milk program 102

$ 499

Programs having foreign relations and defense aspects:
Sales of surplus farm commodities for foreign currencies $1,282
Emergency famine relief to friendly peoples 246
International wheat agreement 72
Transfer of bartered materials to supplemental stockpile 62
Payments to Veterans Administration and armed services for milk and dairy
    products used in excess of normal requirements 40
Value of foreign currencies used by Defense Department for military hous-
    ing and long-term supply contracts 284
Defense food stockpiling 30

$2,016

Investment in REA and FHA loans, subject to repayment: ....$ 448

Long-range programs for improvement of agricultural resources, including
    research, meat inspection, disease and pest control, market development
    and services, protection of soil and water resources, and forest and public
    land management:
Forest Service ....$ 311
Agricultural Research Service 195
Soil Conservation Service 195
Extension Service 77
Co-operative State Experiment Station Service 40
Agricultural Marketing Service, Marketing Research 43
Farmers Home Administration salaries and expenses 39
Expenses and staff offices for other agencies, including Rural Electrification
    Administration (REA), and Federal Crop Insurance Corp. (FCIC) 94

$ 994

Total $3,957

Programs for Stabilizing Farm Income

Agricultural conservation program ....$ 214
Conservation reserve program 294
Land-use adjustment program 27
CCC price support, supply and related programs (less payments to VA and
    armed services for dairy products used in excess of normal requirements) 787
Grain acreage diversion payments 400
Grain price support payments 581
National wool act program 106
Agricultural Stabilization and Conservation Service expenses 115
Sugar act program 84

$2,608

GRAND TOTAL $6,565

* Source: *Des Moines Sunday Register,* March 24, 1963, p. 2–F.

Only the $2,608 million shown in the last part of the table can be properly called farm subsidy.

It is true, of course, that the exports of food at cut-rate prices and donations of food to foreign countries benefit agriculture. But foreign aid in money also benefits certain U. S. industries. The foreign recipients use the dollars to buy machinery and other goods in the U.S. The Food for Peace program is foreign aid and should be classed as such in the federal budget, just as other grants or loans to foreign countries are.

It is also true that food distribution programs, including the Food Stamp Plan, are of some benefit to farmers, although in this case the benefit is very small. But the main benefit is to poor people in this country who receive balanced diets they could not otherwise obtain.

One of the biggest illusions of all is that the vast programs of agricultural research, education and technical assistance are of primary advantage to the farmer.

These public efforts to stimulate more efficient farm production help the consumer directly by lowering the cost of food.

Individual farmers who adopt new methods first tend to gain a temporary benefit from them. But, in the long run, farmers as a group actually suffer a cut in income from this advance of productivity.

The reason for this is that, in a rich country, demand for food is highly inelastic. A 5 per cent increase in total output of food in this country results in a 20 per cent reduction in price. Thus a larger supply sells for less gross revenue.

Programs which tend to stimulate more farm output, therefore, are not a subsidy to farmers but to consumers.

This is the basic reason why production controls, price supports, and other subsidies are necessary. In a sense, the expenditures in the last section of the accompaning table are a consequence of the expenditures for research and education just above them.

Some say that there would have been no surpluses if the government had not supported prices above long-run competitive levels. Against this, others say that since the government financed the research and extension programs that developed the new technology and carried it to the farmer, the government is obligated to relieve the price depressing effects of the resulting increase in production.

One observer, W. W. Wilcox, estimates that foods cost consumers in the United States from $4 to $6 billion a year less now than they would if the prices of farm products had risen as much as prices in other sectors of the economy over the past 8 years. This saving is considerably greater than the cost of the price-support programs.

It is evident then that the *net* cost of the farm programs is a matter of some difference of opinion, as also is the proportion of the money cost of the programs which can properly be charged to agriculture.

PROSPECTS FOR THE FUTURE

The prospects for agricultural production in the United States in the future are not encouraging to farmers. Crop yields are likely to continue to increase faster than population:[7]

With average weather, per acre yields in 1967 would be at least 10 to 20 percent higher than in 1961. More acres (if acreage control programs are not continued) plus more per acre would add up to an increase of one-fourth or more in crop production in 1961. The rate of increase in yields estimated is a little slower than in recent years, when greater use of fertilizer, better plant varieties, more and better chemicals and machinery, and more skillful farming combined to push 1961 crop yields and better products. Despite great gains, we are yet in the foothills of technical progress in agriculture—not at the peak. Unless all signs fail, the ceiling on crop yields is still far in the future.

The spectacular rise in production per acre during the past 10 years has been especially noticeable in the major crops—wheat, cotton and feed grains.

Average yields for the four major feed grains rose from less than a ton per harvested acre in 1950 to 1.32 tons in 1961. By 1967, average yield per harvested acre of about 27 bushels should be expected. This yield has already been reached—in 1958. The possibility of substantially higher yields should not be ruled out.

The average yield of cotton was about 270 pounds per acre in 1950; in 1961 it was 438 pounds. By 1967, average yields of one bale per acre—500 pounds—would not be surprising.

With income levels as high as they are in the United States, total food consumption tends to rise only at about the same rate as population increases. Consumption per person has remained practically constant in the United States since 1950, while per capita income was rising rapidly. United States consumer incomes now are so high that further increases in income add to the demand for some farm products but decrease the demand for others; total food consumption per capita hardly increases at all.

THE PRODUCTION-CONSUMPTION IMBALANCE

The USDA estimates that there is a potential United States crop output increase by 1967 of one-fourth from 1961, but an in-

---

[7] USDA, "Food and Agriculture, A Program for the 1960's," 1962, pp. 22–23.

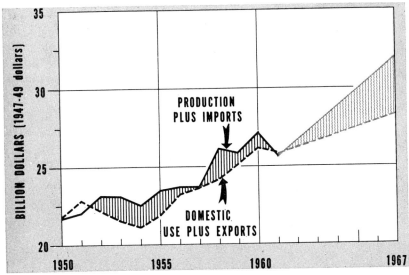

Fig. 1.5. Crops: Estimated production-consumption gap without effective production adjustment programs.

crease of only about 10 per cent in the demand for farm products. The difference may be termed "The Production-Consumption Imbalance."[8] These things are shown in Figure 1.5.

This potential excess of production of farm crops over utilization by 1967, with prices approximately at the 1961 level and with the best obtainable expansion in Food for Peace exports, is estimated at about 12 per cent. If that excess output were put into the market, it would seriously depress farm prices and incomes. If it were to be acquired by the Government in supporting prices, it would create a record burden on the budget.

The agricultural problem, therefore, has been and still is usually diagnosed as a price problem, created by an overly rapid increase in farm output. Price-support and output-control programs were put into effect at various times since the early 1930's in an attempt to solve the problem, yet the problem remains unsolved. We will briefly describe and appraise these programs in the next few chapters in an attempt to determine whether they were well adapted to solve the problem and whether the problem was accurately identified in the first place. Then in succeeding chapters we will consider alternative programs that might do better.

[8] *Ibid.*, pp. 25–26.

Fig. 2.1. Early storage programs. This Carlisle cartoon was published in **The Des Moines Register** in the early 1930's and reprinted in the Sept. 1, 1962 issue. (Courtesy **The Des Moines Register.**)

2

Appraisal of the Price-Support Programs

"The agricultural problem" was first diagnosed in the 1920's and 1930's as a price instability problem. The prices received by farmers varied more than the prices paid by farmers, so price stabilization programs were designed to make the prices of farm products more stable. The biblical concept of Joseph's program of storing the surplus during the seven fat years for use during the seven lean years was adapted to modern times, as indicated facetiously in a cartoon (Figure 2.1) published at the time.

As the industrial depression of the 1930's continued, these price *stabilizing* programs became more and more price *supporting* programs. The diagnosis was simple: Prices are too low, with reference to their earlier relationship (before World War I) to the prices that farmers paid. The remedy was equally simple: Get them up. The concept and phrase "price supports" began to occupy an important place in agricultural thinking and in farm programs.

This was about like diagnosing measles as the red-spot disease, and proceeding to cure it by painting the red spots white. The remedy was merely a program to cover up the symptoms, by a program that could not even cure the symptoms, and which in fact only made the real disease worse.

The stultifying effects of originally diagnosing the farm problem incorrectly as a price problem were compounded by the nature of the price programs that were put into effect to cure the misconceived price disease.

The price-support programs were initiated in 1929 under the Federal Farm Board. This turned out to be a bad time to start that kind of a program. The great industrial depression which also started in 1929 bore prices downward. The Farm Board's attempt to hold prices up by storage operations, unsuited to the job in the first place, failed completely. The Farm Board lost its capital of half a billion dollars—considered a lot of money in those days—and was quietly buried in 1933.

A few months later, the Commodity Credit Corporation (CCC) was set up to do the same job in a somewhat different fashion, using nonrecourse commodity loans to farmers and storage operations of its own on the commodities taken over.

The storage operations of the CCC were conducted on a comparatively small scale at first, at relatively low levels of loan rates. But in 1938, Congress began to prescribe loan rates at certain percentages of parity prices, considerably higher than market price levels. This changed the nature of the programs from price stabilizing to price level raising. The loan rates, the prices, and the quantities of corn placed under loan each year are shown in Figure 2.2 and Table 2.1. The loan rates and prices for wheat at the chief wheat markets over the last few years are given in Figure 2.3 and Table 2.2.

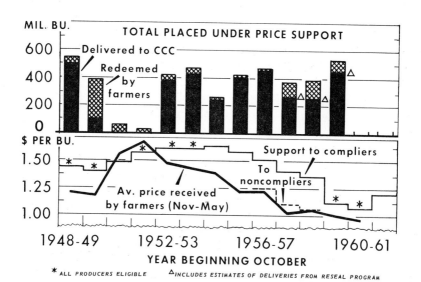

Fig. 2.2. Corn price support operations.

TABLE 2.1

CORN: U.S. LOAN RATES, U.S. AVERAGE FARM PRICES, AND DIFFERENTIALS BETWEEN
THEM; SUPPORT PRICES, AND QUANTITY PLACED UNDER SUPPORT, 1933–61*

Year Beginning October	Announced National Average Loan Rates[a]		Average Price Nov.–May[b]	Placed Under Price Support	Under Loan or Owned by CCC at End of Crop Year
	($ per bushel)	(per cent of parity)	($ per bushel)	(million bushels)	(million bushels)
1933.........	0.45	60	0.45	268	82
1934.........	0.55	68	0.83	20	...
1935.........	0.45	55	0.55	31	...
1936.........	0.55	66	1.06	...	...
1937.........	0.50	58	0.51	61	45
1938.........	0.57	70	0.44	230	258
1939.........	0.57	69	0.55	302	471
1940.........	0.61	75	0.58	103	403
1941.........	0.75	85	0.74	111	197
1942.........	0.83	85	0.90	56	8
1943.........	0.90	85	1.12	8	6
1944.........	0.98	90	1.07	21	9
1945.........	1.01	90	1.15	3	...
1946.........	1.15	90	1.38	26	9
1947.........	1.37	90	2.20	1	...
1948.........	1.44	90	1.20	551	493
1949........	1.40	90	1.18	387	650
1950.........	1.47	90	1.55	54	488
1951.........	1.57	90	1.66	26	306
1952.........	1.60	90	1.47	417	580
1953.........	1.60	90	1.42	471	736
1954.........	1.62	90	1.38	259	870
1955.........	1.58	87	1.21	421	1,060
1956c.........	1.50	84	1.21	477	1,295
1957c.........	1.40	77	1.02	369	1,355
1958c.........	1.36	77	1.05	381	1,400
1959.........	1.12	66	1.00	529	1,800
1960.........	1.06	65	.96	638	2,021
1961.........	1.20	75	.97	658	1,681
1962........	1.20	74	1.04	591	1,491

* Source: USDA, "Agricultural Outlook Charts, 1956," Nov. 1955, Table 35, p. 68; USDA, "Grain and Feed Statistics Through 1954," USDA Stat. Bul. 159, March 1955, Table 48, p. 46; and USDA, AMS, "The Feed Situation," July 1962, pp. 5, 18. Data for 1962 from USDA, ERS, Aug. 1963, pp. 17, 21.

ª Applies to commercial area only in years when acreage allotments are in effect.

ᵇ Average price received by farmers in period when most of the corn is placed under price support. In recent years, loans have been available from time of harvest through May.

ᶜ Loans were made to noncooperators at $1.25 per bushel in 1956, $1.10 in 1957 and $1.06 in 1958.

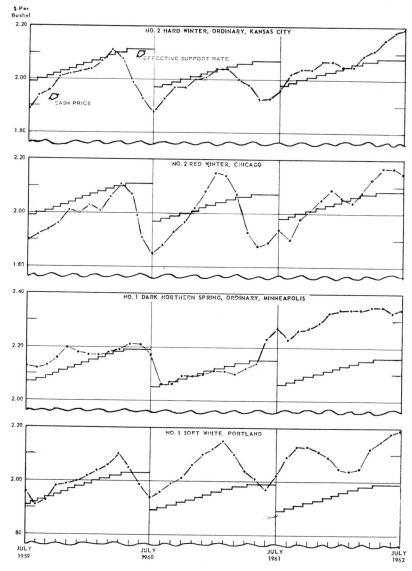

Fig. 2.3. Cash wheat prices and effective support rates. (Source: USDA, **Wheat Situation**, Aug. 1962.)

TABLE 2.2

WHEAT: AVERAGE CASH PRICE PER BUSHEL AT SPECIFIED MARKETS, BY MONTHS,
1959–62*

(Amounts given in dollars)

Year Beginning July	July	August	September	October	November	December
No. 2 Hard Winter, ordinary protein, Kansas City						
1959....	1.89	1.94	1.96	2.01	2.02	2.03
1960....	1.88	1.93	1.97	1.97	2.00	2.01
1961....	1.96	2.02	2.04	2.04	2.07	2.07
1962ᵃ...	2.20	2.17	2.17	2.19	2.22	2.24
No. 2 Red Winter, Chicago						
1959....	1.90	1.92	1.94	1.96	2.01	2.00
1960....	1.85	1.88	1.93	1.97	2.02	2.08
1961....	1.94	1.90	1.98	2.01	2.05	2.09
1962....	2.15	2.11	2.07	2.05	2.10	2.13
No. 1 Dark Northern Spring, ordinary protein, Minneapolis						
1959....	2.13	2.12	2.13	2.16	2.20	2.18
1960....	2.17	2.06	2.06	2.09	2.09	2.10
1961....	2.27	2.23	2.26	2.27	2.29	2.33
1962....	2.34	2.30	2.30	2.34	2.36	2.33
No. 1 Soft White, Portland						
1959....	1.96	1.91	1.93	1.98	1.99	2.00
1960....	1.94	1.96	1.99	2.01	2.06	2.10
1961....	2.02	2.09	2.13	2.13	2.11	2.09
1962....	2.19	2.15	2.13	2.13	2.15	2.17

* Source: USDA, *Wheat Situation*, Aug. 1963.
ᵃ 1962 data for No. 1 instead of No. 2.

ORIGINAL OBJECTIVES OF THE STORAGE PROGRAMS

The original objective was stated in 1933 to operate the programs as price stabilizing programs—to stabilize the prices of farm products against year-to-year variations in production. This could have been accomplished by setting the loan rates for each crop at the level that would have permitted average weather crops to move into consumption. The excess over average weather crops would then have been removed from the market and put into storage to be released back to the market in short crop years. This would have converted the irregular variations in production resulting from irregular variations in weather into a more nearly smooth flow of grain into consumption. This would have stabilized prices to a considerable extent against variations in supply.

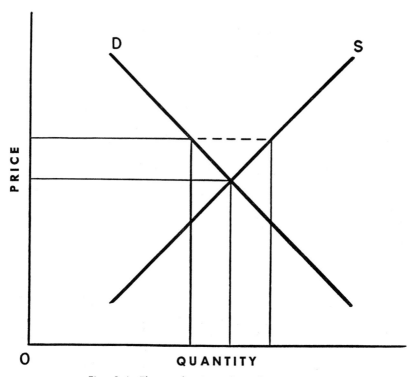

Fig. 2.4. The mechanism of surplus creation.

THE PRICE STABILIZATION PROGRAMS WERE MISUSED AS PRICE RAISING PROGRAMS

In actual fact, however, the programs soon began to go further than this. After the first few years, the objective changed from merely stabilizing prices to "stabilizing them upward." Loan rates were set above average weather crop levels, at certain percentages of parity prices. This raised the level of prices as well as stabilizing them against variations in supply. This high level of prices stimulated production, reduced consumption, and led to the accumulation of unsalable surpluses in storage.

The mechanism that brought about this result is shown in Figure 2.4. The point where the demand and supply curves intersect represents long-run equilibrium. Supporting prices above this level reduces consumption and increases production. The resulting surplus piles up in CCC storage. Storage operations like these are self-defeating. For when the large stocks are returned to the market, as eventually they must be, they depress

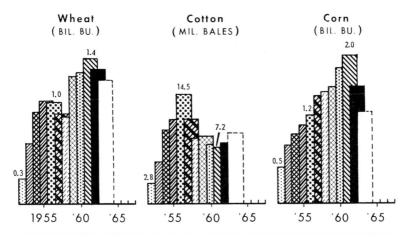

BEGINNING OF CROP YEAR: WHEAT, JULY 1; COTTON, AUG. 1; CORN, OCT. 1.   HEIGHT OF BARS PROPORTIONAL TO VALUE AT
1955 SUPPORT LEVELS.   1963 ESTIMATED ON BASIS OF INDICATED PRODUCTION AND DISAPPEARANCE AS OF OCTOBER 1962

U. S. DEPARTMENT OF AGRICULTURE   NEG. ERS 818X–62 (10)   ECONOMIC RESEARCH SERVICE

Fig. 2.5. Carry-over of wheat, cotton, and corn.

prices about as much as they raised prices when they were originally taken off the market.

During the first 20 years of the programs, this type of operation, as it reached a critical stage, was twice bailed out by wars
—World War II and the Korean conflict—which increased the
demand so much each time that the surpluses quickly vanished.
These events in effect permitted the programs to stabilize prices
to some extent against war-induced variations in demand as well
as in supply. The programs were not planned for this purpose;
variations in demand are too unpredictable and too lengthy to
be handled effectively by planned storage operations. But by
accident, the programs did provide some degree of stabilization
against variations in demand as well as in supply.

After 1952, however, with rapid technological advance and
several years of good weather, the accumulation of surpluses
was resumed on an unprecedentedly large scale, against the will
of the administrators and with no unexpected increases in demand in sight to rescue the programs. Figure 2.5 shows the
size of the stocks in recent years, most of them owned by the
CCC.

In an attempt to stay this accumulation of storage stocks,
the loan rates were reduced to lower and lower percentages of
parity, as the data in Table 2.1 show. The loan rate for corn
dropped from 90 per cent of parity, where the rate had stood
from 1944 to 1954, to 65 per cent in 1960.

But percentages of parity are not appropriate bases for price supports. They take into account only changes in prices, ignoring changes in quantities of product sold and quantities of goods and services purchased; thus they ignore the revolutionary technological improvements in agricultural production practices which drastically reduced costs per bushel through the years.[1]

In 1958, corn producers were offered a choice between (a) the existing program of high supports and restricted acreage and (b) lower supports (the average of the open market prices for corn over the preceding 3 years, or 65 per cent of parity, whichever was the higher) and no acreage restrictions. They voted for the latter. Corn acreage harvested jumped from 73.5 million in 1958 to 84.4 million in 1959, and production rose from 3.8 billion bushels to 4.4 billion bushels. But the restriction to "not less than 65 per cent of parity" and the lag resulting from the inclusion of the supporting effects of the program on prices during the 3-year average periods left loan rates still above long-run open market equilibrium levels. Surpluses continued to accumulate. Not until the emergency feed grains and wheat programs of 1961 and 1962 reduced the production of those crops did the surplus stocks cease to grow and begin to decline.

The stocks were much larger than needed for price stabilization purposes. A Senate Document in 1952[2] after citing "the worst corn production deficits of 850 to 950 million bushels" that took place in 1934 and 1936, went on to say:

> Yields of other feed grains tend to fluctuate in the same direction as do yields of corn, so that the variation in total feed-grain production is about 20 to 25 per cent larger (in tons or equivalent bushels of corn) than in production of corn alone. To cover this additional source of variation (and that in corn yields as well) would have required a total carry-over of 900 million to 1 billion bushels of corn plus the equivalent of another 100 million bushels in the form of reserves of other grains in excess of working stocks.

---

[1] For a full appraisal of parity prices, see G. Shepherd, Staff Paper 10, "Appraisal of Alternative Concepts and Measures of Agricultural Parity Prices and Incomes," in *Government Price Statistics*. (Hearings before the Subcommittee on Economic Statistics of the Joint Economic Committee, Congress of the United States, 87th Congress, 1st Session, Part I, Jan. 24, 1961.) This appraisal is brought up to date in the last three chapters of G. Shepherd, *Agricultural Price Analysis*, Iowa State Univ. Press, Ames, 1963.

[2] "Reserve Levels for Storable Farm Products." 82nd Congress, 2nd Session, Senate Document 130, 1952.

33810973 Sh 48f

C. 1

But this estimate does not pay much attention to the costs of storing the stocks. Karl Fox, then with the USDA, concluded that, when the costs of storage are taken into account, a typical corn carry-over during a period of normal yields should be 600 or 700 million bushels.[3] He added that the CCC should not take action to reduce the corn carry-over below about 500 million bushels, or feel alarmed if corn stocks rose to 800 million bushels as a result of better than average weather. Shepherd and Richards arrived at a round figure of 1 billion bushels of corn equivalent for total feed grains.[4] This includes an allowance of 100 million bushels for feed grains other than corn. This figure, therefore, is about 100 million bushels higher than Fox's upper limit of corn carry-over of 800 million bushels.

More recently, R. L. Gustafson, in his Rule 1 based on maximizing net gain, recommends only about 200 million bushels corn equivalent working stocks when total feed supplies are about average.[5] The recommended quantity when total supplies are large varies with the size of the total supplies.

The stocks of corn, therefore, were nearly twice as large as needed for stabilizing purposes. The corresponding stocks of wheat were more than twice as large as needed.[6]

COST OF THE STORAGE PROGRAMS

The costs of the CCC storage programs rose to high levels. On July 10, 1963, the CCC said in a news release that as of May 31 the total investment of the CCC in price-support loans and inventories amounted to $7,748,330,436—made up of loans outstanding of $2,648,674,459 (including $996,188,492 of loans financed by lending agencies), and the cost value of inventories, $5,099,655,977.

The "realized cost" of "programs primarily for stabilization of farm prices and income" in fiscal 1961 as shown in Table 2.3

---

[3] "Long-range Farm Program." House Committee Print, 1954, p. 39.
[4] Geoffrey Shepherd and Allen Richards, "Effects of the USDA Corn Storage Program on Corn Carry-over Stocks and Corn Utilization." Iowa Agr. Exp. Sta. Res. Bul. 446 (No. Cen. Reg. Pub. 77), 1957, p. 985.
[5] R. L. Gustafson, "Carryover Levels for Grains." USDA Tech. Bul. 1178, p. 19. See also: R. L. Gustafson, "Implications of Recent Research on Optimal Storage Rules." *Jour. Farm Econ.*, May 1958, pp. 290–300. The rules are given on pp. 294–95.
[6] Senate Document 130, *op. cit.*

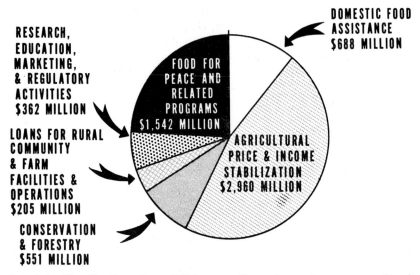

RESEARCH,
EDUCATION,
MARKETING,
& REGULATORY
ACTIVITIES
$362 MILLION

DOMESTIC FOOD
ASSISTANCE
$688 MILLION

FOOD FOR
PEACE AND
RELATED
PROGRAMS
$1,542 MILLION

LOANS FOR RURAL
COMMUNITY
& FARM
FACILITIES &
OPERATIONS
$205 MILLION

AGRICULTURAL
PRICE & INCOME
STABILIZATION
$2,960 MILLION

CONSERVATION
& FORESTRY
$551 MILLION

Fig. 2.6. Classification of net USDA expenditures by major purpose. Fiscal year 1962, estimated. (Source: **Food and Agriculture, a Program for the 1960's.** USDA, 1961, p. 52.)

was $4,128,500,000.[7] The total cost since the programs began in 1932 was $23,975,900,000. The breakdowns for 1961 and earlier years are given in Table 2.3.

The large share of the total appropriations for agriculture that went to the price-support programs in fiscal 1962 is shown in Figure 2.6. The "price and income stabilization" programs took nearly half of the total. The "food for peace and related" programs, undertaken chiefly to dispose of United States agricultural surpluses, took an additional quarter of the total. The "domestic food assistance" programs, also undertaken chiefly to help support agricultural prices, took 10 per cent more. This left less than $1 billion—less than one-sixth of the total appropriations—for the remaining USDA activities.

Only a part of the price-support expenditures went directly to farmers. The rest went to other groups such as storage fees to storage agencies, and indirectly to construction companies for the building of additional storage space. These other agencies received a substantial part of the income transferred from taxpayers. In fiscal 1958, for example, the "realized cost" of the

[7] The "realized cost" is large in recent years partly because it includes the cost of acquiring the large inventory built up in those years. When crops are small, and prices rise enough to pull substantial quantities out of storage for sale on the market, the revenue from those sales would offset a large part of the total costs in those years, and "realized cost" would be relatively small.

TABLE 2.3

REALIZED COST OF AGRICULTURAL AND RELATED PROGRAMS, BY FUNCTION OR PURPOSE, FISCAL YEARS 1932–61*

(In millions of dollars)

Programs Primarily for Stabilization of Farm Prices and Income	1932–61	1954	1955	1956	1957	1958	1959	1960	1961
CCC nonrecourse loan, purchase, and payment programs	6,957.0	372.1	422.6	566.6	874.8	690.0	528.2	513.3	2,019.4
CCC supply commodity export, and other activities	1,146.8	24.7	49.5	70.0	149.1	97.1	132.8	311.8	639.6
CCC interest, administrative, and other general costs	2,471.6	102.7	81.7	195.2	311.7	364.9	195.0	478.1	442.7
National Wool Act Program	294.3	...	0.2	2.0	61.3	57.2	20.0	92.7	60.9
International Wheat Agreement	1,172.7	59.0	99.7	92.3	90.1	82.4	48.3	66.3	76.5
Donations of commodities to other nations—excess of inventory cost over market value	315.8	24.1	37.8	39.5	39.0	43.1	30.7	29.8	71.8
Commodities sold for foreign currencies under Title I, P.L. 480	3,036.1	...	129.5	304.9	497.2	666.2	318.1	501.1	619.1
Removal of surplus agricultural commodities	2,713.7	177.6	58.9	179.1	171.1	125.5	140.9	89.7	203.3
Sugar Act	482.6[a]	11.9[a]	13.0[a]	22.3[a]	23.4[a]	21.3[a]	24.1[a]	21.0[a]	45.2[a]
Soil Bank—acreage reserve program	1,662.3	...	...	3.6	514.7	535.3	608.7	...	...
Acreage allotment payments under Agricultural Conservation Program	2,354.8	...	...	...	...	...	...	...	...
Other, including Agricultural Adjustment Act of 1933, parity payments, and other adjustment and surplus removal programs	2,333.4	36.7	35.1	30.3	28.7	24.8	29.3	32.5	40.4
Total	23,975.9	785.0	902.0	1,461.2	2,714.3	2,665.2	2,027.9	2,094.3	4,128.5

* Source: USDA, CCC records.
[a] Excess of credits—deduct.

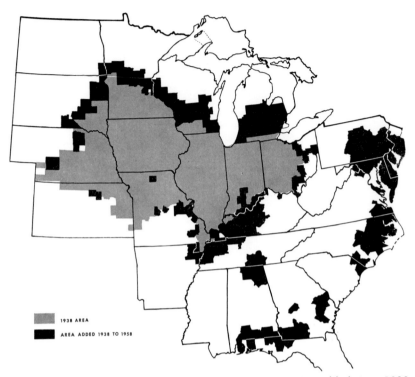

Fig. 2.7. Original 1938 commercial corn area and counties added since 1938.

corn program was $271 million. Of this amount, $110 million —about one-third—went to the grain trade and transportation agencies to cover storage and handling charges. None of this went to farmers. The program thus has been a "grain-trade program" as well as a farm program, and has aided segments of the grain trade as well as farmers.

This is one of the reasons why the grain trade, originally bitterly opposed to "government interference" in the grain business, became reconciled to it as the years went by. A survey, taken in 1957, of Iowa county grain dealers' attitudes toward the federal grain storage program revealed that most of the dealers expressed satisfaction with the program.[8]

---

[8] Geoffrey S. Shepherd, Allen B. Richards, and John T. Wilkin, "Some Effects of Federal Grain Storage Programs on Grain Storage Capacity, Grain Stocks and Country Elevator Operations." Ind. Agr. Exp. Sta. Res. Bul. 697 (No. Cen. Reg. Pub. 114), June 1960.

EFFECTS OF THE FEED GRAINS PROGRAMS ON LOCATION
OF FEED GRAINS PRODUCTION

There was some concern up to 1959 that corn-acreage controls and the denying of loans to noncompliers might be driving some corn production out of the Corn Belt. Some thought, too, that the substitution of corn for controlled crops, such as cotton and wheat, was increasing the corn production outside the Corn Belt—that is, outside of the original "commercial corn area."

Figure 2.7 shows that the commercial corn area did increase in size—more than 60 per cent from 1938 to 1958.[9] Apparently, however, this was merely a result of more counties coming under the definition of a commercial corn county as corn yields per acre rose. The annual county and state production data show that corn production was not "driven out of the Corn Belt." Even corn acreage was not driven out.

The annual corn acreage and production data by counties show that corn acreage and production became more concentrated, not less concentrated, in the original 1938 commercial corn area. Figure 2.8, which illustrates changes in corn acreage, and Figure 2.9, which illustrates changes in corn production, show that the same thing is true of Iowa, Illinois, Indiana, and Ohio, the four states in the heart of the Corn Belt.[10] The figures indicate that this tendency increased even more after 1958 when corn acreage restrictions were removed and new corn rates, which were lower but were available to all producers, went into effect. The tendency for corn production to become more concentrated in the four Corn Belt states continued through the "emergency" feed grains programs of 1961 and 1962. The same thing is true for oats.

Production of hogs also became more concentrated in the Corn Belt, as seen in Figure 2.10, while cattle production just held its own, as shown in Figure 2.11. The changes in hog production are shown in less chronological detail but more geographical detail in Figure 2.12.

---

[9] The "commercial corn area" includes the counties where average corn production during the preceding 10 years was 450 or more bushels per farm and 4 or more bushels per acre of farm land in the county.

[10] The same result is obtained when Minnesota is substituted for Ohio as one of the four Corn Belt states.

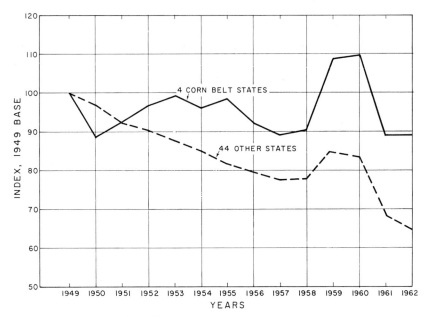

Fig. 2.8. Changes in corn acreage, 1949–62.

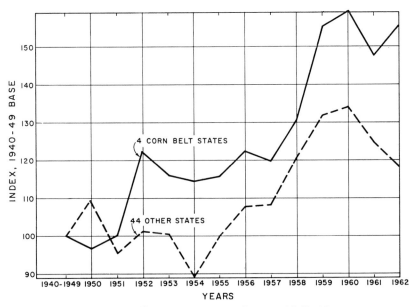

Fig. 2.9. Changes in corn production, 1949–62.

[30]

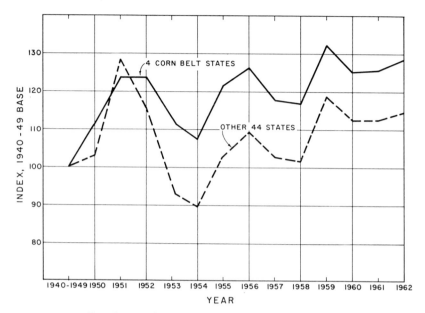

Fig. 2.10. Changes in hog production, 1949–62.

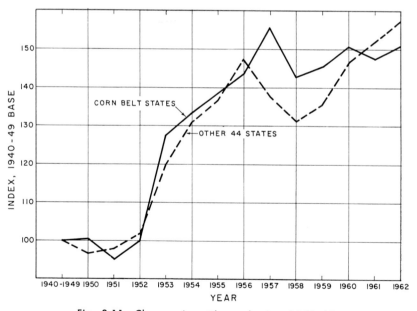

Fig. 2.11. Changes in cattle production, 1949–62.

[31]

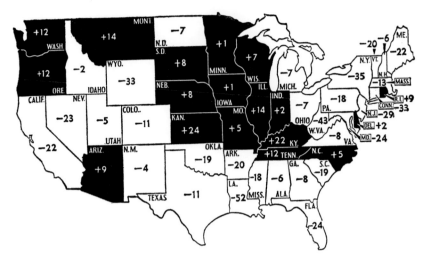

Fig. 2.12. The plus figures in the states colored black show the percentage increase in hog production in 1961 over the 1950–59 average. Minus figures in the other states indicate percentage decrease from the 10-year average. (Source: Taken from an article by Don Muhm, reporting data compiled by B. W. Ebbing of Rath Packing Co., Waterloo, Iowa, published in **The Des Moines Sunday Register**, Section F, Dec. 9, 1962.)

THE PROGRAMS TEMPORARILY RETARDED BUT DID NOT PREVENT A DECLINE IN AGRICULTURAL PRICES

Figure 1.1 indicated that, in spite of the large scale and high cost of the storage programs, the programs were not able to keep prices received by farmers from declining both in absolute terms and relative to prices paid by farmers. The parity ratio declined after the Korean conflict in 1951, until in June 1963 it stood at only 77.

There is some statistical evidence that the storage programs had a temporary supporting effect on agricultural prices. These prices declined, but the evidence indicates that without the programs, prices and incomes would have fallen farther than they did.[11]

This retardation of price decline increased the incomes of feed grains and wheat producers as a group, since the increase in prices was greater in percentage terms than the reduction in production that resulted from acreage restrictions. The effects

[11] Geoffrey Shepherd and Allen Richards, "Effects of the Federal Programs for Corn and Other Grains on Corn Prices, Feed Grains Production and Livestock Production," Iowa Agr. and Home Econ. Exp. Sta. Res. Bul. 459, Aug. 1958. See also: Footnote 13.

of the acreage restrictions on production before 1958 may have been offset, or more than offset, by the effects of the higher and more certain prices.

The raising of the prices of feed grains and wheat also increased the prices of livestock and gross income of livestock producers, since the high prices of feed grains and wheat restricted livestock production. This restriction of livestock production increased income, because the demand for most livestock and livestock products is inelastic. The effect of the programs on total United States net farm income for 1952–59 is indicated by an estimate that the income would have been 34 per cent lower than it actually was if the programs had not been in effect.[12]

Most of the gain in farm income resulting from the corn and other feed grains programs, however, was only temporary. It was attained because quantities of feed grains and wheat were removed from the market and held in government storage. Some of this grain was disposed of abroad under Public Law 480 and other subsidy programs. The major share, however, seems destined for the domestic market. When it is eventually released into domestic channels, it will depress prices and incomes about as much when it comes back on the market as it raised them when it was taken off the market. There will be no net gain over the period as a whole so far as those quantities are concerned. Most of the gain was borrowed from the future, and when the future arrives it will have to be paid back.

REASONS WHY PRICES DECLINED

The basic reason why the storage programs were unable to keep agricultural prices from declining was that the technological agricultural revolution during and after World War II caused production to increase faster than the demand increased. Figure 1.2 showed that agricultural production increased 23 per cent from 1950 to 1960, while population increased only 19 per cent.

---

[12] Geoffrey Shepherd, Arnold Paulsen, Francis Kutish, Don Kaldor, Richard Heifner, and Eugene Futrell, "Production, Price and Income Estimates and Projections for the Feed-Livestock Economy Under Specified Control and Market-clearing Conditions." Special Rept. 27, Iowa State University, Ames, August 1960.

Similar conclusions were reached by the USDA in "Report from the USDA and a Statement by the Land Grant Colleges IRM-1 Advisory Committee on Farm Price and Income Projections 1960–65 Under Conditions Approximating Free Production and Marketing of Agricultural Commodities." Presented by Senator Allen J. Ellender, January 20, 1960.

"During the past 5 years, the annual net additions to stocks of major crops have amounted to the equivalent of a little more than 5 per cent of the harvested cropland."[13]

During the period 1955–57, ". . . about 7 per cent of total farm marketings were diverted from the operation of the normal marketing system by price support and surplus disposal operations."[14]

The increase in production was the basic cause of the decline in prices after 1951. It is obvious that a storage program alone could not solve this kind of problem. It could have only a temporary effect at best.

If there had been no price-support programs, the basic oversupply situation would have shown up as a low-price problem. Instead, the price-support programs caused it to show up chiefly as a surplus stocks problem, partly by encouraging further increases in production through the removal of price uncertainty and guarantee of prices above long-run open market levels, and partly by reducing consumption by livestock.

APPRAISAL OF THE PRICE-SUPPORT PROGRAMS

The USDA experience with price-support programs implemented by storage operations indicates that they are costly, inefficient, and only temporarily and partially effective.

The reasons for this are two:

1. The agricultural problem was incorrectly diagnosed as a price problem in the first place, and

2. The storage programs were unsuited to handle a price problem in any case.

INCORRECT DIAGNOSIS LED TO INCORRECT PRESCRIPTION

The original diagnosis of the farm problem as a price problem, leading to an incorrect prescription, is in fact making the patient worse. It is impeding rather than promoting the adjustments needed to cure the actual disease. The price-support programs are like cough syrup prescribed for a cough that is caused by tuberculosis rather than by a simple cold. They temporarily relieve the symptoms, but in this case they actually make the

---

[13] Sherman Johnson and Kenneth Bachman, "Recent Changes in Resource Use and in Farm Incomes," Chap. 2 in *Problems and Policies of American Agriculture.* (Center for Agricultural and Economic Development, sponsors), Iowa State Univ. Press, Ames, 1959, p. 11.

[14] 86th Congress, 2nd Session, Senate Document 77, 1960, p. 20.

patient worse instead of better. They not only leave the real disease untreated; they accelerate its development.

Storage programs are suitable and workable programs for smoothing out variations in prices caused by variations in production that result from variations in weather. This smoothing out of prices is a valuable objective, and storage programs can attain it. Loan rates set at long-run market equilibrium levels would do the job.

This is the job that the storage programs were originally set up to do—to smooth out the variations in prices about their long-run free market levels. But they have been misused for a different job—to raise those long-run levels also, or at least to keep them from declining or to retard the decline.

The storage programs are completely unsuitable and unworkable for this job. They do not touch the causes of the decline in prices—the overproduction of farm products. Storage programs cannot cope with overproduction. What goes into storage must come out. The overproduction of farm products can only be cured by increasing consumption to match the increased production, or by reducing production to match the existing consumption, or some of both.

Overproduction is not cured by price supports above long-run open-market levels; instead, it is made worse. The high price supports induce still greater production, while at the same time reducing consumption. Both of these together result in the accumulation of large surplus stocks.

The price-support programs clearly lead down a blind alley. A conclusive verdict upon them was rendered in 1962 by one who was in a position to know: [15]

It might be generalized from our past experience that minimum price supports accomplish nothing in the way of an acceptable solution. On the one hand, such supports do not provide farmers with adequate incomes, and on the other hand, they do not induce adjustment, they prevent it.

---

[15] Willard W. Cochrane, "Supply Management—The Way It Works." Address, National Institute of Animal Agriculture, Purdue University, April 9, 1962, p. 3.

3

Effects of the Production-Control Programs

The President and other high officials of the CCC, which operates the price-support programs, originally believed that their price-support operations could be adequately backed up by production controls—that is, by acreage-allotment and marketing quota programs.[1]

These programs were designed to control the supply of farm products by two different methods. For some products, one method was used; for other products, the other method was used; and for still other products, both methods were used.

1. One method of supply control was designed to restrict output *indirectly* by restricting inputs. This method placed a quota not on the product but on one or more of the factors of production. It may be referred to as control of inputs—that is, factor inputs. This method was applied chiefly to the one factor, land. Under the Conservation Reserve, however, the method could be extended to whole farms, thus taking out all three factors—land, capital, and labor—together.

2. The other method of supply control was designed to restrict output *directly* by the use of marketing quotas. These marketing quotas controlled the marketings of the product by placing a sales or marketing quota on each individual grower, restricting to that quota the quantity of the product that he could market. This quantity was usually expressed as a percentage of the quantity the grower marketed in some earlier base period.

---

[1] These beliefs were stated to me in person when I was Acting Chief of the Research Division, CCC, in 1941.

TABLE 3.1

CHANGES IN COMPOSITION OF INPUTS, UNITED STATES AGRICULTURE, 1870–1957*

(Inputs based on 1935–39 price weights)

Year	Percentage of Total Inputs[a]			
	Labor	Real estate	Capital[b]	Total
	(per cent)	*(per cent)*	*(per cent)*	*(per cent)*
1870.........	65	18	17	100
1880.........	62	19	19	100
1890.........	60	18	22	100
1900.........	57	19	24	100
1910.........	53	20	27	100
1920.........	50	18	32	100
1930.........	46	18	36	100
1940.........	41	18	41	100

(Inputs based on 1947–49 price weights)

Year	Labor	Real estate	Capital	Total
1940.........	56	14	30	100
1950.........	40	15	45	100
1957.........	31	15	54	100

* Source: "Productivity of Agriculture, United States, 1870–1958, 1961." USDA Tech. Bul. 1238, p. 11.

ᵃ The use of different price weights prohibits direct comparison of composition percentages for the periods before and after 1940. However, changes in composition within the two price-weight periods, 1870–1940 and 1940–47, serve to indicate the magnitude of changes in composition or input. Comparisons of periods before and after 1940 substantiate the trend in changes of input mix.

ᵇ All inputs other than labor and real estate.

CHANGES IN THE COMPOSITION OF INPUTS IN AGRICULTURE

The *total* of the inputs in agriculture has been increasing only slightly over the past 20 years, but the *composition* of the inputs has been changing rapidly. Table 3.1 shows these changes in percentage form by decades since 1870.[2] Figure 3.1 shows the changes annually, in terms of dollars, from 1940 to 1960.[3]

It is apparent that the input of labor, which used to be the biggest item, has been declining rapidly—from nearly two-thirds in 1870, and more than half in 1940, to only 30 per cent—less than one-third—in 1958.

The input of land has declined moderately, from a peak of 20 per cent in 1910 to 15 per cent in 1960.

---

[2] Ralph A. Loomis and Glen T. Barton, "Productivity of Agriculture, United States, 1870–1958." USDA Tech. Bul. 1238, April 1961.

[3] Harold F. Breimyer, "The Three Economies of Agriculture." *Jour. Farm Econ.*, pp. 679–99, Aug. 1962.

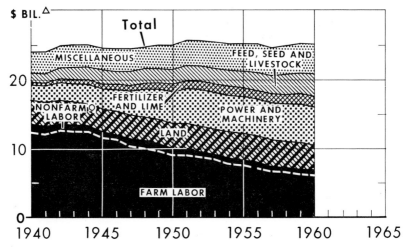

*ANNUAL INPUTS AS COMPUTED FROM QUANTITY-PRICE AGGREGATES.   △BASED ON 1947-49 PRICE WEIGHTS.
○NONFARM RESIDENTS HIRED FOR FARM WORK.   DATA TAKEN FROM U.S.D.A. TECH. BUL. 1238.

U. S. DEPARTMENT OF AGRICULTURE   NEG. AMS 269-62 (4)   AGRICULTURAL MARKETING SERVICE

Fig. 3.1. Inputs of U.S. Agriculture.

The input of capital has risen, offsetting these declines in land and labor, from 34 per cent in 1940 to 62 per cent in 1960.

The most important facts shown by this table and chart are: (1) that land is the least important input in agriculture, and (2) that capital is rapidly being substituted for labor in agriculture, until now the input of capital is greater than the input of the two other factors combined.

INPUT-CONTROL PROGRAMS WERE FOCUSED ON LAND

In spite of the fact that land is the least important of the three main inputs in agriculture, the input-control programs were focused on that factor. No attempt was made to restrict labor or capital. The Farm Credit Administration, indeed, was created to increase the supply of capital; and the 4-H programs had similar effects on labor.

The reasons why the input-control programs focused on the reduction of acres of land and not on other factors were pragmatic and obvious. You can measure acres and enforce a program for reducing them, but it would be difficult to measure capital and enforce a program for reducing it. In addition, it would be difficult to get the political support of the fertilizer, insecticide, and implement manufacturing companies and local distributors, as well as farmers. Similar difficulties would hamper programs to reduce labor and management; the USDA is reluctant to engage in any activity which would be construed as an attempt to "squeeze out the little farmer," or create a scarcity of farm labor and thus raise farm wages to the alleged detriment of the farm operator, or endanger the family farm, or reduce the number of constituents in a Congressman's district.

ACREAGE ALLOTMENT PROGRAMS

The acreage allotment programs turned out to have several weaknesses.

One was that there is enough substitutability among the factors of production in agriculture so that reductions in the one factor were offset to a considerable extent by the increases in the others, for instance capital—particularly fertilizer.

Another feature was that farmers naturally took out their poorest acres. Another was that nonparticipants were free to expand their acreage and production. For these reasons, the reductions in acreage did not have a corresponding reducing effect on production.

Several different analysts of the acreage allotment programs of the 1930's came to the same conclusion—that except for tobacco, the programs did not have much effect on production. The programs after World War II had more effect, but since crosscompliance was not included, the effect was mostly to shift production around from one crop to another.

The 1954 and 1955 corn-acreage programs, for example, apparently had very little effect on total acreage in crops. They also had very little effect on corn acreage; but they did affect total feed grains production by increasing the production of other feed crops.

Table 3.2 shows that the total United States acreage of corn decreased only 1 per cent from 1953 to 1955.[4] The small size of the decrease in corn acreage resulted chiefly from the lack of compliance by many corn farmers. Most of the corn farmers who did not comply with corn allotments intended to feed their corn and, therefore, were not interested in complying for eligibility in the price-support program. Reductions in corn acres made by

---

[4] USDA, ARS, "Effects of Acreage Allotment Programs." Prod. Res. Rept. 3, June 1956. See also: No. Cen. Farm Mgt. Res. Com. "Farmer's Reaction to Acreage Allotments." Ky. Agr. Exp. Sta. Bul. Dec. 1955.

TABLE 3.2

CHANGES IN PRODUCTION, HARVESTED ACREAGE AND YIELDS FOR VARIOUS
CROPS IN THE UNITED STATES, 1953–55*

Crop	Harvested Acreage	Total Production	Yield Per Acre
	(per cent)	(per cent)	(per cent)
Wheat.................	−30	−20	+15
Cotton.................	−31	−11	+28
Corn.................	−1	no change	+1
Rice (1954–55)..........	−28	−17	+16
Oats..................	+4	+30	+25
Barley.................	+66	+61	−3
Grain sorghum..........	+105	+113	+4
Soybeans for beans........	+26	+38	+9
Flaxseed...............	+10	+11	+1
Rye..................	+49	+61	+8
All tame hay............	+3	+7	+3

* Source: USDA, ARS, "Effects of Acreage Allotment Programs." Prod. Res. Rept. 3, June 1956, p. 6.

those who complied with the program were just about offset by increases in corn acres made by farmers who did not comply.

Table 3.2 also shows that the corn program had little or no effect on corn production. But the programs for wheat and cotton had substantial effects on total feed grains production.

Compliance with the wheat and cotton programs was high. Most of the acres diverted from wheat, cotton, and corn went into feed grains production. Iowa corn farmers who complied with corn allotments grew more soybeans and oats. Wheat acres were reduced by 30 per cent. These acres were mainly diverted to grain sorghum in Kansas and to barley in other major wheat-producing regions. The acres which were taken out of cotton production were shifted mainly to the production of soybeans, corn, grain sorghum, and barley. The diversions of acres from allotment crops to feed grains other than corn resulted in a 10 per cent increase in the total production of feed grains. This increase in feed grains production was not necessarily a net addition to the total quantity of grain fed, because some of the wheat would have been fed anyway. But the increase had some depressing effect on feed grains prices.

From 1952 to 1955, the harvested acreage of the crops under acreage controls—wheat, cotton, peanuts, rice, and tobacco—decreased by 33 million acres, but the acreage in other crops increased by 25 million acres. The production of the controlled crops decreased by 12 per cent, but the production of the other crops increased enough to more than offset this, so that total crop production increased. Thus, the producers of these crops transferred a substantial part of their surplus problem to the producers of the nonbasic crops, chiefly the feed grains other than corn, for which price supports were provided without restrictions on production.[5]

THE SOIL BANK PROGRAM

The Soil Bank program initiated in 1955 was more effective in retiring land than the previous programs. Figure 3.2 shows that 28.7 million acres were put into the Soil Bank by 1960, and the total acreage in crops declined by 25.3 million acres, nearly the same amount.

Figure 3.3 shows that the decline in acreage *harvested*, however, was only 12.1 million; this is less than half as much as the 28.7 million put into the Soil Bank. The chief reason for the small reduction in acreage harvested after 1955 is that there was a period of drouth in the Great Plains that year, when acreage abandonment was abnormally high. The acreage abandoned is shown on an expanded scale in the lower part of Figure 3.3. The small decline in acreage harvested after 1955 was chiefly the result of a return to normal weather and normal acreage abandonment. The rest was apparently because some land that was really not used for farming was put into the Soil Bank in some areas.[6]

The effects of the Soil Bank on total agricultural *production* were more than offset by the effects of (1) good weather, and

---

[5] R. P. Christensen and R. O. Aines, "Economic Effects of Acreage Control Programs in the 1950's." USDA, ERS, Agr. Econ. Rept. 18, 1962.

[6] H. E. Conklin and J. V. B. Rice, "The People Who Have Land in the Soil Bank in New York State." Dept. of Agr. Econ., Cornell University, Ithaca, New York, February 1961. See also "Controlling Agricultural Supply by Controlling Inputs," Iowa Agr. Exp. Sta. Res. Bul. IR-3 1963, by the present author *et al.*

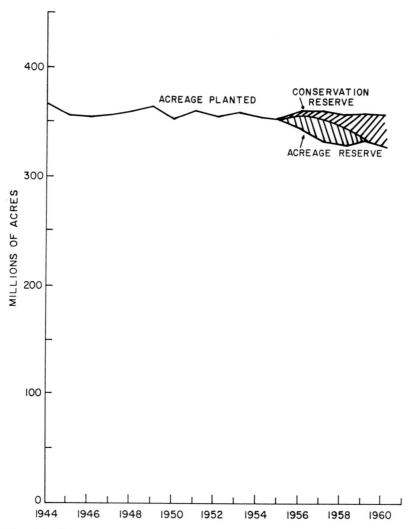

Fig. 3.2. U.S. acreage planted, and acreage in the acreage reserve and Conservation Reserve programs.

(2) new technology on crop yields per acre. Figure 3.4 shows that the program took out mostly land of low productivity in the southern Great Plains, in northern Minnesota, and the Southeast. The data are shown in percentage form by regions in Table 3.3. The percentage participation in these areas ran up to 35 per cent, for example in New Mexico, but in the rich Corn Belt area it was

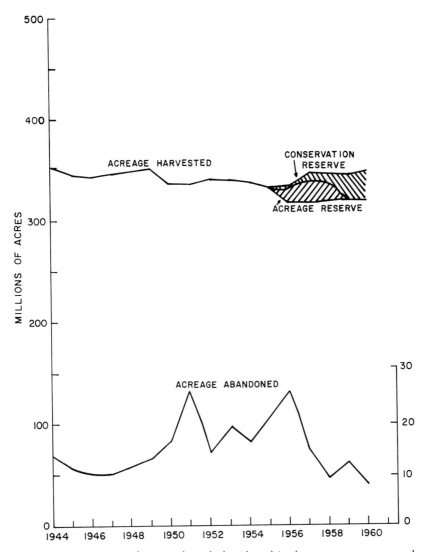

Fig. 3.3. U.S. acreage harvested, and abandoned in the acreage reserve and Conservation Reserve programs.

only 3.1 per cent. The reason for this was that the rental rates differed from state to state according to differences in the productivity of the land, but the range of rates was not as great as the range of profitability. This is shown in Figures 3.5 and 3.6,

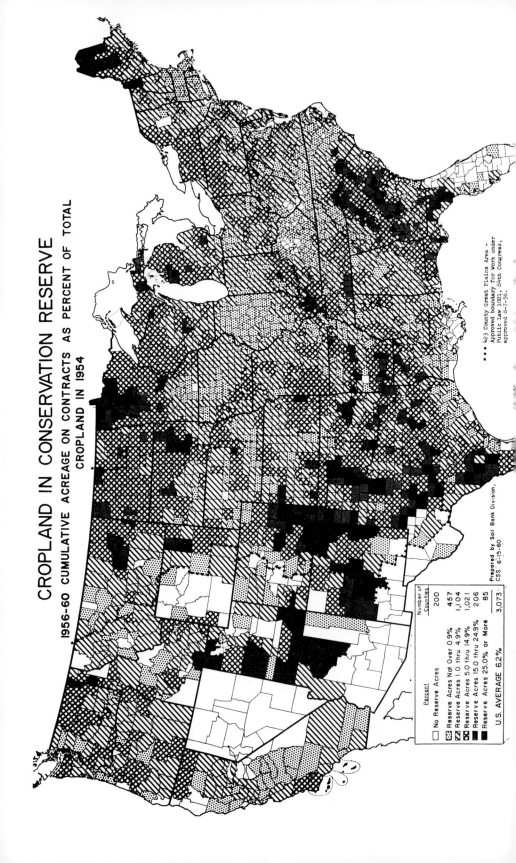

CROPLAND IN CONSERVATION RESERVE

1956-60 CUMULATIVE ACREAGE ON CONTRACTS AS PERCENT OF TOTAL CROPLAND IN 1954

Percent		Number of Counties
☐ No Reserve Acres		200
Reserve Acres Not Over 0.9%		457
Reserve Acres 1.0 thru 4.9%		1,104
Reserve Acres 5.0 thru 14.9%		1,021
Reserve Acres 15.0 thru 24.9%		206
Reserve Acres 25.0% or More		85
U.S. AVERAGE 6.2%		3,073

•••• 423 County Great Plains Area - Approved boundary for work under Public Law 1021, 84th Congress, approved 8-7-56.

Prepared by Soil Bank Division, CSS 6-15-60

TABLE 3.3

PERCENTAGE OF CROPLAND IN THE 1960 CONSERVATION RESERVE[a] AND
THE 1961 FEED GRAINS PROGRAM,[b] BY REGIONS, UNITED STATES[*]

Region	1960 Conservation Reserve	1961 Feed Grains Program
	(per cent)	(per cent)
Northeast....................	5.3	16.3
Corn Belt....................	3.1	23.4
Lake States..................	7.5	20.9
Appalachian.................	3.9	24.7
Southeast....................	9.3	15.6
Delta States.................	10.5	15.7
Southern Plains..............	9.8	26.7
Northern Plains..............	6.7	26.3
Mountain....................	8.2	25.8
Pacific......................	3.0	23.4
United States................	6.2	23.4

[*] Source: USDA, ERS, FED, "Economic Effects of Acreage Control Programs in the 1950's." Agr. Econ. Rept. 18, pp. 11, 50, Oct. 1962. Data on the feed grains program direct from USDA.
[a] Total cropland reported by 1954 Census of Agriculture (6).
[b] Per cent of base acreage for corn and grain sorghums in feed program.

where the rental rates are plotted against the value of land per acre—a good measure of profitability.

The program took out mostly poor land because the range in rental payments per acre was not as great as the range in profitability. The rental payments therefore overpaid the poor land relative to the good land. This was true by states and by counties, and particularly true by farms within counties. On this account alone, the percentage effect of the programs on production was only one-half or one-third as great as the percentage reduction in acres.[7]

The Conservation Reserve program took out 8 per cent of the total cropland used in 1960. The USDA estimates that the total value of the normal crop production at prevailing prices on all land in the program was equivalent to 4.5 per cent of the total farm value of all crops produced in 1960. The estimates of yields on the cropland in the program averaged about 30 per cent lower than those on all cropland in 1960.[8]

---

[7] J. C. Bottum et al., "Land Retirement and Farm Policy," Res. Bul. 704. Purdue University Agr. Exp. Sta., Sept. 1961, pp. 3–4.

[8] Christensen and Aines, op. cit., p. 26.

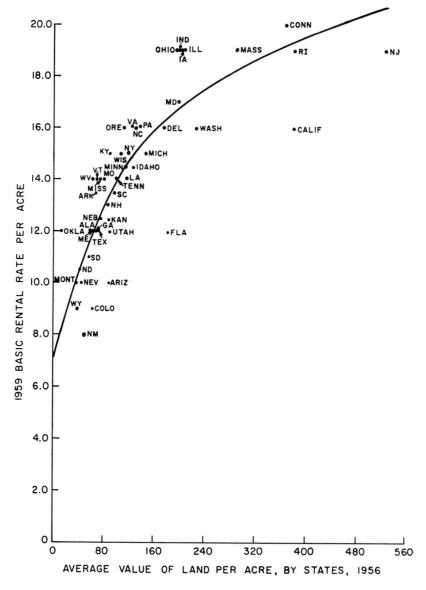

Fig. 3.5. Relation between average value of land per acre by states, 1956, and basic rental rate per acre, 1959.

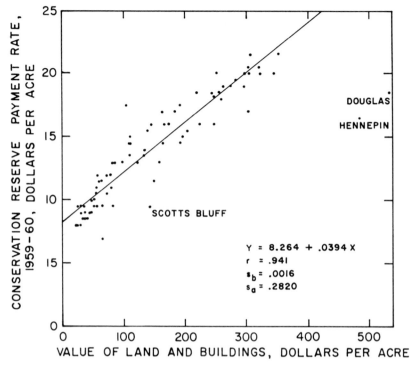

Fig. 3.6. County data from a sample of 80 counties in the Dakotas, Minnesota, Nebraska, and Iowa.

Costs

The "payments approved for rental and conservation measures" (most for seeding to grass) under Conservation Reserve program in 1960 totaled $367 million.

The USDA estimates that the reduction in value of crops produced per dollar of rental payment averaged $2.80 in 1960.[9]

In addition, the government avoided price-support losses on the crops that were not produced. These losses in the 1959 fiscal year averaged $2.70 per bushel for wheat, $1.75 for corn (this is more than the original values per bushel) and for other crops, more than half the amount the government paid for these crops.[10]

---

[9] *Ibid.*, p. 49.
[10] *Ibid.*, p. 27.

TABLE 3.4

RENTAL RATES PER ACRE UNDER THE 1961 FEED GRAINS
AND THE CONSERVATION RESERVE PROGRAMS*

	Range of 1961 Feed Grains Payments at 50 Per Cent Rate		Conservation Reserve 1959 Basic State Rate Per Acre
	(1)	(2)	(3)
Alabama	$12.50 to	$22.70	$12.00
Arizona	7.40 to	38.60	10.00
Arkansas	10.00 to	27.90	13.50
California	24.80 to	56.30	16.00
Colorado	9.20 to	46.10	9.00
Connecticut	40.10 to	47.30	20.00
Delaware	36.70 to	39.80	16.00
Florida	7.00 to	33.70	12.00
Georgia	9.80 to	29.60	12.00
Idaho	23.20 to	51.90	14.50
Illinois	23.10 to	49.70	19.00
Indiana	27.60 to	49.10	19.00
Iowa	24.60 to	43.60	19.00
Kansas	13.90 to	45.50	12.50
Kentucky	20.00 to	40.60	15.00
Lousiana	11.80 to	29.20	14.00
Maryland	27.50 to	45.10	17.00
Massachusetts	27.50 to	46.90	19.00
Michigan	19.60 to	39.00	15.00
Minnesota	15.00 to	40.10	14.50
Mississippi	12.80 to	32.40	14.00
Missouri	23.10 to	42.90	14.00
Montana	7.60 to	49.30	10.00
Nebraska	8.90 to	43.00	12.50
New Jersey	37.90 to	53.90	19.00
New Mexico	10.20 to	36.90	8.00
New York	28.80 to	45.10	15.00
North Carolina	19.80 to	45.90	16.00
North Dakota	8.20 to	19.40	10.50
Ohio	30.30 to	48.30	19.00
Oklahoma	13.20 to	41.00	12.00
Oregon	21.00 to	56.70	16.00
Pennsylvania	34.30 to	47.52	16.00
South Carolina	12.00 to	24.10	13.50
South Dakota	7.70 to	31.60	11.00
Tennessee	17.10 to	43.10	14.00
Texas	8.30 to	60.10†	12.00
Utah	22.50 to	48.50	12.00
Vermont	28.60 to	47.30	14.00
Virginia	18.30 to	42.20	16.00
Washington	29.40 to	57.80	16.00
West Virginia	20.60 to	41.70	14.00
Wisconsin	21.90 to	45.40	15.00
U.S. Average	19.39		14.38
Combined Average	30.93		

* Source: USDA press release, April 14, 1961.
† High rate reflects very limited acreage under irrigation.

THE 1961 AND 1962 FEED GRAINS PROGRAMS

In 1961, the Congress set up an emergency program for feed grains and another for wheat. Under these programs, each corn grower, for example, was offered 50 per cent of the estimated value of the crop per acre if he would keep 20 per cent of the corn acreage on his farm out of production, and 60 per cent for the next 20 per cent up to a total limit of 40 per cent. The level of price support was raised from $1.06 to $1.20, although loans at this rate were available only to participants, and only on the "normal production" on each farm.

The rental rates per acre under the 1961 feed grains program, and under the Conservation Reserve program, are shown in Table 3.4. The United States average rate for the feed grains program, about $31 per acre, was twice as high as the rate for the Conservation Reserve program.

The rental rates for both programs differed from state to state in line with the differences in the productivity of the land. The range of the rental rates for the feed grains program was greater than the range for the Conservation Reserve program. The relation between the two rates, by states, is shown in Figure 3.7. This figure shows that the range of the rates for the feed grains program was about twice as great as the range for the Conservation Reserve program. The feed grains program rates at the low end of the range for each state (in Column 1) ranged from an average of $7 per acre in Florida to over $40 per acre in Connecticut. The rates in Column 2 in some cases were paid for a small number of irrigated acres.

Costs

More than a million farmers signed up in the feed grains program, representing 56 per cent of the base acreages of those crops; 25 million acres were held out of production by participants. Some of the nonparticipants increased their acreage. The net reduction in acres from 1960 to 1961 was 21 million, equal to about 16 per cent. Feed grains production was reduced about 10 per cent. The program cost a little over $800 million.

The emergency programs were extended with small changes in 1962, with similar results to those in 1961.

The 1961 and 1962 feed grains and wheat programs were

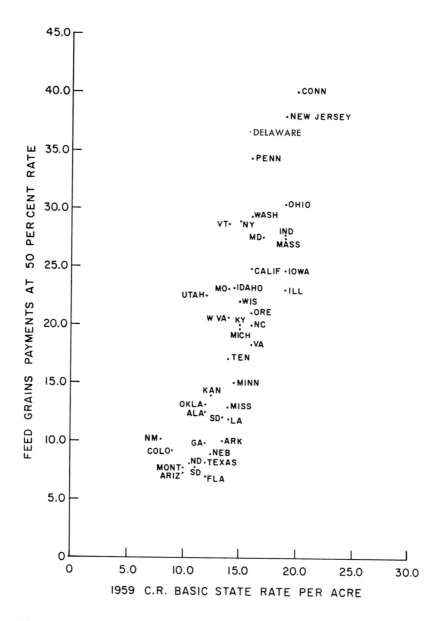

Fig. 3.7. Relation between rental rates for feed grains program and rental rates for Conservation Reserve program. The rates for the feed grains program are based on data in Column 1 of Table 3.4; the data in Column 2 in some cases refer to only a small number of irrigated acres, and therefore are less representative.

effective in reducing production as well as acreage. The 1961 feed grains program reduced feed grains acreage on participant's farms about 25 per cent. The feed grains acreage reduction for the country as a whole was about 13 per cent (nonparticipants increased their acreage). Participants, however, took out their poorest acres and applied more inputs on the acres in crops, and nonparticipants maintained or increased their production, so that the reduction in feed grains production was only about 10 per cent. Stocks of feed grains were reduced also. These things are shown in Figure 3.8.

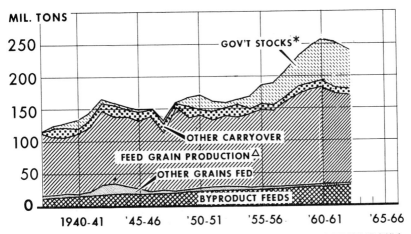

Fig. 3.8. U.S. Government and other feed grains stocks in relation to production, 1937–38 to 1960–62.

The weather in the Corn Belt in 1961 was unusually good for corn. "The 1961 growing season was more nearly optimum for corn than in any (other) year of the study, 1935 to 1961. . . ."[11] This was because of plentiful rains in July and relatively cool August temperatures. If the weather had been about average, feed grains production would have declined more than the actual 10 per cent decline which took place.

---

[11] L. M. Thompson. "An Evaluation of Weather Factors in the Production of Corn." Center for Agricultural and Economic Development Rept. 12T, Iowa State University, Ames, 1962, p. 20.

L. M. Thompson, the author of the study reported above, stated in a later report[12] that the weather in the Corn Belt was above average each year after 1957, and that ". . . had we experienced average weather after 1957 in the Corn Belt, there would have been no surplus corn produced. . . . In other words, *our continued build-up of surplus feed grains since 1957 was associated with a favorable weather cycle.* Just how long this favorable cycle will continue is beyond our present scientific approach to answer. We must continue these studies in order that we can distinguish between the influence of weather and technology. We would make a serious mistake to ignore weather and assign the trend in yields from 1950 to 1960 solely to technology. Our more recent statistical studies show *half this trend to be due to technology and half due to weather.*"

If further research confirms the existence of cycles in the weather, this would cast production controls in a new role. In this role, production controls would supplement storage programs as a means of evening out year-to-year variations in feed grain supplies caused by variations in the weather. In the past, these storage programs have been based on the belief that variations in the weather are random and irregular, and that the average period of variation is short, so that a small crop would follow a big crop within a few years; thus the excess supplies from good years would have to be carried for only a few years before they would be needed to add to a small crop. But if weather comes in cycles, or even in runs of irregular sequences, it might be cheaper to reduce stocks by reducing production for a year or two during a good weather cycle or run—such as that from 1957 to 1962— rather than by continued storage year after year.

Here is a good subject for future research, to determine which method—continued storage, or production controls—would be most effective and cost the least. The study also might show whether there could be developed a new kind of production control, really a Soil Bank in the sense that fertility stored in the soil one year could be withdrawn next year or soon thereafter—if this is possible.

---

[12] L. M. Thompson, "How Weather Has Affected Our Feed Grain Surplus." Reprinted from *Better Farming Methods,* Sept. 1962.

4
Appraisal of the Production-Control Programs

It is instructive to appraise the features of general land re-tirement programs, such as the Conservation Reserve program, in comparison with those of specific commodity programs.

Some of the characteristics of general land retirement programs differ from those of specific commodity programs. For example, acres retired under a general land retirement program cannot be put into another crop, because the acres are completely retired from agricultural production of any kind, except grazing.

In addition, on the 70 per cent of the Conservation Reserve acreage that was retired in the form of whole farms, agricultural production cannot be increased on the rest of the farm, for the whole farm is retired. On the other 30 per cent, however, the situation is the same as under a specific commodity program.

Third, the rental rates in the Soil Bank program were rela-tively high for low-profit farms, so more poor land than good land went into the program; the correlation between land value and percentage participation, with states as units, was -0.5, and it is estimated that the yield per acre on the cropland in the Conservation Reserve averaged about 30 per cent lower than the average for all cropland in 1960.[1] This is not a necessary feature of general land retirement programs; the rental rates could be set more closely in line with profit producing ability, so that good, medium, and poor land alike would go into the program, as in fact it did into the emergency feed grains pro-grams.

---

[1] R. P. Christensen and R. O. Aines, "Economic Effects of Acreage Control Programs in the 1950's." Agr. Econ. Rept. 18, USDA, ERS, 1962, p. 26.

The tendency for poor land to be put into the Conservation Reserve program, and the fact that 70 per cent of this land was in whole farms, caused a drastic reduction in the number of farms and farmers in some low-yield areas. Participation in New Mexico, for example, was 37.8 per cent. This appeared to be in line with long-run goals of the most efficient location and utilization of production resources for the nation as a whole, but it had a severe effect on the community schools, stores, churches, etc., in some of these areas. This was not true of the specific commodity programs, which took a bite out of each participant's farm but did not accept more than 40 per cent of any one farm.

COMPARATIVE COSTS OF THE PROGRAMS

What were the comparative costs of the programs per unit of production reduced?

The costs of land retirement depend not only upon the amount of land that is withdrawn but also upon the accompanying adjustments in the other agricultural inputs. We shall first examine the conditions for Soil Bank participation for the individual farmer and then examine some aggregate aspects of Soil Bank participation.

Conditions for Individual Participation in Land Retirement Programs

For the individual farmer, certain capital and labor inputs are fixed with respect to Soil Bank participation, and others are variable. For example, the depreciation and interest on his machines may be a production cost which cannot be terminated upon entering the Soil Bank, whereas fuel and lubricant costs can be terminated. To make Soil Bank participation more profitable than crop production for the individual farmer, the Soil Bank payment must cover all of his fixed production costs. If the farmer treats all costs as fixed, the government payments must equal the total product on the farm. If the farmer treats land rent as the only fixed cost, the government can eliminate the total product of the farm by paying only for the fraction of the product imputed to land as rent.

The extent to which certain costs are fixed or variable will vary from farm to farm. A farmer who has no off-farm job opportunity may treat his own labor as a fixed cost, whereas a farmer who does have an off-farm job opportunity may treat his own labor as a variable cost. When two farms are similar in other respects and one exhibits lower fixed costs of production than the other, the farmer with the lower fixed costs will find Soil Bank participation profitable at a lower payment rate than will the other farmer.

LAND PRODUCTIVITY AND LAND RETIREMENT

On farms where capital and labor can be most readily transferred out of agriculture, the government eliminates the total product by paying only for the portion of it that is imputed to land as rent. However, rent does not make up the same fraction of total product on all farms. We hypothesize that rent tends to make up a large fraction of total product on the more productive land than on the less productive land. This hypothesis is suggested by the tendency of certain costs, such as seedbed preparation and planting costs, to be approximately the same on soils of differing productivity. If this is the case, a program designed to reduce production at the lower government cost per bushel will tend to take out a higher per cent of the less productive land than of the more productive land. This is illustrated by Figure 4.1 which shows gross product on the horizontal axis and costs on the vertical axis. The line T-T' representing the relationship between total costs and total product is a straight line through the origin under the assumption that economic profit equals zero. Capital and labor costs exceed total product for the submarginal land to the left of point P on the chart but they are less than total product on the more productive land to the right of P. The fraction of total product that is made up by rent is larger for the more productive land on the right side of the diagram than for the less productive land in the vicinity of P. Under the assumption that the government must pay only for the rent earned by land to eliminate total product, production can be reduced at lower cost per bushel on the less productive land in the vicinity of P than on the more productive land further to the right.

Figure 4.2, based on county 1959 census data from a sample of 80 counties in five Midwest states, provides some empirical confirmation of the relationships between costs and productivity hypothesized in Figure 4.1. The region studied included Iowa, Minnesota, Nebraska, North Dakota, and South Dakota.[2] The

---

[2] The data and the methods employed in analyzing them are explained in Appendix A of R. Heifner, "The Conservation Reserve Program as a Means of Controlling Production." Unpublished Ph.D. dissertation, Iowa State University, 1963.

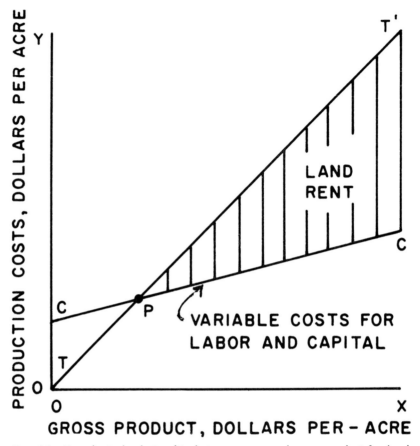

Fig. 4.1. Hypothetical relationship between costs and gross product for land.

cost estimates were constructed from regression analyses of the various individual costs. The figure illustrates the tendency for land rent to be larger in proportion to gross product for the more productive land than for the less productive land in the region.

From the results illustrated in Figure 4.1 some conditional comparisons can be made between the costs for retiring various grades of land. For land with a gross product of $20 per acre the indicated rent constitutes about 15 per cent of gross product. For land with a gross product of $40 per acre the indicated rent makes up approximately 22 per cent of gross product. If production can be controlled by paying only for the rent earned by land, each dollar in payments would eliminate $6.66 worth of production on land with a $20 gross product or $4.54 worth of production on land with a $40 gross product. However, if the pay-

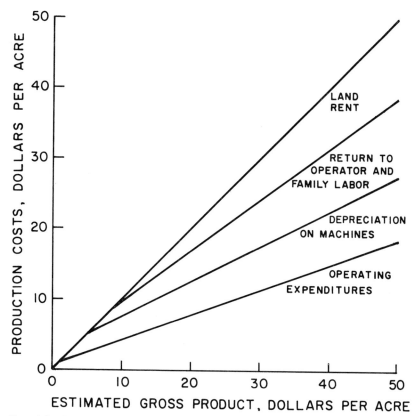

Fig. 4.2. Estimated relationship between costs and gross product, based on empirical data.

ment must cover not only land rent but also part of the capital and labor costs, the production-reduction per dollar of payment is less and there is a decline in the difference in the cost of controlling production on different grades of land. If the government payment must cover machine depreciation and operator and family labor costs in addition to land rent, a dollar of payment would eliminate approximately $1.60 worth of production on all grades of land.

SOME CRITERIA FOR SETTING PAYMENT RATES FOR LAND RETIREMENT

If the object is to reduce production at the lowest possible government cost per bushel of production eliminated, the following condition must be met: The cost of eliminating an additional unit of production on any farm must equal or exceed the cost of eliminating the last unit of production that was eliminated. This requires that the payment offered for a marginal increment of land must be proportional to the production eliminated by retiring this increment of land. If labor and capital are transferred out of agriculture as the land is withdrawn, the payment rate must be proportional to gross product or yield. However, if only the land is removed and the associated capital and labor stay in agriculture, the payment must be proportional to land rent or net product. In reality the situation lies somewhere between these two extremes, i.e., part of the capital and labor are removed and part stay in agriculture. The optimal payment rate is neither exactly proportional to gross product nor exactly proportional to net product but somewhere in between. For a part-farm land retirement program where there is a tendency for the labor and capital to stay on the land, the net product rule is more nearly optimal. For a whole-farm program that effectively removed labor and capital, the gross product rule is more appropriate. This rule would prescribe higher rates for the less productive land and lower rates for the more productive land than would the net product rule. It would result in higher levels of participation in the less productive areas than in the more productive areas.

An alternative goal for land retirement might be to maximize the transfer of capital and labor out of agriculture. This would imply setting payment rates proportional to the value of capital and labor removed, i.e., paying the same price for a dollar's worth of capital and labor removed on each farm. For a part-farm program which has little effect on capital and labor transfer, this goal is not relevant. For a whole-farm program which is effective in transferring capital and labor, this goal implies setting payment rates proportional to capital and labor costs on the various grades of land. In general, this rule prescribes higher rates for the low-producing land and lower rates for the high-producing land than would the gross product rule.

EVENTUAL NET COST OF THE 1961 EMERGENCY FEED GRAINS PROGRAM

The USDA paid out $782 million in rental payments to farmers and incurred administrative costs of $42 million — a total of $824 million—for the 1961 program.

For this outlay, the USDA purchased a reduction in feed grains production estimated at 939 million bushels of corn equivalent. This reduction was about 1.14 bushels per dollar of program cost. With corn at $1 per bushel, this would mean that the program reduced production worth $1.14 per dollar of program cost. This is less than half as high as the estimate of $2.80 for the Conservation Reserve program in 1961 given above.

But this is not the final cost. Much of this initial cost will be offset in future years, because the USDA will incur lower storage costs since it will not have to store the feed grains that were not produced under the program. An additional reduction in cost will result because the USDA will not incur any loss from deterioration of the grain in storage.

The extent of this reduction is indicated in a recent report by the Secretary of Agriculture:[3]

"Grain surpluses are being reduced. CCC holdings of wheat and feed grains are over one billion bushels less than the peak quantities held in 1961 before the new programs were effective. It means the 1964 budget for carrying charges on these grains will be $264 million less than was spent in fiscal 1961—or $770,000 per day—and $813 million less than our costs would have been this year had we done nothing to change the pre-1961 programs."

The final costs of the feed grains program as compared with the cost of a "no controls" program, therefore, will depend on the eventual recovery value of grain which would have been acquired in CCC inventory. No one can say in any exact sense what this would have been. The CCC realized an average of $.995 per bushel for 498.8 million bushels of corn sold to meet 1961 program certificate demands through January 26, 1962. But through experience in earlier years, the realization was considerably lower—only $.53 per bushel. The net cost of the program depends on what the recovery value of the corn and other feed grains will be in the future, and this unknown.

The same sort of thing is true of the cost of the Conservation Reserve program, although the question is more complicated there on account of the larger number of commodities concerned.[4] It is almost impossible, therefore, to make an accurate

---

[3] Orville L. Freeman, speaking at the Farm Forum, Raddison Hotel, Minneapolis, March 4, 1963.

[4] The comparative costs of the Conservation Reserve and 1961 feed grains programs are compared in greater detail in F. A. Kutish and J. W. Uhrig, *Congressional Record*, March, 1962.

TABLE 4.1

Value of Farm Real Estate Per Acre, United States, 1947–62[a] (1947–49 = 100)[*]

Year	Index Numbers
1947	94
1948	101
1949	105
1950	103
1951	119
1952	132
1953	132
1954	128
1955	133
1956	138
1957	147
1958	156
1959	168
1960	173
1961	177
1962	183

[*] Source: USDA, "Farm Real Estate Market Developments." June 1962, p. 26.
[a] Farm land and buildings as of March 1.

and final comparison of the eventual costs of the two programs. The best we can do here is to stay with the estimate given above that the *immediate* costs of the Conservation Reserve program were less than half as high as the costs of the emergency feed grains programs, per dollar's worth of production reduced; this is in line with expectations based on theoretical considerations, and also in line with long-run national goals of efficiency in production.

EFFECTS ON INCOME AND LAND VALUES

Whatever the eventual costs of the acreage-allotment, Conservation Reserve, and emergency feed grains and wheat programs turn out to be, one thing appears evident: Since World War II when these programs have been in effect, farm land values have nearly doubled, but average farm income per farm has hardly increased at all.

From 1960 to 1962, United States total farm net income after expenses increased $1.2 billion. Of this amount, $200 million reflected higher income from farm operations. The remaining $1 billion was larger USDA payments, chiefly under the feed grains program.

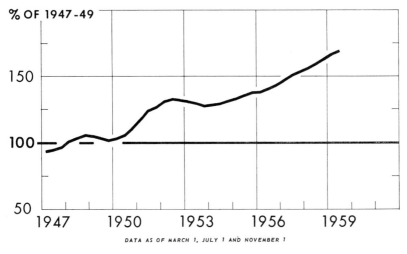

Fig. 4.3. Value per acre of farm real estate—land and buildings.

Table 4.1 and Figure 4.3 show the United States average value of farm land and buildings by years since 1947. It shows that the value has been rising rapidly, until by April 1962 it was 83 per cent higher than it was in 1947–49.

The rise in farm value exceeds the rise in per capita farm income that occurred over the same period. Indeed, up to 1959, per capita farm income from farm sources rose hardly at all. Almost all of the rise in income that did take place came after 1959.

Why Did Land Values Rise?

Land values are determined by many factors—the desire for protection against inflation, for prestige, for security, etc.—but the chief factor usually is the return that the buyer expects to get from the land.

These returns have been affected by the application of new technology and the operation of the price-support, acreage allotment, and Soil Bank programs.

1. The effects of the application of new technology depend on the elasticities of supply and demand and the changes that take place in the location of the supply and demand curves.

The elasticity of the demand for food in the United States is estimated at about −0.2. The improvements in technology moved the supply curve to the right. Under these conditions, gross returns to agriculture would decline.

Gross returns to the individual farm firm, however, would not necessarily decline. If, in the extreme case, only one farmer adopted the new technology, the effect on total production would be negligible, and so would the effect on prices. The demand for any one farmer's product is virtually infinitely elastic. So the gross returns to his farm firm would increase *pari passu* with the increase in its production.

The net returns would increase also, because the marginal cost of the new technology would have been less than the marginal returns; otherwise the new technology would not have been adopted in the first place.

The marginal cost of the new technology in some cases would be close to zero (as in the case of hybrid seed corn, which costs only a very small percentage of the marginal return it brings) or negative (as in the case of such things as diesel tractors where the reduction in total fuel cost is greater than the higher initial and upkeep costs, otherwise the diesel tractor would not be purchased). In all these cases, net returns would increase more than gross returns if only one farmer adopted the new technology.

Obviously, of course, this is only the limiting case at one end of the range of realistic possibilities. The limiting case at the other end of the range is the situation in which all farmers adopt the new technology simultaneously.

This second extreme is used in many discussions of farm policy. It is about as unrealistic as the other extreme, for a great many farmers are limited in their ability to adopt new technology by the topography of their farms, the extent of their education, their managerial ability, and so on.

The actual situation lies somewhere between the two extremes.

Farmers who "get thar fustest with the mostest" with new technology, therefore, face a demand curve which has an elasticity somewhere between infinity and −0.2. The net returns to those with an elasticity in excess of −1.0 could increase, while those below −1.0 would decrease, unless their costs declined more rapidly than their gross returns, which is unlikely.

With the passage of a few years of time, the number of farmers can decline, as in fact it did during the 1950's. This decline in the number of farmers would tend to increase net income per farm, even if total net income for agriculture as a whole were declining, if the decline in the number of families were more rapid than the decline in total net income.

2. The effects of some of the farm programs on net income per farm have been estimated empirically.

Acreage allotments rationed the right to plant acres to certain crops, and the value of these allotments was capitalized into land values. One study estimated that in Pittsylvania County, Virginia, an acre of tobacco allotment accounted for $962 of the selling price of a farm in 1954 and $1,673 of the selling price in 1957.[5] The value of an acre of cropland without the allotment was $22.75. The average sale price of the 203 farms in the sample was $10,242, and an estimated $5,650 (55 per cent of the total value) was paid for the right to grow tobacco on a specified number of the purchased acres. For the $5,650, the purchaser received nothing tangible, but only a franchise to grow tobacco. Similar evidence was found in Greene, Wilson, and Pitt counties, North Carolina.

A study of land values in Kansas yielded similar information on the value of wheat allotments. According to a limited study in two areas in Kansas, the right to grow wheat added substantial value to wheat land. The value added was not of the order of magnitude indicated for tobacco land but was a substantial percentage of the total value per acre.

3. The development of new technology after World War II began to make it profitable for farmers to handle larger farms than before.

The pressure to enlarge their farms may have led some farmers to pay more for an extra 40 or 80 acres than they could for a whole farm; in technical terms, the marginal return for additional acres was higher than the average return for the farm as

---

[5] F. H. Maier, J. L. Hedrick, and W. L. Gibson, "The Sale Value of Flue-cured Tobacco Allotments." Va. Agr. Exp. Sta. Tech. Bul. 148, April 1960, p. 27.

a whole. In the year ending in March 1960, 45 per cent of all sales of farms or tracts of land were for adding to existing farms. The figure in 1950 was only 21 per cent.[6]

4. After World War II, the prices of farm products were high. But farmers could remember the drastic price decline that took place soon after World War I.

At first, farmers were not sure that price supports would be continued at high levels. Land prices at first rose much less, and much slower, than farm incomes.[7] But after the Korean conflict, farmers began to feel more certain that supports would be continued. This feeling of confidence persisted, until the index of land prices reached about the same level as the index of farm income.

APPROPRIATIONS FOR LAND RECLAMATION
PROJECTS TO INCREASE AGRICULTURAL PRODUCTION

At the same time that the one hand of government is trying desperately to reduce agricultural production, the other hand continues to pour forth a stream of irrigation and other forms of land reclamation projects, thus increasing agricultural production.

The size of the Bureau of Reclamation system of irrigation projects is greater than many people realize. In 1959, these projects included nearly 7 million acres of irrigated land, which produced a gross crop value of more than $1.1 billion.[8]

---

[6] Out of a total of 11 regions surveyed early in 1960, the price of land sold for farm enlargement, compared to all land sold, was higher in 5 regions, lower in 5 others, and the same in one region. Source: USDA, ARS, *Current Developments in the Farm Real Estate Market,* Oct. 1960, p. 9.

[7] "We would suspect . . . that the benefits of these programs have had their greatest impact in improving agricultural welfare in those periods in which the uncertainty existing about their continuity was sufficient to preclude them from being capitalized into land values." Walter E. Chryst and John F. Timmons, "The Economic Role of Land Resource Institutions in Agricultural Adjustment," Chap. 17 in *Dynamics of Land Use.* (Center for Agricultural and Economic Development, sponsors), Iowa State Univ. Press, Ames, 1961, p. 263.

[8] *Statistical Abstract of the United States, 1961,* p. 607. Data for 1961 are given, by states, in *Agricultural Conservation Program, Summary by States, 1961.* USDA, 1962.

This value of $1.1 billion is more than 5 per cent of the total value of all crops produced in the United States ($19.6 billion in 1960).[9] This percentage is almost as great as the estimated annual surplus production in recent years (6 to 8 per cent).[10] And $1.1 billion is a little more than the estimated reduction in agricultural production that was achieved by the Conservation Reserve program at its peak in 1960.[11]

The Bureau of Reclamation also handles extensive farm drainage projects. The farm drainage data are put up differently from the irrigation data; no estimates of gross crop value are made for the areas drained. The cost of these drainage operations from 1950 to 1959 totaled $186 million.[12]

These reclamation projects are defended because they add to the productivity of the nation. But in so doing, they create surpluses which lead to programs to *reduce* production in the established agricultural areas, at a cost of billions of dollars. Taxpayers pay twice—once, to finance the reclamation projects to increase production, and again, to finance the production-control programs to reduce production. It may be impartial to subsidize both teams in a football game, but it would be a lot more efficient and less costly to finance only one man to carry the ball unopposed to whatever destination the nation desires, than to have two teams working at cross purposes.

A more rational defense is that many of the irrigation projects are merely by-products of power and flood-control projects which benefit the nation as a whole.

Another argument in defense of these projects is that they increase the production of farm products that are not in surplus—vegetables, fruits, etc.—rather than feed grains or wheat. This argument is only partly true; much of the increase in cotton production in recent years comes from new irrigated areas in the Southwest, particularly California. Cotton production in

[9] *Agricultural Statistics, 1961*, USDA, p. 451.

[10] USDA, "Food and Agriculture, A Program for the 1960's." March 1962, p. V.

[11] "Total value of normal crop production at prevailing farm prices on all land in the (Conservation Reserve) program was equivalent to 4.5 per cent of the total value of all crops produced in 1960. Yield estimates for cropland in the Conservation Reserve averaged about 30 per cent lower than those realized on all cropland in 1960." (Christensen and Aines, *op. cit.*, p. 26.

The total value of all crops in 1960 was $19,586 million (*Agricultural Statistics, 1960.* USDA, p. 454); 4.5 per cent of that figure is nearly one billion dollars.

[12] *Statistical Abstract of the United States, 1961.* USDA, p. 607.

California rose from an average of 1,488,000 bales in 1949–58 to 1,939,000 in 1960—an increase of 451,000 bales.[13] This increase in production resulted almost entirely from an increase in yield per acre; acreage harvested increased only 1 per cent.

Further research is needed to determine the accuracy of another view. This view is that crop production under irrigation is more efficient than existing marginal production on dry land. On this basis, expenditures on irrigation could be classed along with expenditures on research, vocational education, fertilizer, hybrid seed corn, etc.; all of these increase production, but enable farmers to produce more efficiently than before. The nation as a whole benefits from this more efficient production.

Whether the benefits are greater or less than the cost is a complicated question for irrigation experts to answer; the author does not feel competent to deal with it. The answer probably differs from project to project in any case. Pending more research on the subject, this section remains inconclusive; but at least it indicates that the question whether irrigation projects are justifiable is not likely to be answered with a simple yes or no.

ACP SUBSIDIES

Another obvious opportunity to reduce inputs in agriculture would be to reduce the subsidies under the Agricultural Conservation Program.

This program subsidizes a number of conservation practices, most of which in the long run result in an increase in agricultural production.

These subsidies run into large figures. The annual totals for the United States as a whole since 1944 are shown in Table 4.2. They have been running at more than $200 million in recent years. The average payment per payee in 1959 was $204. The relative importance of the different practices subsidized is shown in Table 4.3.

PRODUCTION CONTROLS ONLY A PALLIATIVE

We saw in the preceding chapter that the agricultural price-support programs have not been successful and indeed are not appropriate programs for solving the farm problem conceived as

---

[13] *Agricultural Statistics, 1961.* USDA, p. 62.

TABLE 4.2

AGRICULTURAL CONSERVATION PROGRAM: ASSISTANCE TO FARM-
ERS FOR CARRYING OUT CONSERVATION PRACTICES, UNITED
STATES, BY PROGRAM YEARS, 1944–60*

(Includes assistance under the Naval Stores Conservation Program. Administrative expenses not included. Assistance for
supplemental—emergency—practices included since 1951.)

Program Year	Assistance
	(*1,000 dollars*)
1944	293,867
1945	231,068
1946	267,555
1947	244,748
1948	124,503
1949	223,855
1950	252,006
1951	246,100
1952	226,650
1953	190,496
1954	146,946
1955	192,602
1956	222,032
1957	216,154
1958	219,896
1959	210,296
1960	213,488
1961[a]	238,500

* Source: Agricultural Stabilization and Conservation Service. Data from *Agricultural Statistics, 1962*, p. 640.
[a] Preliminary.

a price problem. Are the production-control programs better on
these scores?

Let us look at the problem analytically, in terms of economic
principles.

Prices are the result of supply and demand. They can be an
evidence or symptom of a disease of supply or demand or both.
When prices are deemed unsatisfactory ("a problem") the
reasons for this are the supply or the demand or both. A *price* program set up to implement the price policy deals with the *results*
or effects of supply or demand, not with the supply or demand
itself. The price program may temporarily alleviate the
symptoms, but it makes the causative supply or demand disease
worse.

This disease is not cured even by production-control programs
to back up the price-support programs. These production-control
programs may seem to be getting at the disease better than price-
support programs, because they deal with production rather than

TABLE 4.3

AGRICULTURAL CONSERVATION PROGRAM: SELECTED CONSERVATION MEASURE PERFORMED, BY PROGRAM YEARS, UNITED STATES AND TERRITORIES, 1955, 1960, AND 1936–60 TOTAL*

Practice	Unit	1955	1960	Total 1936–60[d]
Construction of dams, pits, or ponds (storage type)	Number	69,716	51,946	1,655,013
Construction of nonstorage-type dams, checks and drops	Number	8,102	6,562	3,034,327
Construction of standard terraces	1,000 acres	744	703	25,442
Construction of standard terraces	1,000 miles	37	34	1,380
Establishment of sod waterways[a]	Million sq. ft.	1,553	1,861	29,685
Construction of diversion and spreader terraces	Miles	5,131	4,040	125,593
Field stripcropping[a]	1,000 acres	939	288	104,794
Contour stripcropping[a]	1,000 acres	223	168	5,794
Emergency tillage operations to control erosion on cropland[a]	1,000 acres	12,975	1,246	138,181
Crop residue management[a]	1,000 acres	6,373	7,135	153,640
Regular subsoiling	1,000 acres	153	88	11,824
Tillage operations on range or pasture land[a]	1,000 acres	336	121	3,984
Protection of outlets, inlets and water channels	Number	3,889	10,920	50,286
Protection of stream banks or shores	Projects	1,885	2,266	18,100
Leveling irrigable land to control erosion and conserve water	1,000 acres	375	317	7,158
Lining irrigation ditches	1,000 rods	242	364	2,586
Drainage to permit a system of conservation farming	1,000 acres	1,362	1,658	40,149
Construction of wells for livestock water as a means of protecting established vegetative cover	Number	8,054	9,976	182,488

TABLE 4.3 (continued)

AGRICULTURAL CONSERVATION PROGRAM: SELECTED CONSERVATION MEASURE PERFORMED, BY PROGRAM YEARS, UNITED STATES AND TERRITORIES, 1955, 1960, AND 1936–60 TOTAL*

Practice	Unit	1955	1960	Total 1936–60[d]
Developing springs or seeps for livestock water as a means of protecting established vegetative cover	Number	2,321	3,056	72,607
Installing pipelines for livestock water to improve grassland management	1,000 lin. ft.	2,131	3,608	40,385
Deferred grazing to permit natural seeding to increase vegetative cover[a]	1,000 acres	2,742	3,378	218,155
Control of competitive shrubs on range or pasture land	1,000 acres	1,661	1,921	42,168
Constructing fireguards to protect established cover on grazing land	1,000 lin. ft.	6,856	4,267	984,972
Constructing stock trails through natural barriers to improve grassland management	1,000 lin. ft.	1,341	2,041	36,459
Establishment of permanent vegetative cover[a]	1,000 acres	1,221	2,586	92,018
Establishment of additional acreages of vegetative cover in crop rotations[ab]	1,000 acres	2,052	1,160	247,562
Establishment of annual cover and green manure crops[a]	1,000 acres	7,666	5,982	421,906
Improvement of established vegetative cover for soil protection	1,000 acres	2,165	1,750	13,013
Application of liming materials to permit use of conserving crops[ae]	1,000 tons	15,125	16,249	422,804
Planting trees and shrubs	1,000 acres	150	358	2,991
Improvement of a stand of forest trees for erosion control, watershed protection, or forestry purposes	1,000 acres	133	256	2,342

* Source: USDA, *Agricultural Statistics, 1962*, p. 647.
[a] Includes supplemental (emergency) practices.
[b] Starting in 1950, a portion of the acreage represents an increase over the normal farm acreage.
[c] Standard ground limestone equivalent.
[d] Rounded totals of unrounded data.

with prices. But even they do not deal with supply (the whole curve); they deal only with production (a point on the supply curve) leaving the position of the supply curve unaffected. The oversupply problem is only pushed back, not solved. And the program works against itself; the more it pushes production back and raises prices, so that production becomes more profitable, the more it has to pay farmers not to produce.

AGRICULTURAL PROGRAMS AND THE NATIONAL ECONOMY

The agricultural programs stack up still less well when they are appraised for their consistency with the goals of the nation as a whole.

An appraisal on this basis has been rendered by a leading farm economist, Theodore W. Schultz,[14] in these terms:

". . . what about agriculture? In it the national interest now rides predominately on transfer payments. For these one cannot use the efficiency standard. What then is the appropriate standard? How can one test how well or how badly these transfer payments serve the national interest?

"There are a lot of transfer payments in our society. They are very large. They are not unique to agriculture. We have them in unemployment payments; we have them in social security arrangements. There is a good deal of this in federal appropriations of one sort or another, schooling, health, urban slum rehabilitation. And, of course, the appropriations for agriculture are exceedingly large.

"Let me anticipate the conclusion at which I arrive so you can be on your guard. It can be put as follows:

"1. U.S. agricultural programs are becoming less and less concerned about the efficiency of the economy and the contributions that the agricultural sectors can make to national economic growth.

"2. U.S. agricultural programs are increasingly large income transfer devices; i.e., they are ways of transferring income from the rest of the economy into agriculture.

---

[14] Theodore W. Schultz, "National Security, Economic Growth, Individual Freedom and Agricultural Policy." In *Our Rural Problems in Their National Setting*, Center for Agricultural and Economic Development Rept. 16, Ames, Iowa, Dec., 1962, pp. 2, 3.

"3. But these public transfer payments do not satisfy even the most elementary welfare standards that we applied to other public transfer payments.

"4. The transfer payments for agriculture benefit mainly and ever more largely the owners of farm land.

"5. As income transfers they have a strong regressive effect upon the personal distribution of income among farm families; i.e., those farm families who are already rich and who enjoy high personal incomes by U.S. standards receive the most and more in proportion to the high income they already enjoy than farm families who are really poor. The lowest one-fourth of the farm families in personal income is virtually excluded from any of the income transfers going presently into agriculture."

More recent appraisals made by several other leading economists reach similar conclusions; these are given in "Our Stake in Rural Agriculture, Rural Poverty, and World Trade," CAED Report Number 22, Iowa State University, Center for Agriculture and Economic Development, 1965.

AGRICULTURAL PROGRAMS ARE NOT DIRECTED AT THE BASIC PROBLEM

There is a still more fundamental point. Production-control programs deal only with the production of farm products. Evidence is accumulating that this is really not the basic problem. It is becoming clear that the chief problem is not an excessive supply of farm products; it is an excessive supply of the factors of production, principally farm labor and management.

This evidence is somewhat complicated; it will be presented in the next chapter.

5

Is the Farm Problem an Income Problem?

We have seen that the agricultural price-support, production-control, and marketing-quota programs did not have the desired effects on the prices of farm products. These prices declined below parity in 1952, and continued to decline thereafter until they reached 80 per cent of parity in 1959. They remained at or below 81 per cent of parity thereafter; in June 1963 they stood at 77 per cent.

But this does not mean that farmers now are 23 per cent worse off than they were in 1910–14 (the base period for parity prices indexes). The prices of farm *products*—even relative prices—are only a very inaccurate measure of the economic status of *farmers*. They leave out of account the rapid changes which have been taking place in quantities of goods and services being sold and purchased at these prices.

The economic status of farmers can be more accurately measured by farm income than by prices per unit of product sold and purchased. We need to look more closely at farm income. Perhaps the agricultural price and production programs have been so largely ineffective because the farm problem is not a price or production problem in the first place. Perhaps it is a farm income problem instead. If it is, the farm income data should measure the nature and severity of the problem. They may also suggest more appropriate programs for dealing with the problem.

IS THERE A FARM INCOME PROBLEM?

First, then: Is the farm problem a farm income problem?

Table 5.1 shows that total personal income of the farm population in the United States, from all sources, has been approxi-

TABLE 5.1

TOTAL PERSONAL INCOME, PERSONAL INCOME OF THE FARM AND NONFARM POPULATION,
AND POPULATION ESTIMATES BY RESIDENCE, 1934, 1940, AND 1950–62*

Year	Total Personal Income[a]	Personal Income of Farm Population, All Sources	Farm as Percentage of Total Personal Income	Population[b]		Farm as percentage of total
				Total	Farm	
	($ millions)	($ millions)	(per cent)	(thousands)	(thousands)	(per cent)
1934........	53,575	5,372	10.0	126,374	32,305	25.6
1940........	78,680	7,632	9.7	132,122	30,547	23.1
1950........	228,468	20,376	8.9	151,683	23,048	15.2
1951........	256,692	22,840	8.9	154,360	21,890	14.2
1952........	273,071	22,267	8.2	157,028	21,748	13.8
1953........	288,259	20,036	7.0	159,636	19,874	12.4
1954........	289,825	19,001	6.6	162,417	19,019	11.7
1955........	310,196	18,314	5.9	165,270	19,078	11.5
1956........	332,943	18,582	5.6	168,176	18,712	11.1
1957........	351,423	18,829	5.4	171,198	17,656	10.3
1958........	360,259	20,507	5.7	174,054	17,128	9.8
1959........	383,936	18,976	4.9	177,080	16,592	9.4
1960........	399,199	19,578	4.9	179,900	15,620	8.7
1961........	415,202	20,084	4.8	182,938	14,788	8.1
1962........	439,823	20,535	4.7	185,764	14,300	7.7

* Source: "Farm Income Situation," USDA, ERS, FIS–191, July 1963, p. 37.
[a] Department of Commerce series, excluding Alaska and Hawaii.
[b] Farm population as of April 1 and total population as of July 1 are taken as the closest readily available approximations of their respective annual averages. Estimates exclude Alaska and Hawaii.

mately constant since World War II at about $20 billion per year. Since total United States personal income has been rising rapidly over the past 12 years, from $228 billion in 1950 to $440 billion in 1962, total agricultural income has been declining as a share of total income for the nation as a whole. From 1934 to 1948, agriculture's share was 10 or 11 per cent. After 1948, it began a rapid decline. By 1962, it was down to only 4.7 per cent—less than half as high as it was before the 1950's.

But this is not the farm problem; this decline in "agriculture's share" of total national income is not the thing that concerns farmers. Most farmers recognize that no industry has any fixed share of total national income which it can continue to demand as its own. They know that in a developing and progressive economy, the percentage of the total income that has to be spent

TABLE 5.2

Per Capita Personal Income of Farm and Nonfarm Population, 1934, 1940,
AND 1950–62*

(The averages in this table are derived by dividing appropriate U.S. totals appearing
in Table 5.1 by the population estimates in Table 5.1.)

Year	Of Farm Population			Of Nonfarm Population From All Sources	Per Capita Income All Sources, Farm as Percentage of Nonfarm	Of Total Population From All Sources
	From farm sources[a]	From nonfarm sources[b]	From all sources			
	(dollars)	(dollars)	(dollars)	(dollars)	(per cent)	(dollars)
1934............	99	97	166	512	32.4	424
1940............	161	89	250	699	35.8	596
1950............	622	262	884	1,618	54.6	1,506
1951............	754	289	1,043	1,765	59.1	1,663
1952............	723	301	1,024	1,854	55.2	1,739
1953............	693	315	1,008	1,919	52.5	1,806
1954............	691	308	999	1,889	52.9	1,784
1955............	638	322	960	1,997	48.1	1,877
1956............	642	351	993	2,103	47.2	1,980
1957............	690	376	1,066	2,166	49.2	2,053
1958............	805	392	1,197	2,165	55.3	2,070
1959............	713	431	1,144	2,276	50.3	2,168
1960............	790	464	1,254	2,311	54.3	2,218
1961............	882	476	1,373	2,350	57.8	2,270
1962............	940	496	1,436	2,445	58.7	2,368

* Source: "Farm Income Situation," USDA, ERS, FIS–191, July 1963, p. 39.

[a] Includes returns from farming operations to resident farm operators for their capital, labor, and management, after deduction of farm production expenses (there is no allowance in the item farm production expenses for a return on investment of farm capital). Also includes farm wages and other labor income received by hired farm workers living on farms.

[b] Includes all income received by farm residents from nonfarm sources such as wages and salaries from nonfarm employment, nonfarm business and professional income, rents from nonfarm real estate, dividends, interest, royalties, unemployment compensation, and social security payments.

for food and clothing can be expected to decline. This is a natural concomitant of a rising standard of living. Consumers can only spend a higher share of their income for automobiles, housing, furniture, etc., if they can spend a smaller share of it for food.

The thing that does concern farmers is farm income *per capita* or *per worker* or *per farm operator*—just as labor is chiefly concerned, not with total wages in the United States, but with wage income per worker.

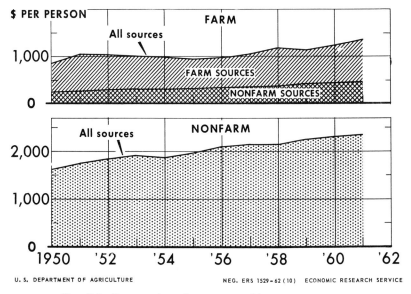

U. S. DEPARTMENT OF AGRICULTURE   NEG. ERS 1529-62 (10)   ECONOMIC RESEARCH SERVICE

Fig. 5.1. Farm and nonfarm personal income per person.

United States Average Farm Income Per Person

The third column of Table 5.2 shows the per capita personal income of the farm population from all sources annually since 1934. Figure 5.1 shows it since 1950. This measure of average farm income is obtained by dividing the United States total realized net farm income from all sources by the total number of persons on farms—men, women, and children—and this is designated farm income *per person* on farms.

This farm income consists of three elements: (1) net cash farm income (cash receipts and government payments, minus production expenses), (2) off-farm income, and (3) nonmoney income, income from food produced and consumed on the farm, and housing provided by the farm.

During the past few years, this personal farm income has been running at about $1,400 per person on farms. Note that this figure includes the income from nonfarm sources as well as from farming. The chart and table show that the farm income from nonfarm sources is more than half as great as the farm income from farm sources. The table also shows that *nonfarm* income per person has run at about $2,400 per person—nearly twice as high as farm income.

These income data tell a different story from the price data given in Figure 1.1 and Table 1.1 in the first chapter of this book. These *income data* show that farm income per person rose slowly after 1950, whereas Figure 1.1 and Table 1.1 show that the *parity price ratio* declined steadily after 1950 about 20 per cent.

The income data differ from the price data in another respect. The price data show the parity ratio at over 100 during the 1940's, but the income data appear to show that most of the time, *farm income runs only about half as high as nonfarm income.* This statement is the one that is most widely quoted when comparisons of farm and nonfarm income are made.[1] The income data appear to show further that per capita farm income from farm sources has risen 45 per cent since 1950, the same percentage as nonfarm income has risen. Per capita farm income from all sources rose 55 per cent over the same period.

These per capita farm income data show that the farm income from all sources is about 50 per cent higher than the farm income from farm sources only. Many farmers have part-time jobs in town which add a substantial amount to their farm income from farm sources.

PER CAPITA FARM INCOMES DIFFER BY REGIONS

Considerable differences exist among per capita farm incomes by regions. Table 5.3 shows that per capita farm income in the Pacific region is more than three times as high as in the East South Central region. It is also higher than the per capita

---

[1] See for example the following three statements:

a. "Average per capita income of farm people is low—$965 compared with $2,216 for nonfarm people in 1959." ("Food and Agriculture, a Program for the 1960's." USDA, 1962, p. 49.)

b. "The income of farm people last year was only 58.6 percent of the per capita income of nonfarm people, even tho farm income rose sharply. Per capita farm income has ranged from 32.4 percent (in 1934) to 63 percent (in 1948) of nonfarm income. Why are farmers paid only half as much on the average as other workers?" (*Wallace's Farmer*, Aug. 18, 1962, p. 13.)

c. In testimony before the House Agriculture Committee on February 7, 1962, Secretary of Agriculture Orville L. Freeman declared that "farm income is too low." He cited these figures: "Farm per capita income averages $986 as compared with a nonfarm average of $2,282; and hourly returns for all labor on the farm, including that of the owner-operator, average 85 cents, as compared with a minimum wage standard of $1.25 and an average of $2.19 in industry."

TABLE 5.3

REGIONAL DISTRIBUTION OF FARM-NONFARM INCOME DIFFERENCES, 1955*

Region	Income Per Capita			Population of Operator Households	Total "Gap" (Col. 3 × Col. 4)
	Nonfarm[a]	Farm[b]	Difference		
	(dollars)	(dollars)	(dollars)	(thousands)	($ millions)
Northeast...............	2,175	1,218	957	1,420	1,359
East North Central.......	2,182	1,082	1,100	3,003	3,303
West North Central.......	1,861	957	904	3,301	2,984
South Atlantic...........	1,521	879	642	3,533	2,268
East South Central........	1,366	751	615	3,105	1,910
West South Central.......	1,577	1,121	456	2,318	1,057
Mountain...............	1,726	1,353	373	725	271
Pacific.................	2,215	2,575	−360	840	−302
United States..........	.....	.....	704[c]	18,245	12,850

* Source: R. H. Masucci, "Regional Differences in Per Capita Farm and Nonfarm Income," *Agr. Econ. Res.*, Vol. 12, Jan. 1960, p. 2.

[a] Estimates of nonfarm income per capita consist of estimated total personal income of the entire population, both farm and nonfarm, as shown in the "Survey of Current Business," Aug. 1958, U.S. Dept. Commerce, less estimated farm-operator family income, divided by the Bureau of the Census estimate of total population July 1, 1955 (excluding armed forces overseas) less estimated population in farm-operator households.

[b] Per capita income of farm-operator households consists of (1) the net income of farm operators from farming, as reported in the "Farm Income Situation," FIS-175, Sept. 1959, plus (2) the off-farm income of farm-operator families, based on data reported in the "Survey of Farmers' Expenditures, 1955," Dec. 1956, USDA, and U.S. Dept. Commerce, divided by the estimated population of farm-operators' households, as reported in the "Survey of Farmers' Expenditures, 1955."

[c] Computed by dividing U.S. total gap by total population of farm-operator households.

nonfarm income in the Pacific region. The significance of these differences is explored in the next chapter.

NET FARM INCOME PER FARM

Another farm income series compiled by the USDA shows net farm income *per farm*. This series differs substantially from the series above which shows *per capita* personal income of farmers.

This operators' realized net farm income *per farm* series is shown in Table 5.4 and Figure 5.2. The dollar figures naturally run about 4 times as large as the farm income *per capita* figures, since they refer to the farm rather than to the individuals on the farm (in most cases, the members of a family).

In other respects, the two series are more nearly similar. They move up and down from year to year in a similar manner.

TABLE 5.4

NUMBER OF FARMS AND AVERAGE FARM INCOME PER FARM, AVERAGE 1910–14,
1920, 1930, AND 1940, AND ANNUAL 1950–62*

Year	Number of Farms	Realized Gross Income Per Farm	Production Expenses Per Farm	Operators' Realized Net Income Per Farm
	(1,000)	(dollars)	(dollars)	(dollars)
1910–14............	6,429	1,181	589	592
1920..............	6,518	2,440	1,355	1,085
1930..............	6,546	1,746	1,055	691
1940..............	6,350	1,738	1,063	675
1950..............	5,648	5,751	3,417	2,334
1951..............	5,428	6,876	4,083	2,793
1952..............	5,198	7,122	4,348	2,774
1953..............	4,984	7,076	4,287	2,789
1954..............	4,798	7,058	4,515	2,543
1955..............	4,654	7,162	4,697	2,465
1956..............	4,514	7,671	5,005	2,666
1957..............	4,372	7,866	5,346	2,520
1958..............	4,233	8,955	5,970	2,985
1959..............	4,097	9,147	6,394	2,753
1960..............	3,949	9,606	6,645	2,961
1961..............	3,811	10,378	7,109	3,269
1962..............	3,688	11,061	7,047	3,414

* Source: "Farm Income Situation," USDA, ERS, FIS–191, July 1963, p. 42.

The farm income per farm data, like the per capita farm income from farm sources, include the return on the farmer's own investment in his farm—equipment, machinery, etc.—plus land and buildings in the case of owner-operators. Interest which the farmer pays on other peoples' funds invested in his farm is a cost which is deducted from his gross income, along with other costs, to yield his net income; but imputed interest on his own funds invested in his farm is handled as part of his net income.

This is an important item. A farmer who owned a typical $100,000 Corn Belt farm would expect a return of about $4,000 on his investment. He might be getting a net income from farming of, say, $7,000. But his return for his labor and management would be only $3,000. If he could get a good job in town paying, say, $5,000 a year, then neglecting differences in costs (above those which are supposed to be taken into account in computing the net farm income—the rental value of the farm home, the

Fig. 5.2. Realized net farm income per farm.

value of the farm-produced food, etc.) he would be ahead financially to sell his farm, invest the money in stocks and bonds averaging a 4 per cent return, and take the job in town. His net income on the farm was $7,000, but in town it would be $9,000.

THE CENSUS DEFINITION OF A FARM

The official USDA figures given in Table 5.4, however, are misleading. They understate the average farm income per person and per farm in the usual sense of the word farm, because "farm" in this case is "farm" as defined by the Census. This definition includes "farms" all the way down to 10 acres in size if the value of sales of agricultural products is $50 or more; it includes places of less than 10 acres if the value of sales or production of agricultural products is $250 or more.

Now most of the "farmers" on these small "farms" are not farmers at all in the ordinary sense of the term. Their chief source of income is a nonfarm job, not farming. Even after 1960, when the Census definition of a farm was tightened up,[2] about 1.3 million of these small farms were classed as noncommercial farms—part-time, residential, or subsistence farms. These were really acreages where city people live, rather than farms. They

---

[2] For an explanation of this tightening up, see "The Farm Income Situation." ERS, USDA, July 1962, pp. 8–11.

constituted more than a third of the total of 3.7 million farms of all kinds in the United States.[3] This large number of "not-really-farms" inflates the number of farms and farmers that is divided into the total United States net farm income, and therefore reduces the "average farm income" substantially below the average income for commercial family farms, with the part-time residential, and subsistence farms taken out.[4]

The inclusion of the noncommercial "farms" along with the real farms might be defended on the grounds that the nonfarm group includes millions of low-income earners too. But the two groups are not comparable in this respect. The percentage of institutional or subsistence part-time workers is much higher in farm groups than in nonfarm groups. And in the case of most nonfarm occupational groups, there is no large "noncommercial" sector analogous to the noncommercial farms that are included in all farms; a man either is employed, generally full time, or is not employed at all.[5]

The first column of Table 5.5, based on 1960 Census data, shows that there were 888,000 plus 404,000 (in round numbers,

---

[3] "The million and a half low-income farmers have long served the statistical function of adding much to the denominator and little to the numerator in the determination of per capita farm income. Their existence thus helps produce a low per capita farm income figure and thereby helps to rationalize farm programs intended to increase over-all farm income. Little attention is paid to the fact that the resulting programs do almost nothing for low-income farmers whose needs they are alleged to serve. The farm policy focus and the outflow of Federal money are excessively concentrated on large operators for whom incomes were already well above average." (Don Paarlberg, "Rural Development Achievements and Shortcomings as Seen at the Federal Level." *Jour. Farm Econ.*, Vol. 43, Dec. 1961, p. 1512.)

[4] Ray Hurley, "Farms and Farmers for Statistical Purposes," AFEA-ASA joint meeting, *Proceedings*, Dec. 1961.

[5] An additional reason why the commonly used USDA average per capita farm income data understate the actual average farm income is that farm families are larger than nonfarm families. The average size of farm families in March 1961, was 4.19 persons, while the average size of nonfarm families was 3.67 persons. (Data from "Current Population Reports—Population Characteristics," Dept. of Commerce Series P-20, No. 116, May 1, 1962, p. 9.) Thus the farm family was 16 per cent larger than the nonfarm family. So the average per capita farm income would need to be increased 16 per cent to make the farm *family* income directly comparable with the nonfarm *family* income.

Some may believe that farmers need bigger family incomes to raise their bigger families. There is some point to this. But one could hardly claim that the cost of raising a family, especially on a farm, is proportional to the number in the family. The marginal cost per child is surely less than the average cost (including in the average, the cost of "raising" the parents).

TABLE 5.5

AVERAGE NET INCOME OF FARM OPERATOR FAMILIES, 1959*

	Number of Farms 1959			Average Net Income of Farm Operator Families			
	Total	Per cent of total	Per cent of sales of farm products	Net cash farm income[a]	Off-farm income	Total cash income	Total income including nonmoney income from farm food and housing
	(thousands)	(per cent)	(per cent)	(dollars)	(dollars)	(dollars)	(dollars)
Commercial farms with sales:							
$10,000 and over............	795	21.5	71.9	6,636	1,978	8,614	9,960
$5,000 to $9,999...........	654	17.6	15.4	2,165	1,567	3,732	5,018
$2,500 to $4,999...........	618	16.7	7.4	1,288	2,077	3,365	4,572
$50 to $2,499.............	349	9.4	1.5	438	525	963	1,476
Other farms:							
Part time[b].............	888	23.9	2.7	176	4,283	4,459	4,890
Part retirement[c].........	404	10.9	1.1	116	1,846	1,962	2,363
Farms with sales $5,000 and over.....	1,449	39.1	87.3	4,618	1,826	6,444	7,763
Farms with sales of less than $5,000....	2,259	60.9	12.7	510	2,589	3,099	3,750
All farms..............	3,708	100.0	100.0	2,115	2,247	4,362	5,275

* Source: *Agr. Econ. Res.*, Vol. 14, Oct. 1962, p. 122. Data from U.S. Census.
[a] Cash receipts from farm marketings, plus government payments, less production expenses.
[b] Value of sales less than $2,500, operator under 65 years of age and either worked off farm 100 days or more, or income of family from nonfarm sources greater than value of products sold.
[c] Value of sales less than $2,500, operator 65 years or older.

1.3 million) noncommercial, part-time, and residential farms in the United States in 1959, nearly one-third of the total of all farms (3.7 million). These 1.3 million noncommercial farms produced less than 4 per cent of all farm output. They added a lot to the numbers of farms and thus depressed the average income (obtained by dividing United States net farm income by the number of "farmers") but they added very little to the income.

The table also shows that if a dividing line is set at sales of $2,500 per farm, 1.6 million farms fell below that level. The off-farm income on these farms, however, is comparatively large, because most of them are not really farms, but only country residences for urban people with urban jobs or other sources of income.

The cutoff point can be set higher than $2,500 gross sales; a farmer really cannot make a living on gross sales of $2,500. Table 5.5 shows the results when the cutoff point is set at gross sales of $5,000. It shows that farmers with gross sales of this amount or more operated only 39 per cent of all the Census "farms," but accounted for 87 per cent of total United States farm sales. Table 5.5 shows that in 1959, these farmers had an average *net* income of $7,763. In 1961, the figure was about $8,000. This is a lot better net income than the misleading figure of $3,414 in Table 5.4 that is usually quoted as the average farm income per farm.

Income Per Farm Worker

Another answer concerning relative farm and nonfarm income is based on a comparison of income per farm worker[6] with the average annual wage per employed factory worker. The data are shown in Table 5.6. These per worker income figures for 1962 were: farm $2,328; factory, $5,021. Conclusion: Income per farm worker is only about half as high as income per factory worker.

This situation appears to confirm the conclusion that is usually drawn from the per capita income figures given in the preceding section—that farm income is only about half as great as nonfarm income. But it also is misleading. The farm workers

---

[6] "The Farm Income Situation." USDA, ERS, FIS-187, July 1962, p. 45. This is total United States realized net farm income from farming, including government payments, divided by the total average number of persons engaged in agriculture during the year, including farm operators and other family workers (except those doing housework only) as well as hired workers.

TABLE 5.6

INCOME OF FARM AND FACTORY WORKERS, AVERAGE 1910–14, 1920, 1930, AND 1940, AND ANNUAL 1950–62*

Year	Persons Engaged in Agriculture			Average Annual Wage Per Employed Factory Worker[c]
	Net income from farming[a]	Number of farm workers[b]	Average annual farm income per worker	
	(*$ million*)	(*1,000*)	(*dollars*)	(*dollars*)
1910–14..........	4,585	13,561	338	547
1920.............	8,860	13,432	660	1,353
1930.............	5,700	12,497	456	1,196
1940.............	5,318	10,979	484	1,289
1950.............	15,863	9,926	1,598	3,033
1951.............	17,958	9,546	1,881	3,294
1952.............	17,218	9,149	1,882	3,492
1953.............	16,692	8,864	1,883	3,664
1954.............	14,917	8,639	1,727	3,665
1955.............	14,206	8,364	1,698	3,936
1956.............	14,765	7,820	1,888	4,097
1957.............	13,803	7,577	1,822	4,243
1958.............	15,530	7,525	2,064	4,301
1959.............	14,239	7,384	1,928	4,590
1960.............	14,641	7,057	2,075	4,665
1961.............	15,478	6,919	2,237	4,802
1962.............	15,598	6,700	2,328	5,021

* Source: "Farm Income Situation," ERS, USDA, FIS–191, July 1963, p. 41.

[a] Realized net income of farm operators including government payments plus total farm wages.

[b] Represents the average number of persons engaged in agriculture during the year, including farm operators and other family workers (except those doing housework only) as well as hired workers.

[c] Average weekly earnings of production workers or nonsupervisory employees in manufacturing, multiplied by 52.

include the family workers, and the farm income includes a good deal of disguised partial unemployment, whereas the factory workers include only *employed* factory workers. The average farm worker's income data therefore understate the actual average income much as the per capita income data do, partly for the same reasons and partly for different ones.

A further comparison can be made between the average *farm operator's* net farm income per farm, shown in Table 5.4, and the average annual wage per employed factory worker. The average farm operator's net income is reduced by the inclusion of the large number (1.3 million) of small "not-really-farms" in the denominator, but this effect is partly offset by the fact that the "farms" also include a number of larger-than-family farms at the upper end of the scale. The latter farms constituted only 4 per cent of the total number of farms in the United States, but at least they offset some of the small farms that were not really farms.

The average farm operators realized net farm income per farm in 1962 was $3,414. This was still below the average annual wage per employed factory worker, of $5,021. It is only when the farms with sales of less than $5,000 per farm are excluded that the average farm income, $7,763, is higher than the average annual wage of factory workers.

One might admit that the USDA average farm income data considerably understate the actual average farm income, but then go on to say that they understate them by a roughly constant percentage, so that they can be used to show the changes in farm income over periods of time, in dollar terms and in relation to average nonfarm income.

This, however, is not true, as McElveen[7] points out in a recent article:

"Average operators' net cash income per farm increased by a fifth during 1949–59 and showed a slight gain even after an adjustment for changes in the cost of living. These and related averages, however, convey the false impression that incomes of individual farmers have made similar gains. The rationale for this interpretation is that fewer farmers mean a larger farm resource base for those who remain in agriculture; thus, the farm income 'pie' can be divided into fewer pieces.

"Actually, the income and farm resources that were contained in the farms that went out of agriculture, even if transferred to the farmers that remain, are too meager to affect appreciably either their farm resource base or their net income. To illustrate this point, the decrease of more than 1½ million in the number of farms marketing less than $2,500 of farm products during 1949–59 was associated with a decrease of only $1 billion in the value of farm products sold from this group. The decline in number of farms in all economic classes of less than $10,000 de-

---

[7] Jackson V. McElveen, "Farm Numbers, Farm Size and Farm Income." *Jour. Farm Econ.*, Vol. 45, Feb. 1963, pp. 9–10, 12.

creased the value of farm products sold from these economic classes of farms by only $2.5 billion. Due to the wide range and extreme right skewness of the farm income distribution, reductions in number of smaller farms over time can cause the mean income to increase even though incomes of the remaining farmers declined. All that is required is a greater proportionate decrease in number of farms (the denominator) than in farm income (the numerator). . . .

"During 1949–59, neither the substantial decline in the number of farms nor the rapid growth in business size of the remaining farms increased real net cash farm incomes. Real income shrank from two-fifths to a fourth of gross receipts because of increased inputs and the decreased value of the dollar. Merely to maintain their farm incomes, farmers had to increase output by two thirds. Thus, despite the increase in farm size, real net income probably declined for all classes of farms. On smaller farms this decline was apparently offset by the increase in all off-farm incomes; but the total income of operator families on farms that marketed products valued at $5,000 or more probably declined sharply. Clearly, unadjusted statistical series on the number of farms of different economic classes are not always reliable indicators of farm income. As this article interprets the data, real net cash farm incomes on the larger commercial farms have decreased rather than increased."

Finally, the breakdown of income by income classes in 1959, given in Table 5.5, shows that the incomes of different farmers cover a wide range. This calls into further question the validity of using United States average farm income data to show the income status of farmers; the average covers such a wide range that it does not mean very much.

The lower part of the table shows that farmers with sales of $5,000 and over, produced 87.3 per cent of the total sales of farm products, and had net incomes per farm operator family of $7,763. This is not a bad income, compared with incomes in the rest of the country. The upper part of the table shows that the commercial farms with sales of $10,000 and over, produced 71.9 per cent of the total sales and had net incomes of $9,960.

This situation leads Ruttan,[8] a competent analyst, to the following conclusions:

---

[8] Vernon W. Ruttan, Discussion: "Farm-Nonfarm Income Comparisons," *Jour. Farm Econ.*, Vol. 45, May 1963, p. 382, 383.

"1. *The net incomes and purchasing power of the approxi-mately 800,000 commercial farm operators who produce close to three quarters of the value of farm output is not low compared to other segments of American society.*

"The data . . . indicate an average net income of just under $10,000 in 1959 for these farm operator families. The median income of all families in the United States in 1959 was under $5,500. When cost of living differentials and capital gains are considered, it seems apparent that the commercial farm operators who produce the bulk of our national food and fiber requirements represent a relatively favored group in American society.

"2. *The net income and purchasing power disadvantages suffered by older farm families relative to nonfarm families has been sharply reduced since the extension of social security to farmers.* The Census Bureau data indicate that prior to 1954 the median income of farm operator families over 65 was less than 40 per cent of the level of urban families and less than 70 per cent of the level of rural nonfarm families in the same age category. By 1960 the median income of farm operator families over 65 had risen to 68 per cent of the level of urban families and to over 97 per cent of the level of rural-nonfarm families in the same age category. Given the differential asset levels of farm operator families reported in Professor Lampman's study, it appears that older farm operator families enjoy a favored welfare position relative to other older families in rural areas and, considering their differential cost of living, are not seriously disadvantaged relative to older nonfarm families . . . .

"The clear implications of these generalizations is that income transfers from the nonfarm sector to commercial farm operators represent a regressive income transfer and are inconsistent with generally accepted principles of equity. Of the income transfer devices with a direct impact on farm income, the extension of social security to farmers appears to have exerted the most significant progressive impact on the distribution of farm income in recent years."

Ruttan's conclusions go a step beyond the conclusions repeated by most observers that farm incomes are low, implying that they are all low. Ruttan's conclusions show that the low-income problem is concentrated chiefly on the small, low-producing farmers. The others are doing alright; yet they get most of the income transferred to farmers by the farm programs. Those who need help least get most; those who need help most get least.

TABLE 5.7

ANNUAL ESTIMATES OF FARM POPULATION, BIRTHS AND DEATHS, AND NET CHANGE
THROUGH MIGRATION AND IN CLASSIFICATION OF RESIDENCE FOR THE UNITED STATES,
1920–62*

(Figures rounded to nearest thousand without being adjusted to group totals)

Year and Area	Farm Population, April	Natural Increase			Net Change Through Migration and in Classification of Residence[a]
		Total	Births	Deaths	
United States					
1920	31,974	485	825	−340	−336
1930	30,529	377	721	−344	−61
1940	30,547	359	662	−303	−788
1941	30,118	383	676	−293	−1,587
1942	28,914	418	700	−282	−3,145
1943	26,186	370	644	−274	−1,740
1944	24,815	353	600	−247	−748
1945	24,420	312	559	−247	+671
1946	25,403	470	710	−240	−44
1947	25,829	443	682	−239	−1,889
1948	24,383	397	611	−214	−586
1949	24,194	392	593	−201	−1,537
1950	23,048	373	555	−182	−1,531
1951	21,890	341	520	−179	−483
1952	21,748	328	508	−180	−2,201
1953	19,874	296	456	−160	−1,151
1954	19,019	268	426	−158	−210
1955	19,078	261	421	−160	−627
1956	18,712	239	406	−167	−1,295
1957	17,656	220	375	−155	−748
1958	17,128	203	355	−152	−740
1959	16,592	184	338	−154	−1,142
1960	15,635	168	314	−146	−1,000
1961	14,803	165	300	−135	−655
1962	14,313				

* Source: USDA, ERS (Farm Population Branch).
[a] Beginning in 1940, includes inductions and enlistments into Armed Forces, and persons returning from Armed Forces. For all years, includes persons who have not moved but who are in and out of the farm populations because agricultural operations have ceased or have begun on the place where they are living.

EVIDENCE OF MIGRATION OFF FARMS

Some indirect evidence concerning farm incomes is provided by population statistics which show the migration of persons from (and to) farms over the past several decades.

The farm population and migration data in Table 5.7 show that the migration varies greatly from year to year. Actually, on the average since 1920, about a million and a half persons a year have been moving off farms into other occupations. About a million persons a year have been moving in the other direction. The net movement off farms, therefore, has averaged half a million or more per year. The net movement varies markedly from year to year; since World War II, the net movement off farms has ranged from about zero up to a figure of 2 million per year (in 1952).

This net migration off farms is some evidence that many real farm incomes were lower than nonfarm incomes. It seems reasonable to believe that farmers pull up stakes and move to town in large numbers only if their incomes are considerably lower than urban incomes.

The following over-all conclusion with respect to farm income, then, appears warranted: The average per capita farm income is not as low in relation to nonfarm income as the widely quoted USDA data imply; per capita commercial farm income actually is considerably more than half as high as nonfarm income. Nearly half of the farmers in the United States have incomes that are substantially higher than factory workers' incomes. But the net migration of farmers to nonfarm occupations has run at a rate of more than half a million per year since World War II. This is pretty good indirect evidence that many real farm incomes are substantially lower than incomes for comparable ability in town.

6
Farm Incomes Are Only Symptoms

The accumulating evidence begins to make clear what the farm problem really is.

The farm problem cannot be accurately diagnosed as a price problem, for prices are only symptoms—not reliable symptoms either—and curing them directly by price programs does not cure the disease that causes the symptoms. It only temporarily covers the symptoms up. The price programs that have been in effect in the United States have done very little to cure the basic farm problem.

The farm problem can be more accurately diagnosed as a low per capita farm income problem. Farm incomes have remained low since the early 1950's, while incomes in most other lines have been steadily rising.

But incomes are only symptoms, too; they merely reveal, more accurately than prices, what the basic farm problem is. Curing these income symptoms directly, for example by income payments, would not cure the basic disease any more than supporting prices will cure the basic disease.

THE NATURE OF THE REAL FARM PROBLEM

The basic disease, the real farm problem, is an agricultural adjustment problem that results from two things:

1. *Continued overproduction* of farm products relative to the demand for them; this keeps *gross national farm income* low.

The increase in agricultural production does not result from any increase in acreage. Figure 1.3 showed that crop acreage in fact has declined. The overproduction results mainly from rapid technological advances and the addition and substitution of

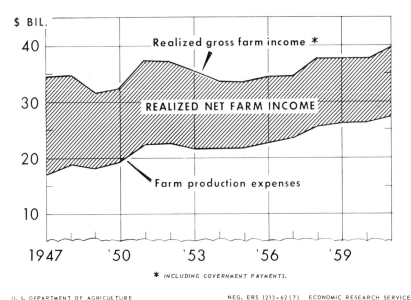

Fig. 6.1. Realized gross and net farm income, 1947–61.

capital resources—machinery, fertilizer, agricultural chemicals, etc.—for land and labor. These are both added to and substituted for labor and land; they cause yields per acre to increase, and also enable one man to handle more acres, thus increasing production per man. This increases gross income per man, and also increases total United States farm production; and because the demand for farm products is inelastic, this limits the rise in total United States farm income to a slow upward climb, as is shown in Figure 6.1.

Production expenses change also, and this affects net income. The use of more efficient production techniques has a tendency to lower some costs, but the increase in the quantity of commercial inputs (i.e., fertilizer) used tends to raise costs. The net effect, as shown in Figure 6.1, is to *decrease* total national net farm income. A corresponding decline in the number of farmers is all that keeps *per capita* net farm income from declining rapidly.

2. *Per capita farm incomes remain low* because of another kind of maladjustment.

This maladjustment is an excessive supply of *farmers*. Along with the overproduction of farm products, a continuous over-

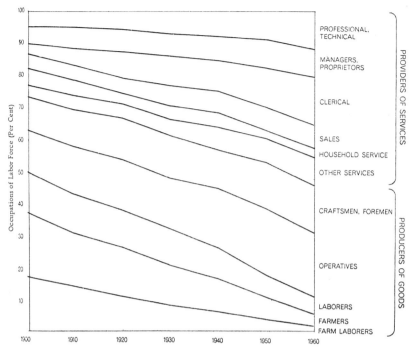

Fig. 6.2. Occupations of labor force (per cent) in the United States by decades, 1900–60. (Source: Philip M. Hauser, "More From the Census of 1960," **Scien. Amer.**, Vol. 207, Oct. 1962, p. 35.)

supply of farmers keeps income *per farmer* low. Earl Heady regards the continuous oversupply of farmers as the chief problem in agriculture. "Agriculture's fundamental problem is not supply of product but supply or quantity of factors," [1] chiefly labor and management.

The large supply of farm operators relative to the demand for them results from two things: (a) the high farm birth rate and the difficulties which impede movement off farms, which keep the supply of farmers excessive, and (b) the decline in the number of farms as they became larger and fewer, and the use of larger implements, which reduces the demand for farm operators.

a. The farm population as a percentage of the total United States population has been declining for many years. Figure 6.2 shows this since 1900, along with the changes in the percentages of other groups.

---

[1] Earl Heady, "Need for Land and Resource Adjustment," Chap. 1 in *Dynamics of Land Use*. (Center for Agricultural and Economic Development, sponsor), Iowa State Univ. Press, Ames, 1961, pp. 2–3.

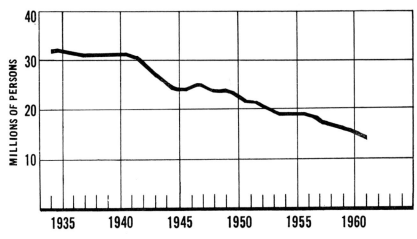

Fig. 6.3. U.S. farm population, 1934–61. (Source of data: U.S. Census.)

The farm population declined particularly rapidly, along with the decline in the number of farms, from more than 32 million persons in 1933 to less than 15 million in 1961, as shown in Figure 6.3; but it did not decline rapidly enough to permit per capita farm incomes to rise during the 1950's. This relative oversupply of farmers keeps the total agricultural income pie divided up into relatively small pieces, and keeps farmers bidding up the rent and price of land. This keeps net income per farmer low. An oversupply of farmers depresses farm incomes per farmer just as surplus farm products depress farm product prices per bushel, bale, etc., of product.

Farm births exceed farm deaths by about 400,000 per year, a rate high enough to result in a continuous increase in the number of farmers if all boys born on farms stay in farming. In 1950, the number of farm children was 68 per cent higher than the number needed to maintain a stationary farm population. According to the 1960 Census, farm women averaged 3.33 children, compared with 2.88 children for rural nonfarm women and 2.26 children for urban women. For the United States as a whole, 2.2 children per woman would keep the total population constant.[2]

b. But we do not need even a stationary farm population. The demand for farmers is declining, and farming practices

[2] Robert C. Cook, "The American Farmer," *Population Bulletin*, Vol. 19, May 1963, p. 54.

have become more laborsaving. Greater mechanization and machinery size have increased the size of farm that a family can handle. The average size of farm in the United States increased from 175 acres in 1940 to 217 acres in 1950 and to 302 acres in 1960. This increase in farm size is likely to continue, with a corresponding decrease in the number of farmers needed to run the farms.

In 1950, the most efficient size of farm (the size of farm with the lowest cost of producing a dollar's worth of crops) under typical conditions in Iowa, with different combinations of machinery available at that time, was about 240 acres. Heady and Krenz show in Table 6.1 and Figure 6.4 that by 1960, with the machinery available then, costs were considerably lower on 350-acre farms than on 240-acre farms; the most efficient size of farm was 50 per cent larger than in 1950. The lowest cost indeed was reached at about 640 acres, a square mile. Most Iowa farms were much smaller than this, the average size in 1960 being about 192 acres, including pasture land. The average number of crop acres per farm was 116 in 1954, rising to 131 in 1959.

Now a 350-acre farm, a little larger than half a square mile, is still a family size farm. Even a 640-acre farm is a family size farm, requiring only one hired man or some short-time summer help in addition to the family.

Some observers are inclined to conclude that since the size of farms has increased substantially in recent years, the number of large corporation farms must have increased and the number of family farms must have decreased.

This is clearly a *non sequitur*. The average size of farms in the United States increased from 217 acres in 1950 to 302 acres in 1960. But this increase was largely a statistical phenomenon; it took place chiefly because a large number of small farms were absorbed into larger units, thus raising the average size of the farms that remained. The situation is similar to the increase in average length of life in the United States over the past 100 years; grownups are not living much longer, but infant mortality has been greatly reduced, and this raises the average age. Figure 6.5 shows that the *number* of small farms has decreased sharply since 1935, and still more sharply in percentage terms since 1950, while the number of large farms increased only slightly from 1950 to 1959. The number of acres that a farm family

TABLE 6.1

Costs Per Dollar of Crops Produced at 1953–57 Prices (Land Costs Not Included)*

Machinery Combinations	Acreage Range That Gives Lowest Costs	Acres at Which Cost Is Minimum	Cost at Minimum
			(cents)
2-plow tractor, 2-row equipment......	0–210 A.	240 A.	52
3-plow tractor, 4-row equipment......	210–370 A.	360 A.	47
4-plow tractor, 4-row equipment......	370–430 A.	400 A.	46
Two 3-plow tractors, 4-row equipment.	430–560 A.	640 A.	45
3-plow tractor, 4-plow tractor, 4-row equipment................	none	680 A.	45
3-plow tractor, 4-plow tractor, 6-row equipment................	560–800 A.	680 A.	44
3-plow tractor, 4-plow tractor, 6-row equipment, combine sheller...	800–960 A.	760 A.	47
3-plow tractor, 4-plow tractor, 6-row equipment, picker-sheller.....	none	760 A.	47

* Source: Earl O. Heady and Ronald D. Krenz, "How Big Will Our Farms Get?" *Iowa Farm Science*, Iowa State Univ., Vol. 16, Nov. 1961, pp. 51–53.

could handle increased, and this was one of the causes of the increase in the average size of farms; but the chief cause was the decline in the number of small farms.

Family farms, in fact, are not defined by size measured in acres. Commercial family farms are officially defined by the USDA as farms where the total labor requirement is less than three man-years. Research shows that family farms, as thus defined, constituted 86.6 per cent of all farms with $5,000 or more of farm marketings in 1954 (up from 83 per cent in 1949).[3] Over this same period, larger-than-family farms decreased in number by 14 per cent. Preliminary estimates for 1959 indicate that these trends continued in the same direction from 1954 to 1959 as from 1949 to 1954.[4]

A LOOK INTO THE FUTURE

The real farm problem, then, is a farmer-adjustment problem resulting from a continual excess of potential farmers being born on farms, and a continual reduction in the number of farmers being needed.

[3] R. Nikolitch, "Family and Larger-Than-Family Farms." USDA Agr. Econ. Rept. No. 4, 1962, p. 1.
[4] R. Nikolitch, "Family Labor and Technological Advance in Farming." *Jour. Farm Econ.*, Vol. 44, Nov. 1962, p. 1067.

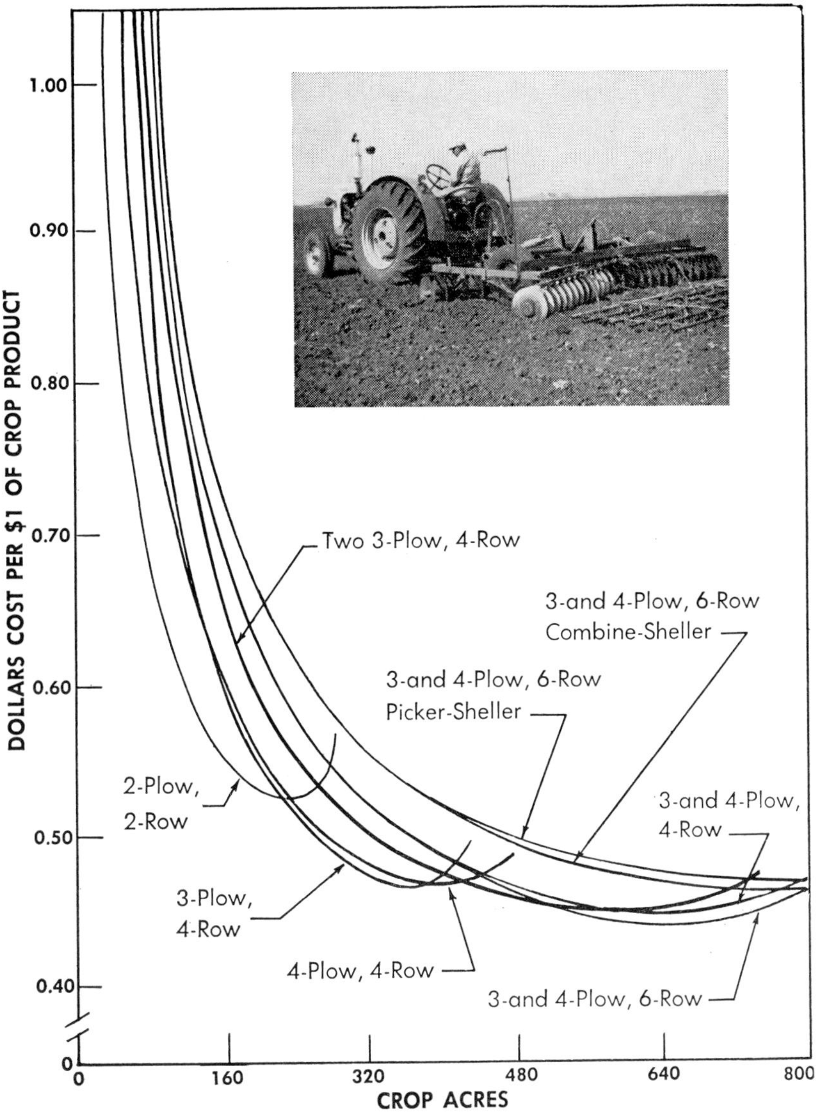
DOLLARS COST PER $1 OF CROP PRODUCT
1.00
0.90
0.80
0.70
0.60
0.50
0.40
0
CROP ACRES
0
160
320
480
640
800
Two 3-Plow, 4-Row
3-and 4-Plow, 6-Row
Combine-Sheller
3-and 4-Plow, 6-Row
Picker-Sheller
2-Plow,
2-Row
3-and 4-Plow,
4-Row
3-Plow,
4-Row
4-Plow, 4-Row
3-and 4-Plow, 6-Row

Fig. 6.4. Average costs of producing $1 worth of crops with eight machinery combinations using current cropping methods. (Source: same as Table 6.1.)

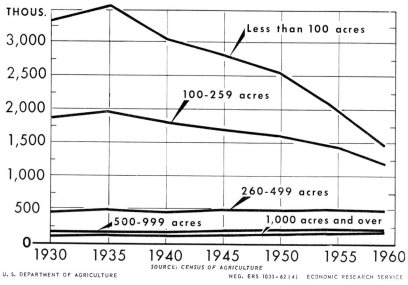

Fig. 6.5. Number of farms by size, United States, by 5-year periods 1930–59. (Source: **Land and Water Resources**, USDA, Washington, D.C., May 1962, p. 25.)

The size of this problem in the past was indicated in Figures 6.2 and 6.3, and the left half of Table 6.2. The size of the problem in the future is indicated in the right half of Table 6.2 and Figure 6.6. The projections are based on a "cohort (age group) analysis"; they show the prospects for the future in relation to the facts of the past.[5]

In this table and figure, the Census data for the past show that the number of farmers in the United States declined nearly 50 per cent from a peak of 6.4 million in 1920 to 3.7 million in 1959. The projections for the future are startling. They indicate that by the year 2,000, less than a million farmers will be needed.

The number of farmers will need to be reduced by nearly two-thirds in the next three decades.

The projections by cohorts are based on the assumption that the numbers in the older age groups will continue to bear the same relation to the numbers in the younger age groups that existed in the past.

---

[5] Marion Clawson, "Aging Farmers and Agricultural Policy." *Jour. Farm Econ.*, Vol. 42, Feb. 1963, pp. 13–30.

TABLE 6.2

Numbers of Farm Operators by Age and Cohort, 48 Contiguous States, 1890 to 1960, and Estimates 1970–2000*

	Total Number of Farm Operators[b]											
	Census of								Projections for[d]			
Cohort[a]	1890	1900	1910	1920	1930	1940	1950	1960	1970	1980	1990	2000
	(thousands)								(thousands)			
2000												40(30)
1990											50(35)	125(80)
1980										60(40)	150(100)	*775(100)*
1970									80(50)	250(150)	*300(150)*	250(150)
1960								62	200(150)	*250(150)*	230(140)	170(100)
1950							164	403	*475(400)*	450(340)	330(240)	225(150)
1940						233	791	806	764(690)	561(500)	382(340)	
1930					372	949	*1187*	980	720(650)	490(440)		
1920				384	1049	*1251*	1157	803	548(500)			
1910			419	1333	*1452*	1428	1000	617				
1900		275	1414	*1588*	1460	1147	745					
1890	219	1194	*1572*	1482	1064	828						
1880	1083	*1410*	1433	994	676							
1870	*1182*	1296	948	584								
1860	1035	865	555									
1850]	1249}	595										
1840]												
Total[b]	4767	5636	6339	6364	6074	5836	5044	3671	2787(2440)	2061(1720)	1442(1005)	985(610)
% farmers not reporting age	...[c]	0.2	0.3	1.3	3.4	4.3	6.2	1.0				

* Source: Marion Clawson, "Aging Farmers and Agricultural Policy," *Jour. Farm Econ.*, Vol. 42, Feb. 1953. Data from: *Census of Agriculture, 1950* and *Census of Agriculture, 1959*.

[a] Years in which operators were 15–24 years of age. Italic figures are number 35–44 years of age, normally the size of each cohort.

[b] Farmers reporting age only.

[c] Farmers not reporting age were allocated (by census) proportionately to age groups.

[d] Figures in parentheses are minimum estimates.

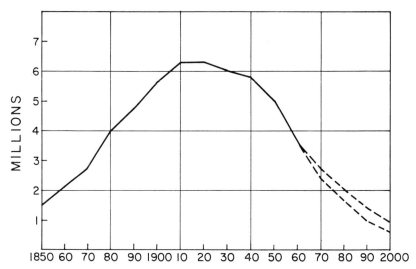

Fig. 6.6. Number of farmers in the United States, by decades, 1850–1960 and projected to 2000. (Source of chart: Marion Clawson, **op. cit.** footnote 5.)

Figure 6.7 shows that this assumption is fairly close to the truth for the earlier cohorts, for the United States as a whole. It is also true for Iowa. But in both cases the slopes of the first and second sections of the lines decrease for the later cohorts. For the Southern states as a group, this decrease is very marked; the slope for the 1950 cohort in fact is negative.[6]

The projections are valid, then, only to the extent to which the assumption of unchanged relationships is valid. To this extent, the projections are based upon the size of the entering group.

The drastic decline in the number of younger farmers in the past is shown in Table 6.2. Figure 6.8 shows the present situation graphically.

One needs to appraise the specific projections shown in Table 6.2 and Figure 6.6 in the light of other collateral facts, some of which point in the same general direction as these specific projections. The decline in the number of farmers in Iowa, to use a fairly homogeneous area, has been less drastic than in the United States as a whole, but it has a good way to go yet before the aver-

[5] G. S. Tolley and H. W. Hjort, "Age-Mobility and Southern Farmer Skill—Looking Ahead for Area Development." *Jour. Farm Econ.*, Vol. 45, Feb. 1963, Figure I, p. 33.

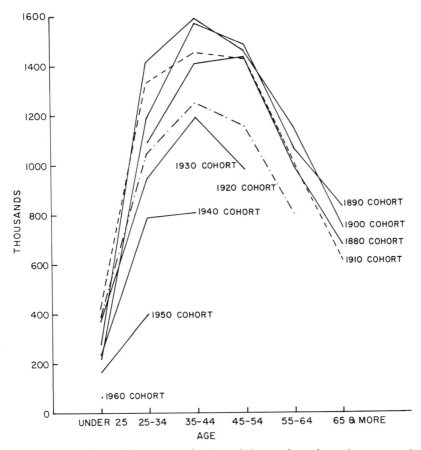

Fig. 6.7. Number of farmers in the United States, by cohorts (age groups),
1880–1960. (Source of data: U.S. Census.)

age size farm (192 acres in 1960) is as large as the optimum size
in 1960 (640 acres). The number of farmers in Iowa would decrease to less than a half of the present number if Iowa farms
were optimum in size; and relentless economic pressure is push-
ing in that direction.

This, then, is the real farm problem: How to ease the prospective drastic reduction in the numbers of farmers so that (1)
those who leave agriculture will be trained for urban jobs, (2)
the incomes of those who remain on farms will not be driven
down to punishingly low levels, and (3) efficient production on
farms will be maintained in line with the goals of the country as
a whole.

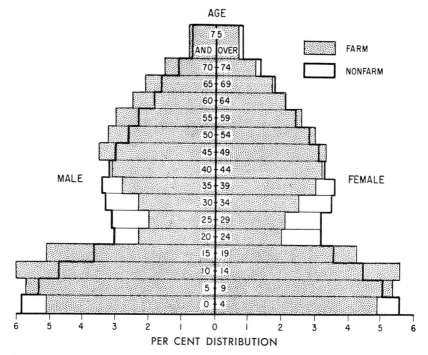

Fig. 6.8. Farm and nonfarm populations, per cent distribution by age groups, 1960. The extensive migration of young people to the city has left the farm population with a narrow "waist" in the ages between 20 and 40, the prime productive and reproductive ages. (Source: Population Reference Bureau, Inc., **Population Bulletin**, May 1963, p. 64.)

INCOMES OF COMMERCIAL FAMILY FARMS BY AREAS

The preceding sections show that the family farm is still by all odds the most prevalent type of farm, and growing more prevalent with the passage of time.

Are data compiled to show the average incomes on these commercial family farms, as distinguished from the somewhat misleading average income on all farms as defined by the Census?

The answer is yes. The USDA has been compiling annual income and cost data for farms of this sort for about 30 years. It compiles them by the type-of-farming areas over the United States shown in Figure 6.9 so that the differences in the average incomes in the different types of farming can be shown as well as the average for the country as a whole.

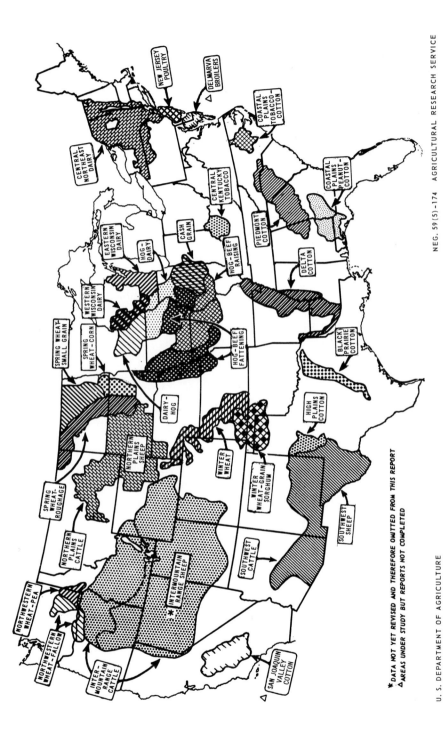

NEG. 59(5)-174   AGRICULTURAL RESEARCH SERVICE

Fig. 6.9.   Location of type-of-farming areas.

U. S. DEPARTMENT OF AGRICULTURE

*DATA NOT YET REVISED AND THEREFORE OMITTED FROM THIS REPORT
△AREAS UNDER STUDY BUT REPORTS NOT COMPLETED

It is necessary to note that these data are not based on all the farms in each area; they are based only on the typical commercial family farms. They thus get away from the distortion of the results when all the farms are included—the one-third or more small tracts that are not really farms at all, but are included in the Census definition of a farm.

These data show the average net "returns to operator and family labor" for each type of farm in each type-of-farming area. This is a little different concept from "net farm income," even when that is defined as the farm income from farm sources only. The net "returns to operator and family labor" are the net farm income from farm sources, minus an allowance for the imputed return on the operator's own investment in land, buildings, equipment, and other capital items on his farm. It is the return to the operator's labor and management, excluding the return on his capital investment on his own farm. It is thus a substantially less inclusive concept than the net "farm income from farm sources," which includes the imputed return on the farmers own investment in his farm along with the return to his labor and management.

DIFFERENCES IN RETURNS AMONG TYPE-OF-FARMING AREAS

Agriculture is a heterogeneous industry, and the commercial family farm data show that the low income problem is more severe in some types of farming than it is in others.

Table 6.3 shows that there are wide differences among farm incomes in the different type-of-farming areas. The average returns to operator and family labor in 1962 ranged from —$2,253 in sheep ranches of the Southwest to $18,643 in the irrigated, large-scale cotton and general crop farms of the San Joaquin Valley in California.[7] In 1961, the lowest returns were made by wheat–small-grain–livestock farms in the Northern Plains; the highest were still those in the Delta.

Furthermore, these differences persist over long periods of time. Figure 6.10 shows the net returns data for two types of farming—hog-beef raising and hog-beef fattening—in two partly

---

[7] This situation is discussed more fully in: G. Shepherd, "Farm Programs for Farm Incomes." *Jour. Farm Econ.*, Vol. 42, Aug. 1960, pp. 639–50.

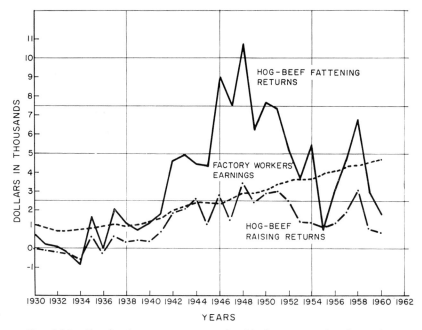

Fig. 6.10. Hog-beef returns compared with factory workers' earnings, 1930–62.

contiguous areas, carried back to 1930, along with the earnings of manufacturing workers.

This Figure 6.10 illustrates the essence of the area farm problem in summary form. It shows that the urban income series rises fairly steadily over most of the period. But the farm returns series jumps all over the place—in the case of the hog-beef fattening series, from roughly three times as high as the urban series in 1948 to only half as high in 1955. The instability of the farm returns series stands out in marked contrast to the stability of the urban income series.

This instability not only is disturbing in itself; high returns in some periods induce high investment in land, for example, which is difficult to pay off in periods of low returns.

The chart shows also that the two farm series differ greatly from each other. In most years, the returns to operator and family labor are about twice as high in hog-beef fattening as they are in hog-beef raising.

TABLE 6.3
Return to Operator and Family Labor, 1956–62*
(using current charge for capital)

Type-of-farming Area	1956	1957	1958	1959	1960	1961	1962 (prelim.)
Dairy farms:							
Central Northeast.	2,658	2,700	2,227	2,102	1,798	2,061	1,099
Eastern Wisconsin, Grade A.	3,116	2,831	2,215	2,994	2,251	3,274	2,551
Eastern Wisconsin, Grade B.	901	804	566	817	386	1,173	667
Western Wisconsin.	2,013	2,150	1,992	1,868	1,763	2,503	2,448
Dairy-hog farms:							
Southeastern Minnesota.	2,496	2,013	1,892	1,190	559	2,127	1,449
Corn Belt farms:							
Hog-dairy.	2,638	3,464	4,173	2,002	1,410	2,700	2,120
Hog-beef raising.	1,376	1,693	2,523	599	123	930	483
Hog-beef fattening.	3,075	4,181	5,764	2,275	619	2,100	4,665
Cash grain.	5,660	2,083	1,962	153	937	2,684	2,395
Poultry farms:							
New Jersey (egg producing).	1,548	420	750	−2,898	2,570	2,261	446
DelMarVa, broiler farms	3,882	1,426	2,983	3,178	3,680	3,265	3,356
Maine, broiler farms.	2,403	1,917	1,906	1,768	1,947	1,926	2,314
Cotton farms:							
Southern Piedmont.	656	600	1,587	734	332	987	910
Mississippi Delta:							
Small	1,468	822	603	1,495	871	1,214	1,159
Large-scale.	14,914	3,453	4,309	20,049	10,918	17,281	17,762
Texas:							
Black Prairie.	−283	440	1,531	711	−49	462	572
High Plains (nonirrig.)	815	4,169	5,800	3,923	5,302	9,790	3,201
High Plains (irrig.)	8,798	6,222	12,195	7,270	7,402	16,540	12,615
San Joaquin Valley, Calif. (irrig.):							
Cotton-specialty crop.	79,433	6,939	7,107	42,437	21,441	−5,026	13,092
Cotton-general crop (med. sized) . .	15,500	14,766	11,949	13,861	8,273	6,550	7,793
Cotton-general crop (large)	44,479	35,880	32,415	44,302	18,304	14,581	18,643
Peanut-cotton farms:							
Southern Coastal Plains.	2,173	1,594	2,592	1,486	2,110	2,998	2,569

TABLE 6.3 (*continued*)

Type-of-farming Area	1956	1957	1958	1959	1960	1961	1962 (prelim.)
Tobacco farms:							
Kentucky:							
Tobacco-livestock (inner)	3,864	2,631	2,934	1,902	1,255	1,798	1,845
Tobacco-dairy (intermed.)	1,863	1,459	1,601	1,408	1,109	1,631	1,493
Tobacco-dairy (outer)	3,100	2,690	2,856	2,409	2,103	2,719	3,040
North Carolina:							
Tobacco-cotton	2,796	1,866	3,371	2,488	4,244	5,049	4,549
Tobacco	2,905	2,061	3,476	2,576	4,469	5,144	4,571
Spring wheat farms:							
Northern Plains:							
Wheat-small grain-livestock	5,298	1,993	3,738	156	1,876	-2,850	7,981
Wheat-corn-livestock	1,594	3,402	4,680	-407	2,436	2,102	2,693
Wheat-roughage-livestock	1,335	2,776	2,489	-984	2,616	-1,421	6,930
Winter wheat farms:							
Southern Plains:							
Wheat	742	2,854	8,605	3,221	4,926	5,305	5,481
Wheat-grain-sorghum	-791	-978	5,368	1,603	7,227	7,245	4,109
Pacific Northwest:							
Wheat-pea	7,341	6,263	407	6,824	281	-73	6,956
Wheat-fallow	5,063	11,189	7,860	7,637	3,326	3,012	7,477
Cattle ranches:							
Northern Plains	-661	905	2,419	1,002	19	1,579	2,659
Intermountain Region	3,216	5,803	9,323	8,054	3,649	4,838	6,785
Southwest	-4,373	-1,187	1,631	536	-2,220	-823	-832
Sheep ranches:							
Northern Plains	2,664	7,130	8,117	3,079	1,992	1,393	6,606
Southwest	-5,985	-1,196	744	402	-2,391	-2,839	-2,253

* Source: USDA, "Costs and returns on commercial farms, long-term study, 1930–57." Stat.Bul. 297, 1961. "Farm costs and returns on commercial farms by type, size, and location." Agr. Inf. Bul. 230, Rev. 1962. Data for 1962 direct from Farm Production Econ. Div., USDA.

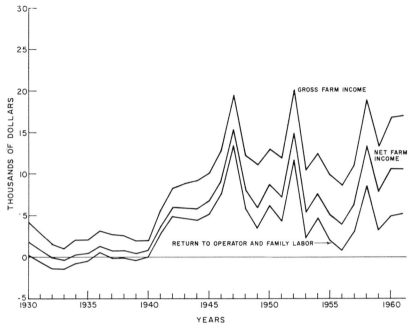

Fig. 6.11A. Returns to operator and family labor on winter wheat farms in the Southern Plains area, 1930–61.

The differences in the farm income situations in the different type-of-farming areas are shown further in Figures 6.11A, 6.11B, and 6.11C. These figures show gross farm incomes, and costs, as well as net returns. These charts clearly show the differences in income level and stability in the different types of farming.

The winter wheat chart shows the violent fluctuations in gross and net income and in returns to operator and family labor that result chiefly from irregular variations in weather; programs to stabilize returns, of a crop insurance or other type, are needed here.

The hog-beef fattening chart shows different character-istics—less variability in returns, with the variability associated with prices rather than with weather; and costs which constitute a much higher percentage of gross incomes than in the case of winter wheat, and which have increased so much that they brought returns down almost to zero in 1955 and 1960.

The cash grain Corn Belt farms are still different; they had very stable gross incomes after 1946, but also had a steady in-crease in costs and in the charge for capital, which brought re-turns in 1959 down almost to zero.

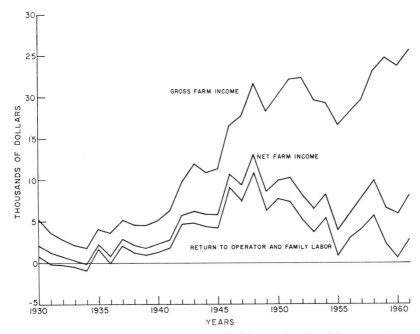

Fig. 6.11B. Returns to operator and family labor on hog-beef fattening farms in the Corn Belt, 1930–61.

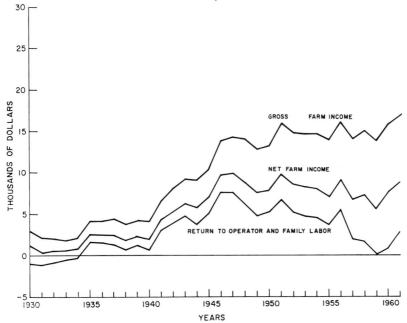

Fig. 6.11C. Returns to operator and family labor on cash grain farms in the Corn Belt, 1930–61.

The net income of these cash grain farmers was still higher than the average annual wage per employed factory worker ($5,021) in 1962; it is the net returns to operator and family labor that declined severely. The owner-operator on this type of farm was getting a decent income—higher than the average employed industrial worker, as shown above—but he was getting it from the property he owned, not from his labor and management.

It is clear from this chart that the charge for capital (which, deducted from net farm income, leaves the returns to operator and family labor) increased greatly from 1950 to 1962. It more than doubled. Why was this?

The charge for capital consisted chiefly of the charge for the investment in land and buildings; this included nearly 90 per cent of the total charge. Did this charge double because the size of the farm increased (more acres) or the value of each acre increased?

Study of the data shows it was almost entirely the latter, not the former. The number of acres increased only from 223 in 1950 to 261 in 1962. But the value of the land per acre increased from $236 to $406.

This raises most interesting questions. Why would farmers, engaged in a type of farming where returns were declining rapidly toward zero, bid up the price of land so far that it left no return on their labor and management? An answer to this question is given in later chapters.

Low Incomes Concentrated in Certain Areas

A still different picture of the farm income problem, by areas, is shown in Figure 6.12. This figure shows three measures of income combined into one—farm income, production, and level of living—by economic areas in the United States. These criteria are spelled out in the lower right-hand corner of the chart.

The heavy concentration of low incomes in the Southeast, with a smaller but still "serious" situation in New Mexico, and "substantial" and "moderate" areas in parts of the Great Lakes states and in the far Northwest, are clearly shown.

This map shows the situation for agriculture, while Figure 6.13 is based on more comprehensive data, showing the situation not simply for agriculture but for the whole population in

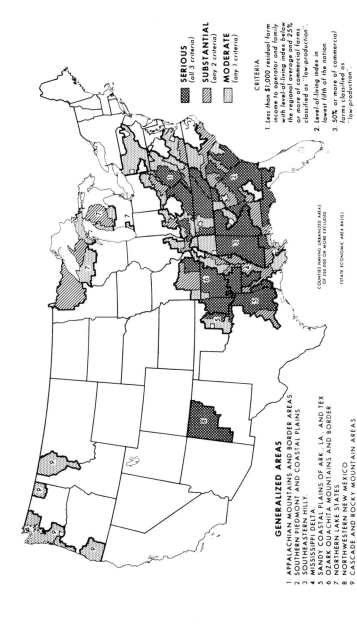

SERIOUS
(all 3 criteria)

SUBSTANTIAL
(any 2 criteria)

MODERATE
(any 1 criteria)

CRITERIA

1. Less than $1,000 residual farm income to operator and family with level-of-living index below the regional average and 25% or more of commercial farms classified as "low-production".

2. Level-of-living index in lowest fifth of the nation.

3. 50% or more of commercial farms classified as "low-production".

GENERALIZED AREAS

1. APPALACHIAN MOUNTAINS AND BORDER AREAS.
2. SOUTHERN PIEDMONT AND COASTAL PLAINS.
3. SOUTHEASTERN HILLY.
4. MISSISSIPPI DELTA.
5. SANDY COASTAL PLAINS OF ARK., LA., AND TEX.
6. OZARK-OUACHITA MOUNTAINS AND BORDER.
7. NORTHERN LAKE STATES.
8. NORTHWESTERN NEW MEXICO.
9. CASCADE AND ROCKY MOUNTAIN AREAS.

COUNTIES HAVING URBANIZED AREAS OF 250,000 OR MORE EXCLUDED

(STATE ECONOMIC AREA BASIS)

PREPARED BY AMS AND ARS

U. S. DEPARTMENT OF AGRICULTURE   NEG. 1804–55 (9)   AGRICULTURAL MARKETING SERVICE

Fig. 6.12. Low income and level-of-living areas in agriculture. (Source: same as Table 6.4.)

TABLE 6.4

PERCENTAGE DISTRIBUTION OF RURAL FAMILIES BY INCOME LEVEL, STUDY AREAS COMPARED WITH ALL RURAL FAMILIES IN THE UNITED STATES, 1956–58*

| Study Area | Net Money Income | | | | | | Total |
| | Less than $1,000 | $1,000 to $1,999 | $2,000 to $2,999 | $3,000 to $3,999 | $4,000 to $4,999 | $5,000 and over | |
	(per cent)	(per cent)	(per cent)	(per cent)	(per cent)	(per cent)	(per cent)
Northwestern Florida..........	29.9	25.6	17.9	8.9	6.2	11.5	100.0
Michigan Cut-Over...........	12.1	13.6	12.1	16.5	15.9	29.8	100.0
Mississippi Clay Hills........	33.1	28.2	18.4	8.7	5.4	6.2	100.0
Missouri Ozarks.............	29.0	26.5	16.6	14.4	6.1	7.4	100.0
North-Central New Mexico....	33.8	22.6	12.4	13.7	6.4	11.1	100.0
Northeastern Tennessee.......	21.7	20.4	15.0	16.0	10.5	16.4	100.0
Northeastern Texas..........	27.2	22.4	17.1	11.4	9.9	12.0	100.0
United States[a].............	10.8	11.2	11.5	13.0	13.5	40.0	100.0

* Source: USDA, "Opportunities for Economic Development in Low-production Farm Areas," Agr. Inf. Bul. 234, Nov. 1960, p. 11.
[a] U.S. Bureau of the Census, "Consumer Income, Income of Families and Persons in the United States: 1957" (14).

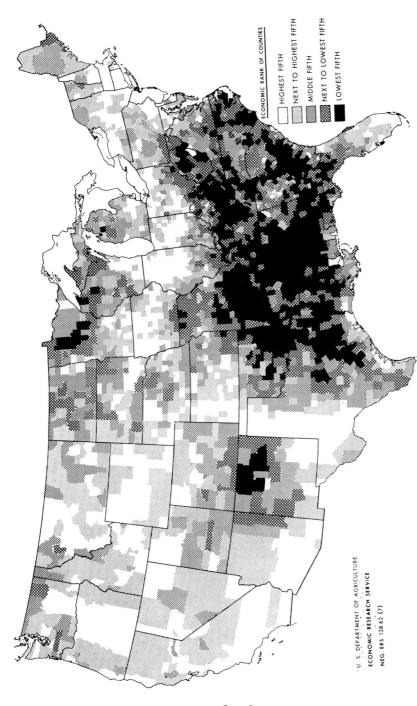

ECONOMIC RANK OF COUNTIES

HIGHEST FIFTH
NEXT TO HIGHEST FIFTH
MIDDLE FIFTH
NEXT TO LOWEST FIFTH
LOWEST FIFTH

Fig. 6.13. Relative economic status of counties, 1960. Index based on equal weighting of (1) median income of all families, (2) proportion of commercial farms in classes V and VI, (3) number of class V and VI farms, (4) farm operator level-of-living index, (5) rate of population change 1950 to 1960, and (6) public welfare case load per 1,000 population.

[111]

each county, with economic rank indicated according to the explanation in lower right corner of chart. The areas in the two maps are closely similar.

The distribution of all families by income levels shows that there are high-income rural families in all areas. Table 6.4 shows a comparison of income distributions in the different areas that were studied. In the Michigan area, about 30 per cent of the families had net money incomes of $5,000 or more. In all other areas, most of the incomes fell below the $2,000 level.

The proportion of all rural families with incomes below $2,000 is two to three times greater in the study areas than in the United States as a whole, again with the Michigan area excepted. The distribution of families by income levels in the latter area is similar to the distribution at the national level.

Comparison of the incomes of rural families in the study areas with all families, both urban and rural, in the United States reveals wide differences in income distribution. Of all United States families, farm and nonfarm, only 15 per cent had incomes below $2,000 and nearly 75 per cent had incomes above $3,000. Similarly, only 10.6 per cent of the urban families had incomes below $2,000. But Table 6.4 shows that in all study areas except Michigan, a higher proportion of commercial farm families than of nonfarm families had incomes below this level. The same comparison held for all farm families. Nearly two-thirds of these families in the Mississippi, Missouri, and Texas areas had net money incomes below $2,000. The proportions of nonfarm and commercial farm families in each area with incomes above $5,000 were similar.

THE LOW FARM INCOME PROBLEM IS NOT "A" PROBLEM

The charts and tables in the preceding sections show that the low farm income problem is not a single problem, affecting all areas alike as prices do. Farm incomes in some areas are very low; in some other areas, they are higher than factory workers' incomes. The maps show the inappropriateness of price programs, covering the whole country, for dealing with the low farm income problem, which is most heavily concentrated in several different geographical areas.

The crucial point is this: The increase in total United States agricultural production causes the prices of farm products to decline. But this decline in prices bears unequally on different kinds of farms and farmers in different areas, because of the different effects of the technological revolution on costs in the different areas.

In areas where topography permits the size of farms to expand, the producers of crops benefit from the technological revolution, at least in the short run. They offset the decline in prices by a decline in costs, so that they can maintain or even increase their net incomes; but the producers in rough areas where fields and farms have to remain small, or those with limited capital or managerial ability, suffer rather than benefit. They cannot reduce their costs enough to offset the decline in prices. The impact of the technological revolution bears unequally on different producers in different areas. The farm income problem is a farm and farmer adjustment problem, and it is an area problem— more severe in some areas than in others, and differing in nature from area to area.

This farm problem is a part of a broad general problem that affects most industries all over the nation, in the cities as well as on the farms of the nation. This broad general problem is the continuous replacement of men by machines in factories, stores, and offices as well as on farms.

Railroads, partly automated now, employ substantially fewer men than formerly, even with all the featherbedding that goes on to keep labor on in obsolete jobs. Further reductions are in prospect. Thousands of small retail grocery stores have been replaced by more efficient large supermarkets and chains, but the government does not feel called on to set up a big program of retail price supports to help retailers, like its farm price supports are supposed to help farmers—and it is a good thing it doesn't. A program of this sort in retailing would be as inefficient and ineffective as it is in agriculture. Factories are not trying to support the prices of their products in an attempt to help those workers who are laid off by automation, and it is a good thing they are not, because it obviously would not help them. Supporting prices or reducing production does not solve this kind of problem.

But most farm programs start from this basis: Average farm income is low, so we must get it up. The programs proceed to do this by supporting or raising the prices of farm products. This raises farm incomes, in the short run, proportionally to sales. This benefits the larger farmers most. But they are the ones who are above average already. Table 5.5 showed that farmers with gross sales in excess of $5,000 had an average net income of $7,763 in 1959. Some of this income reflects return on their investment, and if that return is considered low, other forms of investment are open. But the point is that those farmers with gross sales above $5,000 and average net incomes of $7,763 are the ones who need help least; many of them do not need help at all; yet they get most of the benefit from existing price-support farm programs.

There is real question whether this is either economic or ethical. A large percentage of taxpayers in the United States have net incomes that are considerably lower than $7,763; yet the United States government imposes taxes on them to finance agricultural price support programs, most of the benefits of which go to farmers who already have net incomes averaging $7,763. What kind of economics or ethics is this?

What is needed is a different kind of program, one which would benefit chiefly the particular low-income farmers in particular areas where help is needed most.

Alternative Proposals To Solve
the Farm Problem

Part ■ *2*

We have seen that the farm problem is not a price problem, and that the existing price-support programs are not appropriate means for dealing with it. The farm problem is more accurately diagnosed as a per farmer income problem. Yet even this is only a diagnosis of the symptoms, not of the underlying disease.

The fundamental problem in agriculture is not a problem of an oversupply of farm products depressing their price. It cannot be solved by price programs designed to support the prices of farm products, either by storage programs or by acreage control programs. The farm problem is chiefly a problem of an oversupply of the human factor of production, labor, and management, present in all areas, but more acute in some areas than in others. And this problem is difficult to solve, because a continual oversupply of future farmers is being born, and it is difficult for this continuous oversupply to move rapidly enough out of farming.

We have seen that past and present farm programs have been and are now costly, temporary, and only partly effective. What new and different programs are being proposed for the future, and which ones would be most effective if they were adopted?

The alternative farm programs that are being proposed now cover a wide range, all the way from mandatory (compulsory) acreage reduction programs to control agricultural production—"just like U.S. Steel controls its production"—to abolition of all controls and return to the open market.

Secretary Benson from 1952 to 1960 tried to move in the direction of the latter alternative, and Secretary Freeman in 1962 tried to get legislation through Congress to establish the former. Neither succeeded in reaching his goal.

Which Secretary was moving in the right direction?

Let us appraise the two proposals, the two extremes, and then appraise other alternatives.

7

Returning Agriculture to the Open Market

Agriculture stands now at a fork in the road ahead. It can take one fork and continue or accelerate its current emphasis on restricted output and higher prices; or it can take the other fork in the road and turn toward less restriction and lower prices, at the extreme returning agriculture to the open market. Neither fork (or strictly speaking, tine) provides easy traveling.

The traditional method of controlling inputs in any atomistically (made up of numerous small units) competitive industry like agriculture is to let it be done by prices in the open market. This is one of the methods that is still being advocated now—to abandon government farm programs and return agriculture to the open market.[1]

The general argument for returning agriculture to the open market runs like this: The amount of productive resources committed to agriculture is excessive. In a free market, the excessive production resulting from this excess of productive resources would drive the returns to those resources below the levels they would attain in other occupations. So the remedy is to stop supporting prices and return agriculture to the open market. Prices and returns then would fall. The low returns then would drive the excess resources out of agriculture until the resources would cease to be excessive and their returns would rise to competitive levels—the same levels as they would attain in other occupations.

---

[1] "An Adaptive Program for Agriculture." A Statement on National Policy by the Research and Policy Committee of the Committee for Economic Development, 1962, 711 Fifth Ave., New York 22.

See also L. H. Simerl, "Do We Really Need Price Supports?" *Better Farming Methods*, Nov. 1962, pp. 8–10; and Don Paarlberg, "The Continuing Debate—Supply Management—Bad." *Successful Farming*, Nov. 1962, pp. 33, 80–81.

This general argument may appear merely academic, doctrinaire, and impractical to some, and ruthless, hard-nosed, practical common sense to others. But urgent practical arguments for returning particular crops to or toward the open market have been made by several commodity producer groups.

Cotton in the United States, for example, is described by competent authorities as being "now in the worst competitive position, by far, that it has ever held"[2] because of a change in United States price policy in 1960. This change in policy raised cotton prices; at the same time, rayon and dacron prices, which up to that time had run closely similar to cotton prices, were sharply reduced. The contrasting movements in cotton and rayon prices are shown in Figure 7.1. This figure also shows the sharp rise in rayon staple consumption that followed the decline in rayon prices; meanwhile cotton consumption declined.

Another effect of high domestic prices for cotton shows up in imports of cotton in manufactured form into the United States. These imports have increased from a negligible amount in 1952 to an annual rate equivalent to about 700,000 bales of cotton in 1962.

These imports are manufactured in foreign countries from cotton purchased on a world market in which the biggest influence is the price of our own cotton, which we export at a price 8.5 cents per pound lower than the price at which our own mills can buy it. We do this by means of a subsidy. While domestic prices are held at present high levels, even the present subsidy of 8.5 cents may not be large enough, yet it calls for a quarter of a billion dollars a year from the federal treasury if the United States is to export six million bales.

Horne and McCord continue:[3]

"There is a theory, which we often hear, that it is all right to prop up farm prices to certain preconceived high levels, provided the government is permitted to hold down production to the volume that will sell at those prices. This theory can be pushed too far, and we are on the way toward finding an example in cotton.

"For the catch in this theory is that there is no market volume that we can count upon holding at these prices. We will have a

[2] M. K. Horne, Jr., and Frank A. McCord, "Price and Today's Markets for U.S. Cotton." National Cotton Council of America, Memphis, Tenn., Sept. 1962, p. 26.
[3] Horne and McCord, *op. cit.*, p. 26.

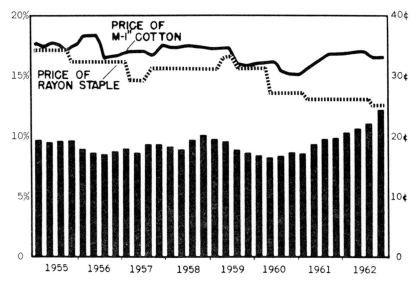

Fig. 7.1. Rayon and cotton prices, and the percentage of rayon to cotton consumption. Sources of data: Consumption—computed from monthly data of U.S. Dept. of Commerce. Man-made fibers converted to cotton equivalent with USDA factors. All data seasonally adjusted. Prices—for cotton (average on designated spot markets), USDA. For rayon staple, Textile Economics Bureau through July, 1959; industry sources thereafter. (Source of chart: M. K. Horne, "The Economic Outlook for U.S. Cotton." National Cotton Council of America, Jan. 28, 1963, p. 9.)

certain market next year and the next and the next, but it will be disappearing rapidly as our competitors eat it up. Eventually this theory of a high price and a smaller market will wind up as a high price and no market, or a pitifully small one."

PROJECTIONS OF PRODUCTION, PRICES, AND INCOMES UNDER FREE MARKETS

How far would the prices of farm products fall under if agriculture were returned to the open market, and how long would agriculture take to adjust to these prices?

Two different sets of projections of prices for United States agriculture under free markets were published late in 1959. One set, confined to the feed-livestock economy, was prepared by agricultural economists at Iowa State University.[4] The other dealt

---

[4] Geoffrey Shepherd, Arnold Paulsen, Francis Kutish, Don Kaldor, Richard Heifner, and Eugene Futrell, "Production, Price and Income Estimates and Projections for the Feed-Livestock Economy Under Specified Control and Market-clearing Conditions," Special Rept. No. 27, Iowa State University, Ames, Aug. 1960.

with the whole of United States agriculture and was prepared in the USDA.[5]

The Iowa State University projections were made on the assumption that price supports for feed grains and wheat would be reduced to the point where no further additions to stocks would be made, and export subsidies would be eliminated, but sales for foreign currency or barter would be continued. The market thus would not be completely free.

The USDA study,[6] made at the request of Senator Allen J. Ellender, assumed that the stocks would be reduced to normal over a period of several years:

Senator Ellender's request specified that the projections should be made under assumptions that all production controls except those on tobacco were removed and price supports were maintained at levels which would permit an orderly reduction over a 7- to 10-year period in the currently excessive stocks of storable farm commodities.

Under these assumed conditions, total farm output would increase to 137 percent of the 1947–49 average by 1965. This would be 20 percent higher than the 1955–57 average of 114 percent. Compared to current indications for 1959, the projected increase would be around 10 percent. The increase above 1955–57 in output of livestock would be 25 percent and that for crops would be 16 percent. The greater increase in livestock output would result from favorable livestock-feed price ratios. Livestock output at the projected level would reduce feed grain stocks by 7 million tons per year and require the use of substantial quantities of wheat for feed.

The projected population figure for 1965 is 195.7 million, an increase of 16 percent from 1955–57. Per capita disposable income at $2,120 in 1965 is 22 percent above 1955–57.

Projected cash receipts from farm marketings at $30.6 billion would be 2 percent higher than the 1955–57 average. Cash receipts from livestock and products at $17.7 billion would be 7 percent higher, and those from crops at $12.9 billion would be 4 percent lower.

Although the projected cash receipts figure is a little higher than the 1955–57 figure, it is 9 percent lower than the $33.6 billion figure for 1958. In that year, a number of unusual factors contributed to an increase in cash receipts.

The projected index of prices received by farmers would be 193 for 1965, 17 percent below the 1955–57 average.

---

[5] "Report From the USDA and a Statement by the Land Grant Colleges IRM-1 Advisory Committee on Farm Price and Income Projections 1960–65 Under Conditions Approximating Free Production and Marketing of Agricultural Commodities. Presented by Senator Allen J. Ellender, Jan. 20, 1960.

[6] Ellender report, *op. cit.*, p. 3.

At 184, prices received for crops would be down a little more than the total index, and prices received for livestock and products at 200 would be down somewhat less than the total.

The projected increase in farm output would imply a per capita food consumption index of about 108 (1947–49 = 100) for 1965, about 5 percent higher than in 1955–57. Per capita consumption of food livestock products would be 8 percent higher with meat, including poultry meat, accounting for all of the increase. Per capita food use of crops would be practically the same as the 1955–57 acreage.

In general, the prices projected by the USDA were higher than those projected by Iowa State University. But both of them were so low that they thoroughly alarmed farmers and farm leaders. Hogs, $11.00 per 100 pounds; beef cattle, $15.00; corn, 80 cents per bushel, or less; wheat, 90 cents per bushel, or less— these projections indicated concretely what a return to the open market would do to the prices of farm products.

The Iowa economists estimated that if the CCC storage programs had not been in effect during the 1950's, average annual cash receipts would have been about $3.6 billion—about 33 per cent—lower. The lowering of net income would have been less than the lowering of total cash receipts in dollars, but it would have been greater in percentage terms.

These estimates indicate that the storage programs raised total cash receipts about 11 per cent, and net income about 33 per cent. These are substantial percentages, especially the gain in net income.

Later estimates made at Iowa State University in 1963 indicated that if open market conditions were instituted in 1963, United States total net farm income would decline from $13.3 billion in 1963 to about $7.5 billion in 1967. This would be a decline of more than 40 per cent.

WOULD THE LAW OF SUPPLY AND DEMAND WORK?

Some observers believe that the projected low open market prices and incomes would shortly reduce production in agriculture. This reduction would be great enough to bring prices up again to levels high enough to bring returns to resources in agriculture up to comparable levels with returns in other occupations. That is, these observers believe that "the law of supply and demand would take care of the farmer."

This is not necessarily true.

The law of supply and demand in the open market is a valid economic concept, but it requires two conditions besides large numbers of producers in order to work as smoothly and quickly to bring about equality of returns as it does in the minds of many who have a knowledge of elementary economics. These two conditions are: (1) perfect or at least reasonably perfect knowledge of opportunities in different occupations, and (2) perfect or reasonably perfect mobility of the factors of production. Economic textbooks spell out these conditions, but often they are forgotten in application. And whenever these two conditions are not met, the law of supply and demand in the open market does not work well. Prices respond quickly and easily, but production responds only slowly and painfully.

These two conditions—perfect knowledge and perfect mobility—are not met at all closely in agriculture.

Imperfect knowledge. Farmers do not have full and accurate knowledge of alternative nonfarm employment opportunities. They hear that urban wages are high, but they also hear that the costs of urban living are high too, and so is unemployment at times; and in most cases they do not have specific information such as that the X company in Y city will take them on next month at Z wages.

Imperfect mobility. In addition, the mobility of farmers is low. The law of supply and demand says that when prices decline, factors of production (land, labor, and capital) move out of production, and production declines until that decline brings prices up to remunerative levels again. But labor and management (farmers) find it difficult to move out of agriculture because of the obstacles to free mobility that stand in the way.

Middle-aged and older farmers, particularly, find it difficult to pull up stakes and get a good job in town. They are not trained for city work, and in any case urban employers discriminate against men over 40. Young farmers can move more easily, but the psychological, sociological, and economic obstacles are still high. Even reducing the flow of potential young farmers into agriculture is not easy. Farm boys in high school are likely to be taking classes in vocational agriculture rather than in vocational industry or commerce. The psychic as well as economic obstacles are hard to surmount.

The situation may be represented schematically in a supply and demand curve diagram with income per farmer (the "price of farmers") plotted up the vertical axis and numbers of farmers plotted along the horizontal axis.

The demand curve, representing the demand for farmers, is inelastic, much as the demand curve for farm products in inelastic. And the curve has been moving to the left as production per farmer has been increasing more rapidly than the demand for farm products has been increasing.

The supply curve for farmers is more complicated than a simple straight or moderately curved line. It has a kink in it at the point of intersection with the demand curve, so that it is very elastic upward to the right, but inelastic downward and to the left. As the demand curve moves to the left, the number of farmers in agriculture tends to remain large, because farmers engaged in farming find it difficult to pull out. Yet if the demand curve were to move to the right—if for example the flow of new technology were cut off—farmers would benefit very little, because the birth rate on farms is high and a continuous excess of farmers is being produced each year. An increase in the demand for farmers would simply be met by a corresponding increase in the number of farm boys who would decide to stay in farming in response to only a small increase in "price" (income per farmer).

Beyond this kinked supply curve lies the further difficulty that a speeding up of migration out of agriculture would not reduce agricultural production proportionately. A small speed-up might not reduce production at all. The remaining farmers in many cases would combine the farms into larger and more efficient units, so that total agricultural production might actually increase rather than decrease. Only if the speed-up were substantial enough to induce transformation of farms into more extensive types of farming would it have much reducing effect on production. And this process is painful and slow.

If agriculture were returned to the open market, then, returns in agriculture would decline from their present supported levels, not just to long-run competitive levels (equal to returns in other occupations) but below those levels. The distance below would be roughly equal to the size of the obstacles to mobility, measured in dollar terms. And this situation would not bring its own cure in a year or two if things were left to themselves.

The process would take a long time. And it would be a grinding, inhumane process if left to itself. It probably would create some poverty pockets or areas in agriculture, perhaps of considerable size, where farmers would be too poor and untrained to be able to move out into better jobs, so that the poverty areas would continue to exist for many years. They would be perpetuated rather than eliminated by low prices.

The working of the law of supply and demand in the open market eventually would tend to drive marginal farmers and areas out of farming. But the obstacles to exit from farming are so great that low incomes in agriculture would persist for many years. Is there not some more humane way of getting the job done?

What is needed is a temporary production control program that would bring about the same kind of reduction in agricultural production and numbers of farmers (in terms of total quantity) and numbers, location, and product-mix, that would result if the open market could bring about efficient reallocations of production and factors of production quickly and painlessly.

That is to say: The open market eventually would maximize efficiency in line with the long-run objectives of society by reducing production and the number of farmers on some farms and in some areas. Therefore, any temporary agricultural production reducing program also should reduce production and the number of farmers on some farms and in some areas—but do it more quickly.

How could the program also do it painlessly? It could do it painlessly by employing the welfare economics principle of compensation.

Welfare Economics Principle of Compensation

Welfare economics recognizes that in a situation where a change in technology benefits some and harms others, it is impossible to measure the good against the harm and say that the one is greater or less than the other. In technical economic terms, interpersonal comparisons of utility (satisfaction) are impossible. No one can prove directly that the benefits of a new invention to one person or group are greater, or less, than the harm to another person or group that is temporarily, or in some cases permanently, thrown out of work by the new invention. But one can prove indirectly whether the benefits are greater than the harm if the person or group that is benefited can fully compensate the person or group that is harmed and still have some of the benefit left. In that case, the invention will have made one person or group better off and no person or group worse off, so there is a net gain to society as a whole.

Programs adopted under this principle, therefore, do not represent a compromise between the benefits of new technology and the disturbance that it creates, but a full attainment of the benefits and a full compensation for the disturbance.

In concrete terms, an agricultural production reduction program that would benefit many and harm none would pay a large enough compensation to secure voluntary cooperation from the farmers on those farms which should reduce production or go out of production. This would indicate that the farmers were fully compensated for the harm they would suffer—the change that they would have to make in their lives, and the temporarily or permanently lower level of incomes that they estimated they would have to accept as a result of the change.

The same principle would apply to the nonfarmers—the local business people, the storekeepers, the bankers, etc.—in the communities where agricultural production would be reduced enough to hurt their business. They, as well as the farmers, could be compensated for the harm they suffered.

If the farms and farmers which moved out of production under this program were more nearly those that were least efficient in agricultural production, compared with their productivity in alternative occupations, the more nearly would the program be in line with the long-run objectives of a growing and developing economy.

It seems evident from the preceding sections that returning agriculture to the open market would not solve agriculture's and society's problem, until the conditions of mobility and knowledge which could render the open market in agriculture effective are established.

To many observers this means that, to put it in positive terms, short-run steps need to be taken to increase farm income by other methods: (1) production control by controlling inputs or outputs, or both, (2) two-price systems, (3) direct payments to farmers, and (4) expansion of the demand for farm products, etc., or all of these until other longer run steps to increase the mobility of the factors of production in agriculture, particularly labor and management, can take effect. Then agriculture can move toward the open market without undue harm to those who are at present trapped in agriculture and cannot easily get out.

These alternatives will be examined in the next few chapters.

8

Proposed Mandatory Production Control

At the other extreme from the free market lies mandatory production control.

Production control in agriculture is being advocated as a means of attaining some bargaining power for agriculture to balance the bargaining power of large units in other parts of the economy.

The arguments whether agriculture is justified in attempting to do this—that is, to gain some bargaining power in relation to other sectors of the economy—have been going on for years. In 1952, a committee of 13 eminent economists recommended that agriculture be returned to the open market.[1] In 1962, the Committee for Economic Development made a similar recommendation.[2] Several farm economists—Karl Brandt, Joe Davis, W. I. Myers, Earl Butz, and Don Paarlberg—feel general agreement with these reports. J. K. Galbraith and a number of other economists, however, hold a different view. They believe that agriculture should develop "countervailing power" to match the monopoly power in the rest of the economy.

The question whether two monopolies are better than one has been discussed by economic theorists as well as laymen. There is some support for the conclusion that they are.[3] Several agricultural economists—Heady, Wilcox, Brandow, Cochrane, and Schnittker—argue vigorously that when monopoly power is so prevalent in the rest of the economy, farmers are entitled to develop some of their own.

---

[1] Farm Foundation Report, "Turning the Searchlight on Farm Price Policy," 1952.

[2] "An Adaptive Program for Agriculture." Committee for Economic Development, 1962, 711 Fifth Ave., New York 22.

[3] T. Scitovsky, *Welfare and Competition.* Irwin, 1951, pp. 415–16.

This view is well reflected in an exchange between H. D. Cooley, chairman of the House Agricultural Committee, and T. O. Yntema, vice-president of the Ford Motor Co., during a discussion of a CED report, which advocated that production controls in agriculture be abolished and agriculture returned to the open market:[4]

"You could sell a lot more cars if you would reduce the price," observed Cooley.

"Some. Not a whole lot more," conceded Yntema.

"The Ford Motor Company controls production?" Cooley continued.

"That's right," Yntema replied.

"Then why is it wrong for farmers to control their production?" asked Cooley.

"Some of them do. They go to work for Ford," said Yntema.[4]

THE CASE FOR PRODUCTION CONTROL

The case for production control in agriculture has been well stated by Earl Heady:[5]

"I believe free markets and absence of any type of production controls currently may be just as unacceptable to farmers as marketing quotas. I believe that wide acceptance exists for land withdrawal on a scale which will cut supply and annual output back far enough that prices can 'be left free in the market,' but with some improvement in level, or certainly without drastic reductions in prices. True, the two million commercial farmers are similar to other businesses in the sense that they are generally profit motivated and respond to prices and adapt inputs and outputs accordingly. But they are dissimilar in the industry sense in that they are unable to manage their surplus capacity and supply to a given set of market prices. Witness other major industries: The steel industry ran at only about half of capacity during the past summer. Prices were well maintained. The petroleum industry has been faced with surplus capacity and inventories over the past several years. But output going to the market has been adjusted generally to a given set of prices. Other examples could be cited where prices are 'determined in the market' but the industry has managed its output so that prices were maintained.

---

[4] *The Des Moines Register*, Aug. 7, 1962, p. 1.
[5] Earl O. Heady, discussion of Karl Brandt's paper at meeting of the Western Farm Economics Association and American Statistical Association, Palo Alto, Calif., Aug. 26–29, 1960.

This same arrangement would be highly acceptable to farmers. They would like this type of 'free market operation,' in contrast to the type which they have. With this ability to adjust industry output to price and still remain competitive with each other in this framework, they would get their return more clearly 'through the market.' They would have to depend less on price support subsidies and would prefer it this way. But we all know that even if we consider the relevant number to be as small as two million, the number is too great for the individual to have any power over the market.

"Because of its extreme competitive structure, is it 'morally wrong' for agriculture to ask for power to manage its output relative to a 'given' price, such as is accomplished in certain other industries? Or, alternatively, we might ask: Is it necessary for all of the 'efficiency guns' to be turned on agriculture? Must it provide the resource savings for meeting all the world challenges which face the nation over the next decades? One would think so when he views the empirical scrutiny to which agriculture is subjected, without similar or parallel analysis and prescription for other industries. The major 'fat' in the economy, which might be used to meet the nation's basic world and internal challenges, is not to be found in agriculture. The industry uses only a small fraction of the nation's resources, if we exclude land which has little alternative use, and its income is even a smaller proportion of national product. Either the 'empirical efficiency guns' ought to be turned equally on other industries, or we should try to give agriculture the same ability to manage its capacity relative to price as exists elsewhere."

John Schnittker states the case for production control in agriculture more dramatically:[6]

"Is it equality of opportunity and equality before the law to grant collective bargaining rights to labor but to decline even to search for similar innovations in farm markets? Is there justice in overt selection or tacit acceptance of output and employment policies, and price and wage policies for much of industry and labor but rejection of similar price and output policies (if they can be devised) for agricultural producers? Do we designate as just, a pricing system which tells us that the value of 800 million

---

[6] John A. Schnittker, "Positive Policies for America Agriculture," Chap. 14B in *Goals and Values in Agricultural Policy.* (Center for Agricultural and Economic Development, sponsors), Iowa State Univ. Press, Ames, 1961, pp. 327, 332.

bushels of wheat a year is $1.5 billion, but the value of a billion bushels accidentally produced in the same year would have been perhaps half a billion dollars less? Is it a contribution to order and stability—to harmonious relationships among human activities—to accept an economic structure for agriculture with distinctly different characteristics than the dominant economic structure and results if not unique, at least unusual? . . .

"Resource owners—farm and nonfarm—covet market arrangements which show promise of doing justice to individual and corporate performance, not modest insurance against disaster. We are gradually achieving such arrangements in the United States. Unemployment insurance is important, but it is not a substitute for collective bargaining against a backdrop of full employment. Farm income insurance may be an appropriate supplement to farm output and price policies but is not likely to be a substitute for them."

PROPOSED MANDATORY PRODUCTION CONTROL

The production-control programs discussed in the preceding chapters were all voluntary. Farmers were offered cash rent or other forms of inducement to participate.

Farmers who wished to participate did so as individuals. Other farmers, who did not wish to take part, were free to stay out. Many of those who stayed out increased their production, thus offsetting part of the reduction made by those who came in. Payments had to be made high enough to offset the greater production a farmer could undertake if he stayed out.

Accordingly, the question began to be raised whether acreage reduction should not be made mandatory on all the producers of a commodity, like some marketing agreements are, if two-thirds of the producers voted in favor of it. It was believed that this would be more equitable among producers, and cheaper to operate, than the preceding and current voluntary programs.

Mandatory production control was proposed by one of its leading advocates, Willard W. Cochrane, in these words:[7] "By supply control I mean the conscious adjustment of supply to demand, commodity by commodity, year after year, to yield prices in the market that have already been determined as fair by some responsible agency. And I have reference to a permanent set of

---

[7] Willard W. Cochrane, "Some Further Reflections on Supply Control." *Jour. Farm Econ.*, Vol. 41, Nov. 1959, pp. 697–98.

institutional controls to deal with a chronic condition of overproduction in agriculture. Further, since every commodity of any importance in agriculture is produced by many hundred to many thousand producers, it follows that a specific aggregate adjustment can only be achieved by consistent adjustments on each of these many farms. Finally, since unanimous agreement in collective action is virtually impossible, it also follows that the will of the majority must be imposed upon the minority in any effective supply control process in agriculture."

INTEGRATION IMPLEMENTED BY VOLUNTARY CONTRACTS NOT SUFFICIENT FOR SUPPLY CONTROL

O. P. Blaich supports Cochrane's belief that mandatory controls are necessary for effective supply control. He draws on his experience in California with voluntary contracts between growers and processors, to point out that these contracts are not sufficient for supply control. Integration implemented by voluntary contracts will not do the job even when a large percentage of the growers are under contract.[8]

The hops industry is a good example where the use of contracts between brewers and hops growers has failed to achieve full market price stability. A large share of the hops is produced under contract from one to three seasons in advance. But, some growers and brewers each year find it more appealing to deal outside of the contract market. This inelastic supply and demand condition generates a tremendous price instability in the "free market" which in turn is transmitted to the contract market because the contractors follow the "free market" quotations to a large degree.

To some extent, the hops market demonstrates that supply-management through voluntary contracts does not work in industries that have a competitive structure. Some means of guaranteeing full participation and of preventing leakages to the market is needed to gain the desired price effects.

But, the general problem in agriculture is even more complex than the case of hops. The price for most food commodities is formed in the sphere of influence of forces that determine the price level for all food. Thus, attempts to balance the supplies of a particular commodity cannot ignore the existence of all close food substitutes.

---

[8] O. P. Blaich, "Is Integration the Answer?" *Better Farming Methods,* Aug. 1962, pp. 13, 24–26. The rest of this section is adapted from this article.

Any maladjustment in the production of substitutes can be as injurious to the price stability of a particular product as if that product's own quantity were to vary in the market. Here too, vertical integration is no help; a contract between a grower of peas and a vegetable canner, for example, cannot control the quantity of all food products that substitute for peas.

Thus, it is obvious that vertical integration *per se* cannot be the answer to the income problem of commercial farm producers as long as the structure of the industry remains principally atomistic and competitive.

Even if all farm food was produced under contract, there is still no individual incentive for food handlers to regulate the total number of contracts that are let. Control of the aggregate production of all food is the critical factor because the demand for food is so inelastic that a very small change in quantity marketed will cause a wide swing in the food price level.

Thus, if a "proper" balance is to be achieved between supply and demand, then some form of horizontal integration, some form of producer collaboration, will be needed in addition to any vertical arrangements that may be used to facilitate the market.

The power of horizontal integration in achieving price and income stability was discovered by the crude-oil producers back in 1933. During the early part of this century, crude-oil prices had gyrated violently from year to year and from one period to another. Every time a flush new field was brought into production, the price of crude oil fell to lower and less profitable levels than before. The crash of 1931 was the final straw. The discovery of oil in Texas and Oklahoma sent prices tumbling from one dollar to less than ten cents per barrel.

Before 1931, prorate laws had been passed in several oil-producing states. However, oil moved freely in interstate commerce so that aggregate control was impossible. Moreover, each state limited its control for fear that it would lose its share of the market without a gain in price.

In 1933, however, the Industrial Recovery Act authorized the Federal Bureau of Mines to prorate crude-oil production among states, among oil fields, among pools, and among producers. This was the ultimate in supply management.

From the oil producers' limited and short-run point of view, it worked. How good it was for the nation as a whole is another matter.

Between 1925 and 1933, annual crude-oil prices had fluctuated between 65 cents and $1.88 per barrel. But, after prorationing, prices held fairly stable as aggregate supplies were kept in balance with consumer demand. During the 1933 to 1946 period, annual average prices varied only between $1 and $1.21 per barrel. After that, it rose steadily to reach $3 in 1958.

The problem in agriculture is very similar to that experienced by the crude-oil industry. In farming, every time a new surge of technology hits the industry, an excess supply of food is produced and farm prices are depressed severely. Thus farmers, too, might want to consider the power of horizontal integration, the power of cooperative action, to stabilize the level of food prices and farm incomes.

DO FARMERS WANT MANDATORY CONTROLS?

A mandatory land retirement program of this sort is no idle dream. It actually reached the stage of proposed legislation in 1962, but was defeated in the House by a narrow margin.

The reason for considering this mandatory feature is that without it, nonparticipants increase their acreage and production of the crop and nullify part of the reducing effect of the program. Accordingly, rental payments have to be set high so as to induce high participation and keep numbers of nonparticipants low; in addition, the percentage acreage reduction has to be set high, since part of the reduction will be reduced by the increase in acreage and production by the nonparticipants.

In May of 1963, wheat producers voted on a compulsory acreage reduction program—compulsory in the sense that if two-thirds of them voted in favor of the program, it would be compulsory on them all, those who voted against it as well as those who voted for it.

In similar referenda for this kind of program each year for several years preceding 1963, the wheat growers had voted in favor of the program. But in 1963, the campaign was developed as an issue whether wheat producers wanted more government management of agriculture, or less. Taking the proposed wheat program as a specific case under this broad issue, farmers voted overwhelmingly against the program, and thus by inference voted for less government management of agriculture; the vote was only 48 per cent for the program, and 52 per cent against (66.7 per cent for the program was required for adoption).

The vote did not mean that wheat producers wanted the government to get completely out of their operations. Wheat producers knew before they voted that if they did not vote for the program, the 1964 program would provide loan rates at 50 per cent of parity (about $1.25 per bushel) for producers who voluntarily chose to comply with the acreage allotments applicable to their farms. There would be no other inducements, however, for producers to reduce their acreages in wheat.

It was possible, of course, that new legislation would be passed, providing for more government management than this, before these "standby provisions" would go into effect. But since wheat producers had voted against government management, it seemed unlikely that any new program would be very stringent.

The wheat vote does not necessarily signify a long-run aversion of wheat growers to government management. Tobacco and rice farmers also voted down quotas once, but then voted them back in again after one disastrous year. The 1963 referendum may well be only a skirmish in the big battle over wheat.

ESTIMATED EFFECTS AND COSTS OF A MANDATORY PROGRAM

What might be the effects and costs of a mandatory land retirement program of this sort? And what difficulties might stand in the way?

The mandatory feature applied to programs that would take out parts of farms like the current feed grains and wheat programs, would have one obvious and immediate effect: It would prevent nonparticipants from expanding their acreage and offsetting part of the reduction affected by the participants. The programs would not "hold an umbrella" of price supports over nonparticipants as well as participants; there would be no nonparticipants.

Accordingly, the percentage reduction required by the program could be set lower than with a purely voluntary program. Under the 1961 feed grains program, for example, the government paid for, and participants took out, 25.2 million acres; but nonparticipants increased their acreage, and the net reduction was only 20.4 million acres. If the program had been mandatory, the government would have had to pay for only the 20.4 million acres.

At $31 per acre, this would have reduced the cost of the total rental payments $142 million, that is, from $782 million to $640 million. This is a substantial sum; it amounts to a reduction of about 18 per cent.

In addition to this reduction in numbers of acres paid for, a mandatory program might get along on a lower rental rate per acre than a voluntary program, or, on no rent at all.

It is difficult to estimate how much lower the rate might be under a mandatory plan than under a voluntary plan. Under a voluntary plan, the rate has to be high enough to provide more income than the other alternative of staying out of the plan and increasing production. But under a mandatory plan, the second alternative would not be open; the only alternative would be no program at all, and this would be less attractive than the alternative of staying out of a voluntary program and capitalizing on the beneficial effects of the participants' reduced production. Accordingly, it seems likely that a compulsory plan could get along with lower rental rates than a voluntary plan.

One other consideration, however, might work in the opposite direction. The rental rate would have to be high enough to induce two-thirds of the producers to vote for the plan. Under the 1961 voluntary feed grains program, producers representing about 50 per cent of the feed grains producers signed up. The rate under a mandatory plan would have to be high enough to get the percentage of farmers who would vote for the plan up to two-thirds. This would tend to offset some of the reducing effect on the rate of the other considerations given above.

It would be possible to cut this Gordian knot simply by legislation. That is, legislation might be passed similar to the earlier voluntary acreage allotment programs, under which the government did not make rental payments at all. The inducement to participate consisted in the fact that participants were eligible for CCC loans at rates above open market levels, while nonparticipants were not eligible.

This form of reward could not be used under a mandatory plan, since there would be no nonparticipants then. But some form of reward might be needed to induce congressmen to vote for the plan and farmers to support it. Perhaps the direct payments tried out on a small scale in the 1963 feed grains and wheat programs (at 18 cents per bushel) could be used.

Direct payments might work better than price supports above long-run market levels, for two reasons:

1. They would not reduce consumption, since prices would seek their own levels in the marketplace.

2. They would have less stimulating effect on production, if they were limited, as the 1963 direct payments are, to base quantities. If the payments were limited to base quantities, farmers would get the benefit of increased returns (prices plus payments) on their base quantities, but the lower open market prices on quantities in excess of their base would be marginal prices which would offer less inducement to increase production than the prices plus payments for the base quantities.

Thus a mandatory program (1) would cost substantially less than a voluntary program; (2) would share the burdens and benefits of the program more equally among producers; and (3) could make good use of direct payments limited to base quantities.

FLEXIBILITY

One of the offsetting features of the mandatory plan is its inflexibility. It would compel all producers of the crop concerned to cut their acreage by the same percentage. This would impose a rigidity on the cropping pattern that would be ill adapted to the perpetual changes that require each individual farmer to make the adjustments on his particular farm that suit that farm best.

Carroll Bottum puts it in these words:[9]

"Much more flexibility and freedom is possible under a voluntary program than under a compulsory program.

"A percentage of a crop or a group of crops or of all cropland must be retired on every farm under a compulsory program. If a percentage of a grain crop or a group of crops are retired, a historical base is necessary. This is particularly objectionable to farmers. The base years may catch one farmer with a large base acreage while another on the same type land may be caught with a small base acreage. One farmer for personal reasons may be contracting his operations while another may be in an expanding phase of his business. Each man must meet the same regulations.

"Under a voluntary program, each farmer is free to decide whether or not he participates in the program. If the program catches him with a low base or in an expanding phase of operations, he may stay out of the program.

[9] Carroll J. Bottum, "Land Retirement in Agriculture." National Agricultural Forum, Dec. 11–12, 1962, *Proceedings*, pp. 73–74.

"Under a voluntary approach, land may be retired on either a whole farm or partial farm basis. Likewise a voluntary program may be geared to retire the below-average grades of land or be geared to retire more land in one area than another.

"Our studies show that a program which retires both whole farms and partial farms costs less from the Treasury than one which retires only partial farms.

"Under a mandatory program where a part of the land on each farm is retired, the tendency is to return this land to production whenever the program is discontinued. Under a voluntary program it is more possible to direct the program towards the land that should, from the economic standpoint, be retired or shifted into other uses. The whole farm approach offers this opportunity. Once it's converted into grass, timber, recreation and other uses, it is less likely to be withdrawn and placed back into agriculture."

LAND RENTAL PROGRAMS ARE COSTLY AND INEFFICIENT

Land retirement programs that take out good, medium, and poor land alike, like the 1961 and 1962 feed grains and wheat programs, are not efficient in reducing total agricultural productive capacity in line with long-run goals of efficiency and economic growth. Mandatory programs would be still less in line. Programs of the Soil Bank type that take out chiefly poor land are better suited to that purpose. These Soil Bank type programs are, for example, analogous to the meat packing industry closing down its least efficient plants temporarily, rather than reducing operations at all of its plants, efficient as well as inefficient. Also, as shown in Chapter 3, they cost less per dollar of production reduced.

Programs of the Soil Bank type, however, are still a costly and relatively inefficient way to take out the poorer grades of land. They do it on a rental basis, with contracts running from 5 to 10 years in length. This is analogous to the meat packing industry closing their least efficient plants for 5 to 10 years, and leaving them to stand idle during that time, and doing nothing to reemploy the workers at those plants during this period at their other plants or retraining them for other jobs.

If the excess capacity problem in agriculture were likely to continue for only 5 or 10 years, then the present type of Soil Bank program would be appropriate to deal with it. But the problem is referred to as "chronic." It is likely to extend as far as can be seen into the future. In that case, governmental purchase would be more effective than rental. This would be analogous to the packing industry selling their plants to others who would put them to other uses.

Government purchase would put the government in a position to make the best long-run alternative use of its land, rather than simply leaving it idle. The government could put the land into recreational areas, into forest for timber production, into long-range urban development, and so on.

GOVERNMENTAL PURCHASE OF LAND

Earl Heady has estimated that if the $8.1 billion loss on operations of the CCC from 1933 to 1960 had been used to buy land at $100 per acre, 81 million acres could have been purchased.[10] The $213 billion of price support and conservation expenditures would have bought 213 million acres at $100 per acre, or half that many acres at $200 per acre. If this land had been held out of production, this would have solved the farm surplus capacity problem, and the government could recoup most or all of its costs by selling the land later for other uses. In that case, the annual cost would be only the comparatively small annual interest charges until the land was sold.

One disadvantage of a land purchase program is the slow rate at which it would proceed. Only about 11 million acres come on the market for voluntary sales or transfers per year. The government would need to proceed slowly—not necessarily at a small percentage of this 11 million acres, because the government purchases would be a different element and would in most cases be focused on different land from that which ordinarily comes on the market—but still slowly, so as not to drive up the price of land unduly. To use a rough figure for illustration, say 5 million acres of purchases per year, it would take 12 years before 60 million acres were purchased.

A government purchase program would necessarily be a long-run program, because of the permanent nature of the purchase operation. It should, therefore, be in line with the nation's long-run objectives of economic development and efficiency. What kind of purchase program would this be?

---

[10] Earl Heady, *Agricultural Policy Under Economic Development.* Iowa State Univ. Press, Ames, 1962, pp. 555–56.

One answer might be: a program that would retire the poorest land—the least productive (low-yield) land in the physical sense. If this basis were chosen, a lot of the dry land in the Western Plains would be retired.

But this program would not necessarily make economic sense. The land might be yielding a net return of only $5 per acre. But if one farm family could handle 2,000 acres, the family would be making a good living, which would be cut off by government purchase and retirement of the land.

A manufacturer with many plants who needed to retrench might consider closing down the least efficient ones. But this would not necessarily be the best course for him to follow. The least efficient plants might have no alternative uses, whereas some of the more efficient ones might be easily convertible to other uses. The guiding principle, therefore, would be to close down the plants which could be converted to other uses with the least reduction in net income to the company as a whole.

Thus, the land to be retired would not simply be the least productive land; the net returns from its alternative (nonagricultural) use might be zero. Again we can use dry land in the Western Plains, yielding a net return of $5 per acre, as an example. Its alternative (nonagricultural) use might be zero. But land in the Southeast yielding $8 per acre might yield $5 per acre in forest, or in use for recreational purposes. The nation would be better off to retire from crop production this land in the Southeast and put it into trees than to retire the dry land in the West and put it to no use at all.

Thus, the land to be retired would not necessarily be the poorest land, but rather the land where the alternative (nonagricultural) use would bring a return most nearly equal to its present return, whether that return be high or low. This land would as likely be in one place as in another, in one value bracket as another, and in one yield bracket as another.

The government purchase program that would reduce crop production with the least idling of productive resources, therefore, would be one that not merely took land out, but took it out and put it into nonagricultural uses that were the closest possible to full agricultural use of the land. The measure of fullness of use in this case would be net return.

If for example, the government purchased land and only let it lie idle, then the least idling of resources would be attained by idling poor land. But if the purchased land could be put to productive nonagricultural use, still less idling of resources might be attained by buying good land and putting it to a nonagricultural, but still almost as highly productive, alternative use.

What might some of these alternative uses be?

Homesites

In some areas, one alternative use might be sites for homes. This represents an intensive use, more valuable in most cases than use for crops. But it is very small in percentage terms, and not much can be done in any case to expand it.

Forestry

Another possible use is forestry, for the production of wood.

Wood is one product that is in short supply rather than surplus. Timber requirements by the year 2,000 are projected to be double what they are now.

It is estimated that by the year 2,000, the nation will need nearly 12 billion cubic feet of saw logs for lumber compared with 6,419,000,000 used in 1952; 7,125,000,000 cubic feet of logs for pulpwood compared with 2,697,000,000 used in 1952, and 1,478,000,000 cubic feet of veneer logs and bolts compared with 451 million in 1952.[11]

The United States Forest Service believes that the key to future wood supplies rests with 4 million owners of small timber tracts. These owners hold about 55 per cent of the nation's commercial forest land. But most of this land is producing far below its capacity.

The U.S. imports only 10 per cent of the timber consumed, and there is little likelihood of a substantial increase from Canada or other countries.

Figure 8.1 shows that land in forests amounted to 746 million acres in 1959. This was two-fifths more than the 458 million acres in cropland. The figure also shows, however, that the USDA projection of use by 1980 is slightly less, not more, than the use in 1959. A USDA estimate of the number of acres of cropland "that might be converted to trees" by 1980 under government easement and rental programs designed for the purpose is shown in the fifth row in Table 8.1 to be 19 million acres.

---

[11] Report by R. E. McArdle, Chief, United States Forest Service, *The Des Moines Sunday Register,* March 30, 1958, p. 11-G.

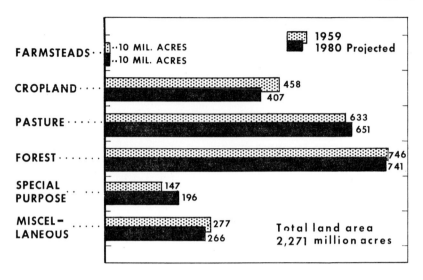

U. S. DEPARTMENT OF AGRICULTURE   NEG. ERS 1035-62 (4)   ECONOMIC RESEARCH SERVICE

Fig. 8.1. Present and projected major land uses. (Source of data: USDA, Land and Water Resources, 1962.)

Income-producing Outdoor Recreational Uses for Land[12]

There is strong interest in developing opportunities for outdoor recreation on farms to help meet the growing needs for recreation, to help provide employment and income to rural people and an income-producing use for some rural land not now needed for crops.

Title IV of the Food and Agriculture Act of 1962 authorized the Farmers Home Administration to make loans for a recreation enterprise in the same way it makes a loan for a dairy or other productive enterprise.

The Soil Conservation Service has been directed to help rural people through technical assistance and planning to establish income-producing recreation on farm land.

---

[12] This section is adapted from M. L. Upchurch, "Policies To Promote Basic Adjustment in Land Use" from *Our Rural Problems in Their National Setting*, Committee for Agricultural and Economic Development Rept. 16, Ames, Iowa. Dec. 1962, pp. 68, 69.

TABLE 8.1
Projected Land-use Adjustments*
(In million acres)

Change	20-Year Projection	First 5 Years	Second 5 Years	Third 5 years	Fourth 5 Years
Cropland:					
To urban....................	6.0	1.4	1.4	1.6	1.6
To public facilities.............	1.0	.3	.3	.2	.2
To recreation, open space, wildlife....................	5.0	2.0	2.0	.5	.5
To pasture...................	36.0	25.0	7.0	3.0	2.0
To forest....................	19.0	6.5	6.5	3.0	3.0
Total......................	68.0	35.2	17.2	8.3	7.3
Pasture land:					
To cropland.................	10.0	.5	.5	3.0	6.0
To urban....................	5.0	1.2	1.2	1.3	1.3
To public facilities.............	1.0	.3	.3	.2	.2
To recreation, open space, wildlife....................	6.0	1.5	1.5	1.5	1.5
To forest....................	8.0	2.0	2.0	2.0	2.0
Total......................	30.0	5.5	5.5	8.0	11.0
Forest land:					
To cropland.................	7.0	.5	.5	2.0	4.0
To urban....................	5.0	1.2	1.2	1.3	1.3
To public facilities.............	2.0	.5	.5	.5	.5
To recreation, open space, wildlife....................	7.0	2.0	2.0	2.0	1.0
To pasture...................	11.0	2.5	2.5	3.0	3.0
Total......................	32.0	6.7	6.7	8.8	9.8
Miscellaneous:					
To urban....................	5.0	1.2	1.2	1.3	1.3
To public facilities.............	1.0	.2	.2	.3	.3
To recreation, open space, wildlife....................	5.0	1.3	1.3	1.2	1.2
Total......................	11.0	2.7	2.7	2.8	2.8

* Source: USDA, Land and Water Resources, May 1962.

Existing programs should be reviewed and changed as necessary to keep land use more nearly in balance with requirements. Exceptions would be made for assistance in enlarging inadequate family-type farms.

In 1961, 25 million acres were in the Feed Grains Program and 28.4 million acres were in the Conservation Reserve. Conservation Reserve contracts will expire on 16.8 million acres in the next 5 years and on 11.6 million acres in the second 5 years. As contracts expire these lands will be eligible to participate in any Department of Agriculture land diversion program. There are about 600,000 cropland acres under contract that have been shifted to grass in the Great Plains Conservation Program. Contracts in the Great Plains Conservation Program will expire on 300,000 acres in the next 5 years and on 300,000 acres in the second 5 years. These lands also will be eligible to participate in land diversion programs.

The Agricultural Conservation and Stabilization Service can help develop recreation on farm land through the old line ACP cost-sharing practices, at least to the extent of providing habitat for game and fish, and through the new cropland use adjustment program. Recreation is one of the approved uses for land shifted out of crops, and cost-share payments for some recreation improvements will be provided.

The potential market for outdoor recreation opportunities on both public and private land is growing. Studies made by the Outdoor Recreation Resources Review Commission, projections by the Forest Service and National Park Service, and other studies point to expanding demands for recreation. The Forest Service expects a threefold increase by the year 2,000 in visits to forests for recreation. Other projections are comparable.

The extent to which demands for outdoor recreation can be met by farm people on farms is a moot point at present. Examples of outstanding success can be cited—the Pennsylvania dairyman who traded his milk cows for a golf course, the New Hampshire farmer who developed a ski slope, and many farmers who provide hunting and fishing opportunities to paying guests. It is too early to say how much and what types of these activities and land uses will be successful as economic enterprises. Experience with the market and with the unique qualities of successful management is still rather limited.

While efforts are being made to expand recreational use of farm land, public recreation resources are expanding too. Careful thought needs to be given to the relationships between public and private sectors of the business. Public recreation can complement private ventures as well as the other way around.

9
Marketing Quotas and Marketing Agreements

Marketing quotas which restrict output directly are considered by some observers to be superior, with respect to allocative efficiency, to controls which restrict inputs. A method of control which reduces output rather than resource inputs would leave farmers free to make the most efficient use of their resources. With output quotas, producers would be able to combine available resources within their individual farms at lower costs and in more efficient ways than if inputs like land or feed grains were restricted.

Marketing quotas for farmers have been applied in the United States through two different procedures: (1) marketing agreements and orders applied to handlers, who then worked out quotas and prices to individual farmers, with the government acting as referee, as in the case of milk; and (2) direct government programs, where the quotas and prices are worked out by the government, as in the case of wheat; in this case the marketing quotas were tied in with the acreage allotment (production control) program for wheat.

MARKETING AGREEMENTS

Marketing agreements developed first in Scandinavia and England, next in California, and then in the United States as a whole.

They developed out of producers' cooperatives' early attempts at "commodity control." Some of these cooperatives had endeavored to increase the total returns of their members by limiting shipments. The fatal weakness in this procedure was that even when the cooperative included in its membership a large percentage of the farmers producing the product, the "outsiders" who did not belong to the cooperative increased their shipments instead of reducing them; they benefited from the cooperative's actions without bearing any of its costs. As a result, the program of limiting shipments quickly broke down.

This soon led to legislation to correct the situation. This legislation provided for restriction of marketing wherever two-thirds of the farmers controlling two-thirds of the acreage of a crop were in favor of control. The significant feature of these programs for prorated restriction of marketing was that whenever a program was approved by the necessary two-thirds of the producers and the program went into effect, it became binding on *all* producers, even those who may have voted against it.

Federal Marketing Agreement Programs

Marketing agreement programs on a federal scale, analogous to the state programs in California, were developed shortly before World War II.

The usual procedure for initiating a marketing agreement program in a market begins with a request from some group in the market for a program and for its consideration at a public hearing. This request may be made by producers or handlers; but in most instances, it comes from producers' cooperatives.

Once a hearing is called, it is the responsibility of producers, handlers, and others in the market to supply the testimony and evidence necessary as the basis for further action. Each provision of a proposed marketing agreement and order must be justified. The hearing affords all interested parties an opportunity to take part in the development of a program with sound and workable provisions for the particular market. Frequently producers do not have the necessary factual information with which to justify their proposal. Handlers usually do have this information. Too often, however, they have been unwilling to cooperate by taking part in the hearing and furnishing the facts for the record. Since handlers are the ones who are subject to regulation under a marketing agreement program, the submission of pertinent data by them to show the extent to which they would be helped or injured by each specific provision of a proposal certainly is in their own interests.

Marketing agreement programs apply only to handlers of agricultural commodities (dealers). They apply to farmers' cooperatives as handlers of a product, but they do not apply to farmers as producers. The programs operate through marketing agreements and orders issued by the Secretary of Agriculture. Marketing agreements are contracts between the Secretary and the handlers of the product who sign the agreement; orders are regulations issued by the Secretary which make the terms of the "agreement" compulsory upon all handlers of the product.

Ordinarily, before a marketing agreement can go into effect with an order, the agreement must be signed by handlers of at least 50 per cent of the volume of the commodity handled in the prescribed marketing or producing area, and the issuance of the order must be approved by at least two-thirds of the producers, by number or by volume of the commodity. If more than two-thirds of the growers vote for the agreement, it becomes binding upon all producers alike, those who did not vote for the program as well as those who did. If less than 50 per cent of the handlers sign the agreement, the order may be issued by the Secretary anyhow, with the approval of the President.

The marketing agreements have been applied in two major fields—dairy products (mostly milk) and fruits and vegetables.

Purposes

The main purpose of agricultural marketing order programs is to increase producers' net returns. To achieve this objective, marketing orders include various types of provisions: control of volume marketed; quality, size, grade, pack, or container regulation; advertising and sales promotion; research and investigation; and the prohibition of unfair trade practices. Each order may include one or more of these provisions. Which ones are included depends on the particular order and the legislation on which it is based, federal or state.

Legislation varies among those states which have enabling legislation for marketing orders. Most states having enabling legislation do not provide for volume control of supplies going to market, and limit their marketing order provisions to quality, size, or pack regulation; advertising and sales promotion; or research and investigation. Under federal marketing orders, permissive provisions include volume control, both within a given season or from season to season; quality, grade, size, pack or container regulations; research and investigation; and the prohibition of unfair trade practices; but the provision of advertising and sales promotion is not permissive.

Marketing orders under federal legislation are not permissive for all crops. Under current federal marketing legislation, orders are not permissive for even all processing crops. There are exceptions such as olives, asparagus, and grapefruit segments, and in the Agricultural Act of 1961 the list of commodities was further expanded to include turkeys, turkey hatching eggs, apples in 15 states instead of 3, and cherries and cranberries for canning and freezing. Thus, the unprocessed fruits and vegetables list has been widened, but not completely opened. In fact, the major canned fruits and vegetables are still explicitly prohibited from having orders under federal enabling legislation.

Volume Control[1]

Under certain conditions, limiting the total shipments to market during the season may increase farm price and income—at least in the short run. An important condition concerns the proportion of total flow to market covered by the marketing order. For such a program to raise prices effectively, the marketing order should cover all or a sufficient amount of the product being marketed during the control period. But even if the marketing order covers enough of the total market, so that prices can be increased by limiting total volume shipped within the season, this does not mean that producers' total returns are necessarily increased. Whether or not they are depends on the nature of the total seasonal demand for the product. If consumers respond to the increase in prices by buying relatvely less of the product— that is, by buying competing products or doing without—the total returns will be no greater; in fact, will be even less. The situation is different if consumers are not too sensitive to price changes in the product; or, if the decrease in net purchase is proportionately less than the increase in price, then producers' total returns will be increased by a rise in price—at least in the short run. It is for these reasons that marketing order analysts are concerned with price, income, and cross elasticities of demand, both short and long run.

There are still other aspects to volume control as a means of raising producers' total returns for the season. Marketing orders

---

[1] This section is adapted from Sidney Hoos, "Possibilities and Consequences of Improving Income to Farmers Through Marketing Agreements and Orders." Paper given at a seminar, Farmers in the Market Economy, Center for Agricultural and Economic Development, Iowa State University, Ames, May 13–16, 1963.

do not provide for control of production. Hence, continued restriction of the volume marketed, if it does result in higher returns to producers, can lead over time to an expansion in production. This, in the longer run, is apt to defeat the attempt to raise producers' total returns. Thus, if the excess supply problem that the industry faces is temporary or seasonal, a marketing order can help. But marketing orders by themselves are not likely to solve chronic surplus problems. An order may, in fact, prolong the chronic surplus by retarding needed production adjustments in the industry.

Analysis and experience indicate that crops which meet the following general conditions are more likely to be successful with marketing orders if the programs are reasonably modest in their objectives:

1. The nature of the demand for the product at the farm level must be of a certain type if volume control is exercised—the demand should be price-inelastic, with not too low income elasticity, and the demand cross-elasticities should not be high.

2. On the supply side, the price elasticity and the cross-supply-elasticities must not be high. The modifying adjectives "high" and "low" cannot here be pinpointed other than to note they are used in a relative sense and in comparison with agricultural products in general.

3. A community of mutual interests, in particular in marketing problems, must exist among the participating growers and/or handlers.

4. The production of the product is rather concentrated in particular areas which are sufficiently small so that there is considerable similarity of production and marketing conditions among the growers.

5. Some actively interested organization such as a farmers' cooperative or other commodity group participates through educating the growers about the program, urging them to vote, sponsoring able men to sit on the administrative boards, encouraging the adoption of amendments to meet changing needs, and nourishing acceptance of the view that the operation and survival of the program is vital for the benefit of the grower individually as well as the group.

The institutional and organizational conditions are at least as necessary as the economic ones. More than a few marketing orders have failed because the institutional and organizational criteria were not met, although the necessary economic criteria existed.

If these are necessary conditions, then it is clear that all crops at all times cannot have successful agricultural marketing order programs—only certain crops under certain conditions. If this were more widely appreciated, there perhaps would be fewer frustrated experiences and disappointments among various growers and handlers. In some of those crops the real problems may be of such a nature that a marketing order is probably not the answer. Agricultural marketing orders have a big and difficult enough job without burdening them with the types of problems for which they are not appropriate action tools.

MARKETING QUOTAS

Marketing quotas are a device to distribute reductions in the total marketing of a product among producers of that product.

Marketing Quotas To Restrict Marketings

Marketing quotas which restrict output directly are considered by some observers to be superior, with respect to allocative efficiency, to controls which restrict inputs. "A method of control which operates on output rather than on resource inputs would lead to more efficient use of resources and would be more equitable as among producers. With output quotas, producers would be able to combine available resources within their individual farms at lower costs and in more efficient ways than if resources like cows or feed grains were restricted. Producers in varied situations would be subject to less discrimination if they happened to have command over more or less of any one kind of resource."[2]

Marketing quotas for farmers have been applied in the United States through two different procedures: (1) marketing agreements and orders applied to handlers, who then worked out quotas and prices to individual farmers, with the government acting as referee, as in the case of milk; and (2) direct government programs, where the quotas and prices are worked out by the government, as in the case of wheat; in this case the marketing quotas were tied in with the acreage allotment (production control) program for wheat.

---

[2] "A Study of Alternative Methods for Controlling Farm Milk Production and Supporting Prices to Farmers for Milk and Butterfat." 84th Congress, 1st Session, House Document No. 57, Jan. 5, 1955, p. 21.

Negotiable Marketing Quotas

One of the objections to marketing quotas is that they would freeze production patterns and hinder the continuous adjustments that are desirable in our dynamic economy. In order to meet this objection, a program involving the use of negotiable marketing certificates has been advocated in recent years by several economists.

"Marketing quotas should be transferable to permit readjustments in production among growers. This would reduce one of the significant criticisms of the use of controls. It would add to the problems of administration but once established the significance of the gains in efficiency would more than offset any additional cost of operations." [3]

Willard Cochrane outlined a proposal for negotiable quotas in these terms: [4]

1. It would be the responsibility of Congress to determine and set forth fair or parity prices for agriculture, as it does now. But in this scheme of things the role of parity prices has changed. No longer would parity prices serve as pegs on which to support farm market prices; rather they would serve as guides in the setting of national sales quotas. Thus, in the determination of parity prices for agriculture, the Congress would, in fact, be determining fair prices for both consumers and producers, and the needs and interests of both groups would have to be considered.

2. The United States Department of Agriculture would set national sales quotas for each principal agricultural commodity in amounts which the USDA had estimated would clear the market at the predetermined fair or parity prices. In practice this might mean the establishment of national quotas on each principal farm commodity moving into the marketing channel destined for human consumption (say 15 to 25 commodities). And these national sales quotas would, of course, vary from year to year as demand conditions changed, or as Congress redefined parity prices. To avoid, or to minimize, the difficult problem of integrating production controls vertically, national sales quotas would not be established for commodities typically consumed on farms, sold among farms, or sold to farms (e.g., feed grains, feeder cattle, baby chicks).

3. Each farmer at the inception of the program would receive a market share, his pro rata share, of the national sales quota for each commodity, based probably on his historical record of production. The farmer's share might be received in small denominational units, to which, for purposes of exposition, we give the name, marketing certificates. And once the program was in operation it would

---

[3] O. C. Stine, "Agricultural Production Control," *Policy for Commercial Agriculture—Its Relation to Economic Growth and Stability.* Joint Economic Committee, 85th Congress, 1st Session, Nov. 22, 1957, p. 691.

[4] Willard W. Cochrane, "The Case for Production Control Restated," *Policy for Commercial Agriculture—Its Relation to Economic Growth and Stability.* Joint Economic Committee, 85th Congress, 1st Session, Nov. 22, 1957, pp. 721–22.

be illegal for a farmer to market any commodity having a national quota except insofar as he had marketing certificates to cover the quantities involved. The number of marketing certificates would not be increased, or decreased, from year to year with changes in the national sales quota for a particular commodity. Rather each farmer could market an announced percentage of the face value of each of his certificates—a percentage in accordance with the national sales quota for the year. By this device the awkward problem of issuing and confiscating marketing certificates would be avoided for the bulk of agricultural production.

4. Each marketing certificate would be negotiable. Each farmer would be free to buy or sell marketing certificates as he saw fit. By this device freedom of entry and exit would be maintained within a controlled agriculture; by this device the individual farm operator would be free to expand production, or contract it, in light of local conditions, as total output was adjusted to demand at a defined fair price. The value of operating in a stabilized agriculture where product prices and returns were relatively certain and relatively good, and where long-range production plans could be formulated with reasonable assurance of materializing would, of course, get capitalized into these marketing certificates. The price of these certificates would become the cost of doing business in a stabilized agriculture.

Carroll Bottum appraised marketing quotas as follows:[5]

"If farmers were in favor of complete market quotas, farm marketings could be limited and prices and incomes to the agricultural industry could be raised. If the quotas were nonnegotiable, such a program would tend to freeze the agricultural pattern of production. Therefore, many have proposed that these quotas should be negotiable. If they were negotiable, then the producers on the better lands and on the better operated farms would tend to bid up the value of the quotas, and marginal farms would tend to be squeezed somewhat the same as with free prices. Assuming such a program worked effectively, it would raise the gross income to agriculture but over time, it would probably result in some of the gains being bid into the quotas or more people staying in agriculture. Some lands would probably go out of crop production.

"It does not appear likely that farmers at this time wish to subject themselves to such a high degree of control as would be necessary under this approach for the gain it offers."

[5] J. Carroll Bottum, Agricultural Editors Economic Conference and Workshop, Iowa State University, Ames, May 14–15, 1959.
Roland W. Bartlett registers an adverse opinion in "Should We Have Marketing Quotas To Improve Prices Paid Producers?" *American Cooperation.* American Inst. of Cooperation, 744 Jackson Place, Washington, D.C., 1959, pp. 225–36.
See also, Lyle P. Schertz and Elmer W. Learn, "Administrative Controls on Quantities Marketed in the Feed-Livestock Economy." Univ. Minn. Agr. Exp. Sta. Tech. Bul. 241, Dec. 1962; and W. Butcher and Earl Heady, "Negotiable Feed Grain Output Quotas," *Jour. Farm Econ.*, Vol. 45, Nov. 1963, pp. 780–88.

10
Multiple Price Programs

Under the open market, and also under most price-support programs, producers all get the same price, except for differentials in time, place, and form.

More complex multiple price programs are in use in many milk price areas, by which the different prices received for the different classifications of milk (uses to which the milk is put, such as fresh fluid milk, manufacturing milk, etc.) are carried all the way back to the individual producers.[1] Multiple price programs of this nature are being proposed for other commodities.

A form of multiple price system has in fact been in effect with a number of export crops since World War II. Exports of wheat and cotton, for example, have been subsidized by substantial amounts, which vary from year to year, and from program to program, sufficient to move the commodities into export channels at prices much below domestic prices. The different prices in effect for wheat in 1956–57 are estimated in Table 10.1. ". . . during 1953–57, virtually all American wheat was exported under some type of subsidy or concession associated with official efforts to keep domestic wheat prices at artifically high levels in the face of record heavy wheat stocks." [2]

---

[1] These milk price plans are described and analysed in E. S. Harris, "Classified Pricing of Milk." USDA Tech. Bul. No. 1184, 1956, and in G. Shepherd, *Marketing Farm Products—Economic Analysis.* Iowa State Univ. Press, 1962, Chap. 24.

[2] Helen Farnsworth, "Wheat Under Multiple Pricing: A Case Study," *Policy for Commercial Agriculture—Its Relation to Economic Growth and Stability.* Joint Economic Committee, 85th Congress, 1st Session. USGPO Nov. 22, 1957, p. 563.

TABLE 10.1

INDICATED MULTIPLE PRICES PER BUSHEL OF REPRESENTATIVE AMERICAN WHEATS,
1956–57 AVERAGES AND APPROXIMATIONS*

Form of Price	No. 2 Hard Winter (Kansas City)	No. 2 Soft Red Winter (St. Louis)	No. 1 Dk. Northern Spring (Minne- apolis)	No. 1 Soft White (Portland)
	(dollars)	(dollars)	(dollars)	(dollars)
Terminal loan rate.......	2.30	2.30	2.34	2.21
Domestic market price....	2.28	2.23	2.31	2.41
International Wheat Agreement export price..	1.56	1.50	1.45	1.50
Barter basis Foreign currency net price: Sec. 402, Mutual Security............	1.25	1.20	1.16	1.27
Public Law 480, title I..	.64–1.06	.61–1.02	.60–1.00	.65–1.80

* Source: Helen Farnsworth, *op. cit.*, p. 560. Footnotes to the table omitted.

The Treasury costs for this program for wheat are high, running at about half a billion dollars a year. Indirect costs also are
high.

MILK PRICE PLANS

Two-price or multiple price systems have been in effect for
a good many years with milk. Fluid milk prices in the Midwest
usually run about 40 cents per 100 pounds above the price of
surplus milk which is diverted to manufacturing purposes.[3]

Two-price systems for milk were developed because fluid
milk producers believed that the prices they received were being
beat down by the milk dealers, who were usually large in operational size and small in numbers in each milkshed and thus were
in an oligopsonistic position. The producers formed themselves
into "bargaining associations" which were designed to meet the
oligopsonistic power of the dealers with monopoly power of their
own, and enable them to take advantage of the differing elasticities of demand for fluid milk and manufacturing milk. But milk
is irregular in flow and highly perishable, so instead of bargain-

[3] Milk dealers in the Chicago area in March 1960, for example, paid
farmers $3.39 per 100 pounds for milk for fluid purposes, but only $2.99
for milk for manufacturing purposes, out of the same cow. (Supplement
for 1961 to "Federal Milk Order Market Statistics." USDA, Stat. Bul. No.
248, Nov. 1962, pp. 88, 89.)

ing to set the price from day to day, the two groups meet only at infrequent intervals to work out a formula which would set prices from month to month automatically in response to changing supply and demand.

Multiple price systems are also used for some specialized fruits and nuts, as in California. They have not previously been used with such nationally produced products as cotton or wheat, except in the form of export subsidies, as shown above. What is new in present proposals is the plan to use two prices for *domestic* sale, *carried back to the individual producer.*

TWO-PRICE PLAN FOR WHEAT

A formal two-price program for wheat was incorporated in the Food and Agriculture Act of 1962.

The level of price support (the commodity loan rate) for wheat of the 1963 crop was $2 per bushel for participating producers (those who agree to divert part of their wheat acreage, in accordance with the provisions of the program). The rate to "cooperators who are not participating producers" was $1.82 per bushel. The 18 cents difference between these two rates was represented by negotiable certificates, prorated according to each producer's wheat acreage allotment.[4]

PRINCIPLES OF PRICE DISCRIMINATION

Multiple price systems of this sort follow the principle of maximizing total revenues by price discrimination. In a market which can be separated into two or more separate submarkets with different elasticities of demand, total revenues are maximized if sales are pushed in the different markets to the points, not where prices (average revenues) are equal, but where marginal revenues are equal.

The effects of multiple price plans of this sort depend upon the relative elasticities of the domestic and foreign demands. If the foreign demand is more elastic than the domestic demand, dumping goods at lower prices abroad increases the total returns from the sale of the goods in the two markets.

This is true even if the demand in the foreign market is less elastic than unity, and the dumping therefore reduces the total value of the goods sold on the export market. The increase in the

[4] Rept. No. 2385, House of Representatives, 87th Congress, 2nd Session, Sept. 17, 1962. "Food and Agriculture Act of 1962." Conference Rept., p. 11.

total value of the goods sold on the domestic market is greater than the decrease in the total value of the goods sold on the export market.

Conversely, if the foreign demand is less elastic than the domestic demand, dumping goods at lower prices abroad decreases total returns.

And finally, if the foreign demand has the same elasticity as the domestic demand, dumping goods at lower prices abroad has no effect on total return.

These principles of export dumping are illustrated graphically in Figure 10.1.[5]

In the absence of any dumping operations, the price for the goods sold on the domestic market is 8.0, the same as the price of the goods sold on the export market. The amount consumed domestically is 260 units, and the amount exported is 120 units. Total returns from the sale of the commodity are 260 units domestically consumed multiplied by a price of 8.0, or 2,080; plus 120 units exported multiplied by the price of 8.0, or 960, a total return of 3,040 units of value.

The solid lines in Figure 10.1 show what happens under an export-dumping plan when the export demand is more elastic than the domestic demand. The domestic price rises from 8.0 to 11.3. The quantity domestically consumed declines from 260 to 220 units. The quantity remaining for export increases from 120 to 160 units, depressing the export price from 8.0 to 6.4. The total returns then consist of 220 units sold at a price of 11.3 or 2,486; plus 160 units exported at a price of 6.4, or 1,024, a total of 3,510. This is 470 value units more than the total returns without dumping.

The dashed curves DD′ and ED′ represent a different situation. In this case, the export demand is less elastic than the domestic demand. Returns from the sale of the crop in the domestic market are 220 units sold at a price of 8.7, yielding a total return of 1,914. Exports of 160 units are sold at a price of 3.7, giving a return of 592. The combined receipts from the sale of the domestic and exported portions of the commodity, under these circumstances, are 2,506. This is 534 value units less than the total returns without dumping.

---

[5] Figure 10.1 and the arithmetic in the next few paragraphs are taken from F. L. Thomsen, "Export-Dumping Plans." *Jour. Farm Econ.*, Vol. 22, pp. 446–47 and 453–54. A somewhat different form of exposition, though based on the same chart and arithmetic, is given in Thomsen's book, *Agricultural Prices*, McGraw-Hill, 1952, pp. 217–18.

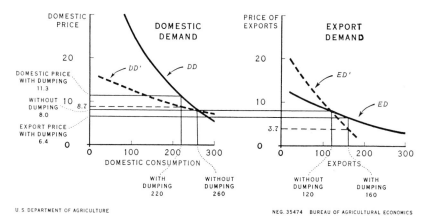

Fig. 10.1. Effects of dumping under different conditions of elasticity of demand.

This type of diagram shows clearly just what happens under the conditions given, and how the relative elasticities of the domestic and export demand determine the results. The diagram does not show directly, however, to what point dumping should be carried in order to maximize the total returns from the sale of the crop in the two markets.

That point can be shown by drawing in the marginal revenue curves based on the average revenue curves (demand curves) shown in the diagram. That will show the point directly, without requiring any arithmetical computations. All that is necessary is to locate the two points, equidistant to the left and right of the domestic and export quantities that would be sold under open market conditions, where the marginal revenue in the two markets would be equal.

It would be easy to draw these marginal revenue curves in the diagram if the average revenue curves were straight lines, simply by bisecting the horizontal distances from two points on each average revenue curve to the Y axis for that curve, and running a line through the bisection points. The average revenue curves in the diagram, however, happen to be curved, so the job is geometrically more complicated, requiring that a series of tangents be drawn in. The diagram is already rather filled up with lines. The principle of maximizing total revenue by equalizing marginal returns can most easily be demonstrated by starting from scratch with a new diagram, similar to the one shown, but with straight-line average revenue curves. One neat method of doing this is to superimpose the export part of the diagram on the domestic part, and add the two amounts together. Another way is to put the two charts back to back.

Application to Conditions in the United States

The analysis presented above shows the principles involved. The application of these principles to the situation in the United States, however, is an additional problem in itself.

The conclusions stated in the analysis are valid only if all the crop (including both the domestic and export portions) is bought and sold by one agency, and the gains and losses are reflected directly back to the growers without the agency itself taking any gain or loss.

Conditions in the United States do not meet this requirement. A crop is bought and sold by domestic mills, etc., and exporters. They all pay the same price (but the exporters recoup their losses that result from selling at lower prices abroad from the federal government). Domestic farmers gain; they get higher prices for their grain. Domestic consumers lose; they pay correspondingly higher prices for their grain, flour, bread, etc. The United States government also loses, by the amount of the subsidy it pays on the quantities exported.

A TWO-PRICE SYSTEM PROVIDES LESS INCENTIVE TO INCREASE PRODUCTION

One of the results of supporting prices above open market levels is that this leads farmers to increase production. A two-price system where the two prices are carried back to the individual producer can avoid this effect. In the two-price plan for wheat in the Food and Agriculture Act of 1962, the lower price for each producer's production above his (high-price) quota is intended to be not high enough to induce an increase in production.

This situation is shown in simplified form in Figure 10.2. The high price for the quota quantity would cut the supply curve above the intersection point with the demand curve, but it does not get out that far. The high price applies only to the relatively small quota quantity. The quantity produced in excess of the quota receives only the lower price. In principle, each farmer

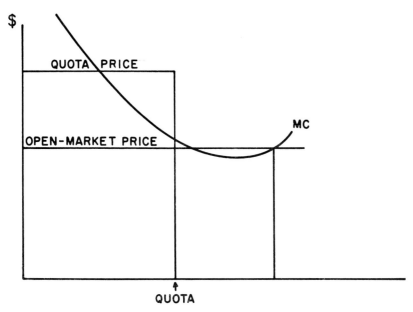

Fig. 10.2. A two-price system reduces the incentive to increase production.

carries his total production out to the point where his marginal costs equal the marginal (nonquota) price. Yet he still is able to get the high price for his quota quantity.

This indicates that a two-price system may appear to be a means for escaping the present dilemma in agriculture: (1) If prices continue to be supported at high levels, that provides an incentive for farmers to overproduce; this involves the government in expensive and dead-end storage programs to withhold the excessive production from the market, or adds to the expense of paying farmers not to produce the excess. (2) If price supports are lowered, that reduces farm incomes.

A two-price system which kept price supports high for, say, two-thirds of each farmer's previous production would maintain his income on that two-thirds, while the lower price for the rest of his crop would remove the incentive to increase production.

Two-price systems, however, can at best be considered only a temporary stopgap. There are several reasons for this:

1. The quota quantities would have a tendency to freeze production patterns, in a world where continuously changing technology requires continuously changing production patterns.
2. They would be regarded by other countries as subsidizing production in the United States, and those other countries would believe themselves justified in putting countervailing duties on our exports to them.
3. In addition, two-price systems would alleviate the low farm incomes without making any other change in the low-income farmers' situation. A two-price program would not pay these farmers to move off the farm; it would pay them to stay. Many of these farmers would be those who prize the non-monetary values of farm life highly enough to offset the lower money incomes they receive on the farm. If their money incomes fell lower than 20 per cent below the income they could earn in town, many of them would move to jobs in town. But if income payments make up part or all of the gap, they would stay on the farm. Their symptoms, low incomes, would be relieved, but the causes of their low incomes would persist unchanged. The problem would only be covered up; it would not be solved.

For these reasons, two-price systems are only temporarily effective, unless they include a clear understanding, spelled out in the legislation, that the higher of the two prices would steadily be reduced over the next few years to the same level as the lower price. This would give farmers time to plan readjustments.

11

Direct Payments to Farmers

Direct payments to farmers have been proposed as a possible means to support or increase farm incomes. They are, in fact, in use in the wool program, and they were included on a small scale in the 1963 feed grains program.

There are two different forms of direct payments—commodity payments (at so much per unit of the commodity) and income payments (per farmer).

Commodity payments. Under this plan, a guaranteed level of prices for each major farm product would be established by the USDA ahead of time. No restriction would be placed upon production or marketings. Then whenever the United States farm average price, or some other price representing the national average, fell below the guaranteed level, the USDA would make up the difference by direct payments to farmers.

In the case of corn, for example, the guaranteed price might be $1.00 per bushel. If the actual average price one month fell to 80 cents, then 20 cents per bushel would be paid to each producer who sold corn that month, regardless of the price he received for his corn at the elevator. This would bring the returns to the average producer up to $1.00.

Each producer would have as much incentive as ever to get the best price he could when he sold his corn, because he would get a payment of 20 cents per bushel, regardless of the price he received for his particular sale. He would simply have to present some authoritative evidence of the total number of bushels he had sold—a copy of his sales slip, for example—and receive a direct payment at the rate of 20 cents per bushel.

Income payments. The second form of direct payments is income payments. These payments are made, not to bring returns per bushel up to a predetermined level when the open market price fell below that level, but to bring *farmers' incomes* up to a predetermined level when those incomes fell below that level.

We will consider these two kinds of direct payments separately below.

DIRECT COMMODITY PAYMENTS

The great advantage of direct commodity payments to farmers is that they leave prices to seek their own equilibrium level in the market place. This has three effects:

1. It keeps products moving through into consumption. This frees the federal government from the costs involved in trying to support prices by purchase and storage operations.
2. It reduces or eliminates the need for costly subsidies designed to move exports into foreign markets—subsidies which in many cases are offset by countervailing duties imposed by foreign governments, so that our subsidies in effect are simply piped from our treasury into theirs. In these respects, direct payments make more economic sense than purchase and storage operations.
3. The great *disadvantage* of direct payments is that they only "cure" the symptoms; they leave the basic disease to run on unchecked, or actually made worse. If the low incomes are caused by an excessive number of farmers dividing up the total income pie, then direct payments to farmers will not reduce the numbers of farmers; they are more likely to increase them. When the basic disease is a maladjustment of productive resources, direct payments tend to perpetuate the disease, not to cure it.

The effects of direct payments and their cost would depend mainly on the level of the base price and how producers responded to direct payments. The base price level would depend on the purpose of the program. The two chief objectives in most peoples' minds appear to be to raise the long-run incomes of producers, or to reduce cyclic variations in production and prices like the 4-year hog cycle.

If the objective were to raise the long-run level of incomes for hog producers, for example, the base price would need to be set higher than the long-run level of market prices. But this would result in increased hog production, in response to the higher prices and to less price uncertainty. This would tend to drive hog prices down, making larger direct payments necessary. The larger payments would have to be made on increasing numbers of hogs. This would continue until public criticism of the growing size of the payments forced a reduction in the base price.

The long-run income-raising objective does not seem practical for hogs and other perishable products. It would be similar to the experience with corn and other feed grains, where the original price stabilization program for corn was converted into an income-raising program by setting the loan levels above long-run average prices rather than a little below them. The income-raising objective is incompatible with the stabilization objective, as shown by the accumulation of huge stocks of grains, cotton, dairy products, etc. It does not seem reasonable to go through an analogous process with hogs.

The Food and Agriculture Act of 1962 included a special kind of direct payment. It was a payment of 18 cents per bushel on the normal yield of the acreage devoted to feed grains or wheat. A feed grain producer with a 100-acre base, for example, who diverted 20 acres to conservation received 18 cents per bushel on the normal yield of the remaining 80 acres. On the production above that level, he got no payment.

This is a form of two-price system, under which the lower price for additional production acts as a restraint on production. This form of direct payment has some advantages, but it is subject to the same shortcomings as the two-price plans analyzed in the preceding chapter.

Direct Payments on Lightweight Hogs

In view of the foregoing considerations, a different proposal has been suggested to help hog producers—to make direct payments only on lightweight barrows and gilts, say from 180 to 200 pounds, to induce farmers to market their hogs at lighter weights and thus reduce total pork production.

Direct payments on these lightweight hogs would stabilize hog prices by supporting hog returns at the bottom of the cycle in two ways: (1) direct payments would add directly to hog producers' returns, and (2) if they induced farmers to market their hogs at lighter weights, this would result in a short-run reduction of the total tonnage of pork going to market. Since the demand for hogs is inelastic, hog prices would then increase, as would total returns to the producers.

But an interesting problem then would arise. The price differentials between light and heavy hogs would change as the percentage of light hogs in the run increased, and this change in differentials would offset part of the direct payment.

The differences between the prices of different weight hogs result from the relative supply and demand for hogs in the different weight groups. If the payment on 180–200 pound barrows and gilts induced farmers to market more of their hogs below 200 pounds, then the differentials between the prices of different weight groups would change. The prices of the lighter hogs would decline relative to the prices of the heavier hogs. This would offset part of the direct payment on the 180–200 pound hogs, and this would reduce the inducement to bring hogs in to market at 180–200 pounds.

Effects on Price Differentials of Making Payments On 180–200 Pound Hogs

If the direct payments on 180–200 pound barrows and gilts were large enough to induce farmers to market all their barrows and gilts at 180–200 pounds, that would reduce the average weight of barrows and gilts from about 225 to about 190 pounds. This would reduce the total tonnage of barrows and gilts about 15 per cent.

But the payment would have to be very large to bring about this reduction. The charts in Figure 11.1 show the relationship at Chicago between the ratio of the percentage of hogs 200 pounds and under in the receipts to the percentage of 240–270 pound hogs in the run, and the price differential for those two weights of hogs, by months, separately by years from 1956 to 1959.[1]

This period from 1956 to 1959 covers one full hog cycle. It shows that as the relative percentage of lighter weight hogs in the receipts increases, the price premium for these lighter weight hogs relative to heavier hogs decreases and then becomes negative.

---

[1] Geoffrey S. Shepherd, Donald D. Rohdy, James W. Gruebele, and William Dobson, "Analysis of Direct-Payment Methods for Hogs To Increase Hog Producers' Incomes." Iowa State Univ. Agr. and Home Econ. Exp. Sta. Res. Bul. 514, Feb. 1963.

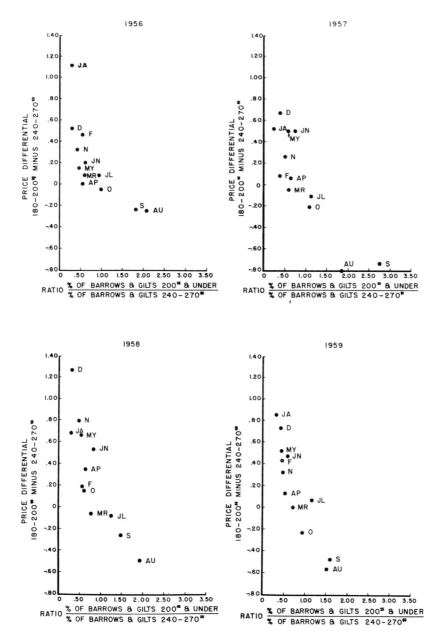

Fig. 11.1. Relationship of the ratio of percentage of hogs 200 pounds and under and percentage of hogs 240–270 pounds to the price differential between 180–200 and 240–270 pound hogs, at Chicago, separately by years, 1956–59. (Source: G. Shepherd, D. D. Rohdy, J. W. Gruebele, and W. D. Dobson, "Analysis of Direct-Payment Methods for Hogs To Increase Hog Producers' Income." Iowa State Univ. Agr. and Home Econ. Exp. Sta. Res. Bul. 514, Feb. 1963, p. 811.

The effect changes from one year to another. The regression was about 80 cents in 1958 and about $1.10 in 1959. That is, an increase of 1 in the receipts ratio caused approximately an 80-cent decline in the price differential in 1958, and $1.10 in 1959.

If the plan had worked, then, and had increased the relative number of 180–200 pound hogs coming to market, that would have depressed the relative price of 180–200 pound hogs at the rate of about 80 cents, for an increase of 1 in the ratio in 1958, and about $1.10 in 1959. This would have wiped out some of the effectiveness of the payments.

Suppose, for example, that a change in the ratio of 1 had resulted from a direct payment of $1.00 per 100 pounds on light-weight hogs. Then in 1958, 80 cents of the $1.00 would have been offset by the change in the market differential against it. In 1959, the change in differential, $1.10, would have more than offset the payment.

This system thus would be self-equilibrating. To the extent that a payment for marketing hogs at lighter weights was successful, and induced farmers to market more of their hogs at lighter weights, the relative price of the lighter weight hogs would decrease, and this would nullify part or all of the payment. The incentive to market hogs at lighter weights would thus decrease to the point where a new equilibrium would be reached.

Short-Run and Long-Run Effects

In the short run, the program could reduce total pork production nearly 4 per cent. This would increase prices about 8 per cent, which would increase total gross income from hog sales nearly 4 per cent.

This increase in income would increase profits. Since no change would have taken place in over-all competitive conditions, hog production would increase until about the same tonnage of pork would be produced as before, or a little more, since the direct payments would lower pork prices to consumers a little and lead to a small increase in pork consumption. Hog weights would be lighter, but the number of hogs would be greater. Hog producers' incomes would consist mostly of returns from the market-place, and partly of direct payments. Their incomes would be a little greater than before, since pork consumption would be subsidized; consumers would eat a little more pork than before; the government would be paying out substantial sums in the form of

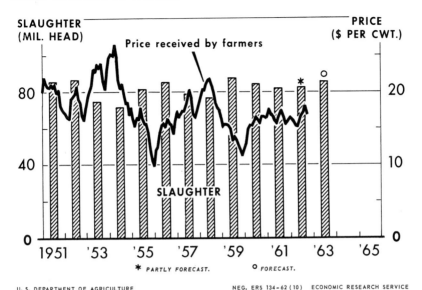

Fig. 11.2. Changes in hog slaughter and prices received by farmers, 1951–62.

direct payments. There would be a small benefit to producers, and some benefit to consumers, since they would get their pork at slightly lower prices and their pork consumption would slightly increase.

Direct Payments To Stablize Incomes

The corn storage program was an attempt to stabilize corn prices and incomes. It was originally set up in the belief that stabilizing the flow of corn into consumption would also stabilize livestock production and prices. This stabilizing effect was expected to be most pronounced for hogs; the bulk of the nation's hogs is produced in the Corn Belt on corn-producing farms, and corn makes up about 80 per cent of their feed.

There is some evidence that the corn program does have a stabilizing effect on corn prices and consumption. It is able to cushion hog production against the irregular shocks from variations in corn production caused by irregular variations in the weather. But it does not appear to have had a stabilizing effect on the cyclic movements of hog production and prices from 4 to 6 years in length. Figure 11.2 shows that hog prices varied cyclically through the 1950's much as they did before World War II.

Stabilize Hog Prices?

The cyclic behavior of hog production results from producers' errors of expectation or estimation of hog prices. Most producers seem to base their expectations on current prices. The length of the cycle is determined by the time involved before farmers change their hog production in response to prices—plus the time of gestation and the growing period for hogs.

Most producers wait until hog prices have remained high or low for several months or a year before they decide to produce more or fewer hogs in response to high or low hog prices. Then 10 to 12 months go by from the time the sows are bred until the time when pigs from the sows can be marketed. As a result, hog production and prices tend to move in about 4-year cycles. That is, high hog prices cause high production a year or two later; this high production causes low hog prices; these low prices cause low hog production a year or two later, and so on.

How can this cycle be broken?

The United States is primarily a price-directed economy. So a possible point of attack would be to stabilize hog prices in the belief that this would stabilize hog production. Stabilization programs for corn and other feed grains have helped stabilize the denominator (the price of corn) in the hog-corn ratio. What is needed now is to stabilize the numerator (the price of hogs).

So long as hog production continues to vary cyclically, variations in hog prices are necessary to clear the market. Stable prices are needed to guide hog producers to stable production; but, at the same time, varying prices are needed to clear the market.

These two things could be accomplished at the same time if prices were left free to vary and clear the market, while hog producers were, in effect, guaranteed a fixed price announced in advance. Then if the market price fell below the level, the difference would be made up by a direct payment.

If the objective were only to reduce cyclic variations in hog production and prices, the base price should be set a little lower than the long-run average price. This is because most hog producers would produce more for a guaranteed price of, say, $15 than they would for an uncertain price that later turned out to be $15.

There are several different methods setting the level of the base price.

Parity prices. Parity prices for hogs are computed monthly like the prices for the other important farm products; but they are not used as the basis for hog price supports, since hogs are perishable.

The parity price for hogs on June 15, 1963, was $22.40. Parity prices have been above the actual market prices of hogs most of the time since 1949. If parity prices had been used as the base price below which direct payments would have been made, hog production would have increased considerably. And market prices would have fallen so low that payments would have had to increase substantially. This probably would have caused a drastic lowering of the base price—perhaps abandonment of the whole program. Percentages of parity substantially below 100 might work better. But parity prices take any changes in technology into account so slowly that other alternatives need to be considered.

A moving average of market prices. This could be used if the period were enough to average out the effects of cyclic movements. With hog production price cycles running about 4 years in length, a 4-year moving average of market prices would be a minimum to average out the effects of the cycle. But there would still be a lot of variation in the 4-year average, since each cycle is somewhat irregular within itself, so an 8-year moving average might be better.

The chief shortcoming of moving averages, however, is that *they project the past into a future that is never quite the same as the past.*

The current level of the 8-year moving average is higher than hog prices are likely to average in the next few years. The past 8-year period includes several years when hog prices were higher than their normal relation to corn prices; much corn was going under government loan and into CCC stocks rather than into hogs. This cannot go on forever, and sometime this movement of corn into CCC stocks will have to stop. The relation between corn prices and hog production and prices then will be different from the relation in the recent past.

Changes affecting both supply and demand are only slowly assimilated into a moving average. So the 8-year average is always at least 4 years behind the times. What is needed is a base price which reflects recent and prospective developments in technology and in demand more accurately than 4- or 8-year moving averages.

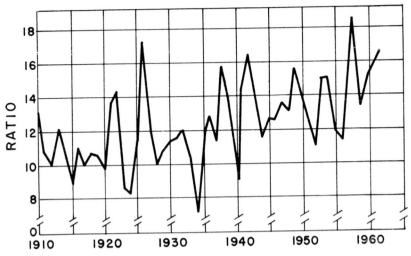

Fig. 11.3. Average hog-corn ratio, 1910–61.

A 14:1 hog-corn price ratio base. One of the most important factors affecting hog production is the hog-corn price ratio. Normally, when hog prices are high relative to corn prices, hog production is more profitable than when the hog-corn price ratio is low, and hog production expands. Similarly, a low hog-corn price ratio leads to a reduction in hog production, and an average ratio leads to an average production. In recent years, as Figure 11.3 shows, this ratio has averaged about 14:1; in earlier years, it averaged about 13:1.

The national average farm price of corn from 1958 to 1963 was about $1 a bushel. With average weather, the average price is likely to continue to run at about this level. The price usually runs lower than the loan rate when feed supplies are large. This by itself would indicate that a level of about $14 per 100 pounds would provide about a 14:1 hog-corn price ratio. This is the ratio which, in the past, has led neither to an increase nor decrease but to an average production of hogs.

But it is still likely that producers would respond more to a guaranteed price than to uncertain prices which might average out the same as the guaranteed level. So it might be necessary to *reduce* the guaranteed price by some figure such as 10 per cent to avoid an increase in hog production resulting from the elimination of price uncertainty. This would mean that the base level for hog prices would need to be, not $14, but perhaps $13 to avoid stimulating an increase in hog production.

DIRECT INCOME PAYMENTS TO STABILIZE INCOME

A different form of direct payment program has been proposed: To stabilize individual farmer incomes by direct *income* payments *per farmer* rather than by commodity price stabilization operations or direct commodity payments per unit of product—per bushel of wheat, per pound of cotton, etc.

For this purpose, two income objectives may be considered.

1. One objective would be to keep each farmer's net income relatively stable at about its average level over a period of years, no matter how low or high that average level might be. If a small-scale farmer's average net income were, say, $2,000, and drought or some other calamity reduced it some year to $1,200, that farmer would receive a direct income payment from the federal government of $800. If a large-scale farmer's income fell from its average of $20,000 to $10,000, he would get a direct income payment of $10,000.
2. A different objective would be to maintain some minimum subsistence level of, say, $3,000, to be applied to every farmer regardless of the size of his average income. On this basis, whenever the income of any farmer fell below $3,000, it would be made up to $3,000 by a direct income payment from the federal government. The objective here would be welfare, up to a subsistence level.

The first objective would be to keep every farmer's income stable, regardless of its level. This would permit every farmer to produce to the limit of his technical know-how, without having to keep a margin of safety against uncertain returns. This would benefit society as a whole as well as the farmers concerned.

A major shortcoming of the proposal is its probable high cost, and the high payments that would be made in many cases to farmers who were already well off getting, say, only $10,000 instead of their average $20,000. There probably would be plenty of charges that the government would be helping some farmers maintain their normal two Cadillacs instead of being reduced to only one.

The second direct payments objective has a strong welfare flavor. It would provide payments only to those who needed them, in terms of reference to some minimum standard.

This kind of income payment program is advocated by Boris Swerling. The payments under this program would be based not upon sales, but upon the extent to which individuals' net incomes fell below the average of the preceding five years. And the maximum base income would be some figure such as $3,600.[2]

In the past, farm policy has been led astray by the cult of national aggregates and averages. For purposes of political coalitions, it may be appropriate to speak in terms of a conglomerate agriculture or even of a broader commodity alliance. As a factual matter, diversity of income and of price experience is an important characteristic of agricultural enterprises in situations short of major commodity inflation or serious recession. From year to year, as net farm income rises or falls, the fortunes of particular farm operators diverge widely from the national experience; particular commodities move strongly against the national trend; and there is a wide difference between the income experience of individual producers of the same commodity in different regions or localities. This pattern of diversity distinguishes cattle-ranching from livestock-feeding, dairy farms in eastern Wisconsin from those in the northeastern states, even the production, respectively, of early and late potatoes. The effort to attain parity for "agriculture," though it has presumed that income would be diverted from other economic groups, has in fact accentuated the divergence of interests within agriculture. Reductions in permissible acreage have set western and southwestern cotton growers against those in the Southeast; statutory minimum allotments for cotton and wheat have put pressure on moderate-sized operators; and the farm bloc has split on the question whether corn has received more favorable treatment than cotton and peanuts.

The appropriate orientation for policy is toward the well-being of farm people, not the prosperity of a monolithic agriculture or a just price for cotton or wheat. Changes in aggregate farm income, by which one recent proposal would gauge the need for farm aid, do not provide sufficiently accurate signals for the purpose. Nor can the flow of federal farm assistance be appropriately related to the state of aggregate demand or industrial employment, after the recent lesson that the agricultural sector can sag in a thriving economy and can prosper during mild recession. Even movements in the per capita income of the farm population from all sources fail as a precise guide for policy: as the number of subsistence and part-time farmers has declined, a factor that formerly tended to depress the per capita figure now introduces an opposite bias. Social measures might well take more accurate account of the individual farm enterprise and the individual farmer rather than referring to misleading averages, and the contribution of earnings from off-farm sources must not be ignored.

Later, Swerling elaborated on his proposal a little further:[3]

---

[2] Boris C. Swerling, "Income Protection for Farmers: A Possible Approach." *Jour. Polit. Econ.*, Vol. 67, April 1959.

[3] Boris C. Swerling, "Positive Policies for American Agriculture." Chap. 14A in *Goals and Values in Agricultural Policy*. (Center for Agricultural and Economic Development, sponsors), Iowa State Univ. Press, 1961, pp. 312–14.

If one is impressed by the malfunctioning of commodity programs, conscious of economic realities that have contributed to recent difficulties, and cool to the merits of policy proposals most widely discussed, he is under some obligation to devise alternative arrangements. May I presume to restate here a different and much more modest approach for protecting the income of farm operators. This measure attempts to apply standard principles of social insurance, along the following lines:

1. As with unemployment insurance, benefits would be related to the income experience of the individual farm operator during the recent past.
2. Social security practices would be followed in establishing an upper limit on the amount of insured income, and there would accordingly be a modest ceiling on the total benefits enjoyed by a particular individual.
3. Benefits would accrue only to growers who suffer an abnormal reduction in income, not to prosperous and distressed individuals indiscriminately.
4. Specifically, a grower would draw benefits if his farm earnings in a given year fell more than, say, 25 per cent below the average of the preceding 5 years. The maximum base income would be set at $4,800 net, equivalent to some $15,000 gross.
5. The right to benefits would attach to the person, not to farm land or to the farm enterprise, and would accordingly not be transferable.
6. Benefits would not be conditional upon the production of particular commodities or even upon continued employment in agriculture.
7. Benefits would be scaled downward as off-farm sources of income rose, but at the same time contingent protection would be afforded to persons shifting from farming to other occupations.
8. The plan would be contributory and compulsory, but the federal government would subsidize the program by making premium payments on some matching basis . . . .

Outside agriculture, income-maintenance programs have typically been guided by the principle of a social minimum or have sought to pool risks in order to soften the distress caused by adverse economic developments beyond any individual's control. In this spirit Congress has enacted minimum wage, unemployment insurance, and social security legislation. Remember that the urban labor force does well if unemployment insurance covers half a man's earnings for a 26-week period, and recall also the considerable number of farm people who now enjoy this degree of protection on the off-farm portion of their earnings. By standards of social insurance, 75 per cent of base represents a generous level of income support, but even higher figures would avoid adverse side effects that result from corresponding percentages of statutory parity.

A strong feature of this proposal is that it would not involve large government payments to large and successful operators who do not need them.

One objection to the proposal, however, comes immediately to mind: Many farmers making a net income of, say, $3,000 might be planning to move to a better paying job in town. But if they were offered a guaranteed income under Swerling's proposal of $3,600 (or in his later paper, $4,800) a considerable share of the small-scale farmers would be likely to decide instead to remain on their farms, take life a little easier (or for that matter much easier) and let their farm income decline, knowing that it would be made up to $4,800 by direct income payments.

This objection is avoided in the case of direct commodity payments (per unit of the commodity) by making those payments uniform for all producers when the *average United States price* declines below the "support" price, regardless of the price each producer got for his products. Thus, each producer has the same incentive as ever to get the highest price he can, in the open market, and to produce as much as he can. But if this feature were included in the direct *income* payments plan, when the *average United States net income* declined below the "support" level ($4,800) to, say, $4,000, then all producers would receive an income payment of $800. This payment would not be needed by the large-scale producers with a net income of, say, $20,000, but it would not be enough for the small-scale producer with an income of, say, only $2,000. Direct income payments to each farmer when *his* income fell below a specified figure would remove the incentive for a substantial number of farmers to earn all they could.

In addition, this proposal would rectify the low farm incomes without making any other change in the low-income farmers' situation. The program would not pay these farmers to move off the farm; it would pay them to stay. Many of these farmers would be those who prize the nonmonetary values of farm life highly enough to offset the, say, 20 per cent lower money incomes they receive on the farm. If their money incomes fell lower than 20 per cent below the income they could earn in town, many of them would move to jobs in town. But if income payments made up part or all of the gap, they would stay on the farm. Their symptoms, low incomes, would be relieved, but the causes of their low incomes would persist, unchanged. The problem would only be covered up; it would not be solved.

12

Prospects for Increasing Domestic Demand for Farm Products

Expansion of demand, or increased food consumption, is one of the most commonly proposed solutions to the farm problem. Proponents of this idea maintain that increased consumption would sell more farm products, raise prices of farm products, reduce surpluses, and improve the diets of consumers all at the same time.

In examining this proposal, it will be helpful first to show what has been happening to the demand for food and fiber in recent years, as a basis for projecting what is likely to happen in the future. Perhaps this will show that the demand will soon catch up with the supply; perhaps it will show the reverse—that demand will fall farther behind.

We will deal first with the domestic demand for food and fiber in the United States, and in the next chapter with the foreign demand.

It is difficult to measure changes in demand. Changes in prices or in quantities consumed, alone, do not measure changes in demand; they may merely measure changes in supply, the demand remaining unchanged. A decline in prices, for example, may result not from a decline in demand, but from an increase in supply, cutting an unchanged demand curve at a lower point.

It is necessary first of all to understand what has been happening to per capita consumption of food in the United States.

CHANGES IN CONSUMPTION

The annual per capita consumption of food in the United States has remained close to 1,500 pounds since World War I.

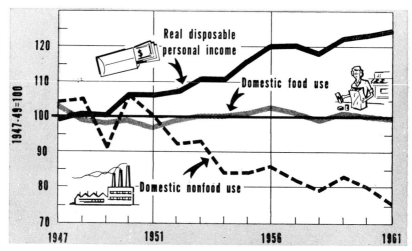

Fig. 12.1. Index of per capita consumer income and consumption of farm products. (Source: USDA, **Food and Agriculture, A Program for the 1960's,** p. 15.)

Apparently, the capacity of the human stomach now is no greater than it was 50 years ago. It may be less, since a higher percentage of the population is engaged in sedentary occupations.

In the United States, appetite does not depend on the level of income. Consumers with low incomes are still above the subsistence level, and they eat almost the same number of pounds as high-income consumers. Figure 12.1 shows that per capita consumption has remained relatively stable since World War II, even though incomes have increased, foods have been improved, diets have changed and extensive promotion and advertising have been undertaken.

Although the per capita consumption of food has been relatively stable, drastic changes have been taking place in the consumption of individual commodities. Figure 12.2 shows that the per capita consumption of meats, poultry, eggs, fruits, and vegetables have increased significantly since 1910, while the consumption of cereals has decreased 30 per cent and the consumption of potatoes has decreased 50 per cent. As a result of these shifts, fewer calories are consumed, though the total poundage per person has remained roughly constant. The caloric intake has declined chiefly because working hours are shorter and the work is less strenuous.

Most Americans obtain as much food energy from their diets as they need. The opportunity for expanding demand lies pri-

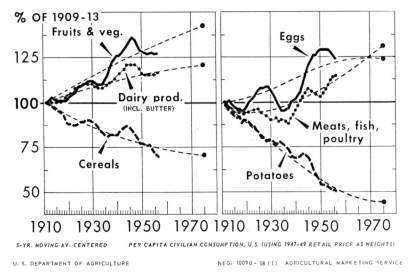

Fig. 12.2. Trends in U.S. eating habits, with projections to 1975. Five-year moving average centered. Per capita civilian consumption, U.S. (Using 1947–49 retail prices as weights.)

marily in the direction of substituting high value foods, measured in terms of resources used, for those of low value. For example, the production of livestock products requires five to ten times as much farm resources as the production of the same quantity of calories from basic cereal products. Recent trends in our eating habits show that consumers are changing toward high quality food products that use greater quantities of agricultural resources.

Some of these increases in consumption have been associated with relative price declines. These shifts in consumption are sometimes incorrectly considered as changes in demand, but they are only increases in consumption, not in demand; the demand may not have increased at all. Since the demand for food is inelastic, this kind of increase in consumption actually causes a decrease rather than an increase in total farm income.

CHANGES IN EXPENDITURES

Changes in expenditures (in prices multiplied by quantities) come closer to measuring changes in demand than either prices or quantities alone. But they are an accurate measure of changes in demand only if the elasticity of demand is unity. Where the demand is inelastic, as it is in the case of food in the United

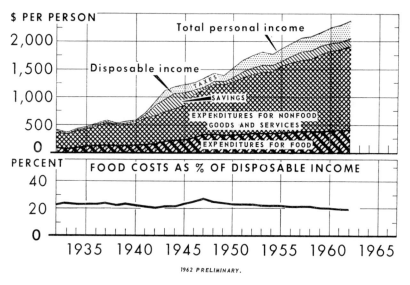

U. S. DEPARTMENT OF AGRICULTURE   \.NEG. ERS 592-63 (1)   ECONOMIC RESEARCH SERVICE

Fig. 12.3. Food costs and consumer incomes, 1932–62.

States (about −0.2)[1] an increase in supply will cause a decrease in expenditures, though demand may not have changed at all.

Furthermore, increased expenditures at the consumer level in the form of payment for increased marketing services do not necessarily increase the demand at the farm level; they may actually decrease it.

Expenditures, however, are a useful index of demand, if quantities also can be measured. Changes in expenditures, after adjustment for changes in marketing costs, also provide a direct measure of changes in receipts by farmers.

Table 12.1 and Figure 12.3 show that per capita expenditures for food have been rising since 1930, but that the percentage of disposable income spent for food has been declining slightly. The percentage would have declined more rapidly, more nearly in conformity with Engel's Law, if the make-up of the food had re-remained constant, as shown in the right-hand column of Table 12.1, where the most recent figure is only 14.1 per cent.[2]

---

[1] G. T. Barton and R. F. Daly, "Prospects for Agriculture in a Growing Economy," Chap. 3 in *Problems and Policies of American Agriculture.* (Center for Agricultural and Economic Development, sponsors), Iowa State Univ. Press, Ames, 1959, p. 33.

[2] For a more detailed discussion of this subject, see Chapter 4 of G. Shepherd, *Marketing Farm Products,* 1962, and Chapter 1 of *Agricultural Price Analysis,* 1963, Iowa State Univ. Press.

TABLE 12.1

PER CAPITA FOOD COST AND EXPENDITURE RELATED TO DISPOSABLE PERSONAL INCOME, UNITED STATES, AVERAGE 1935–39, ANNUAL 1946–60*

Year and Quarter	Disposable Personal Income	Total Expenditure for Consumer Goods and Services	Food Expenditure			Cost to Consumer of Fixed Quantities of Food Representing 1935–39 Average Annual Consumption Per Person	
			Actual	Percentage of		Actual	Percentage of disposable income
				Disposable income	Total expenditure for goods, services		
	(dollars)	(dollars)	(dollars)	(per cent)	(per cent)	(dollars)	(per cent)
1935–39...	514	493	118.6	23.1	24.0	118.6	23.1
1946...	1,136	1,040	288	25.4	27.7	201	17.7
1947...	1,181	1,148	318	26.9	27.7	244	20.7
1948...	1,291	1,216	328	25.4	27.0	256	19.8
1949...	1,271	1,214	311	24.5	25.6	243	19.1
1950...	1,369	1,286	313	22.8	24.3	245	17.9
1951...	1,473	1,359	346	23.5	25.5	274	18.6
1952...	1,520	1,400	356	23.4	25.4	279	18.3
1953...	1,582	1,458	355	22.4	24.4	271	17.1
1954...	1,582	1,466	355	22.4	24.2	270	17.1
1955...	1,660	1,554	358	21.6	23.0	265	16.0
1956...	1,742	1,605	370	21.3	23.1	267	15.5
1957...	1,804	1,666	381	21.1	23.4	276	15.5
1958...	1,826	1,684	387	21.2	23.5	288	15.8
1959...	1,904	1,770	384	20.2	21.8	282	14.8
1960...	1,937	1,818	386	19.9	21.4	285	14.7
1961...	1,983	1,840	386	19.5	21.0	288	14.5
1962...	2,060	1,905	394	19.1	20.6	291	14.1

* Source: Supplement for 1961 to "Consumption of Food in the United States, 1909–52," USDA Handbook No. 62, 1962, pp. 57–59, and "Marketing and Transportation Situation," USDA, August 1963, pp. 2, 14.

TABLE 12.2

FEDERAL FOOD DISTRIBUTION PROGRAMS: COST OF FEDERAL ASSISTANCE TO SCHOOL
LUNCH AND SPECIAL MILK PROGRAMS AND TO INSTITUTIONS AND NEEDY PERSONS,
1944–61

(Data in millions of dollars)

Year Beginning July 1	Idemnity Plan Cost	School Lunch Distribution Under Section 6	School Lunch Distribution Under Sections 32, 416	Special Milk Program	Institutions and Needy Persons, Food Distribution Under Sections 32, 416
1944	42	..	6	..	7
1945	51	..	6	..	2
1946	60	6	2	..	3
1947	54	13	19	..	14
1948	59	14	21	..	14
1949	64	17	38	..	24
1950	68	15	35	..	25
1951	66	16	17	..	7
1952	67	15	52	..	17
1953	67	15	94	..	61
1954	69	13	70	17	97
1955	67	15	100	46	135
1956	84	15	132	60	104
1957	84	15	76	66	109
1958	94	43	67	74	137
1959	94	61	71	80	75
1960	94	61	72	84	174
1961	99	69	113	89	253

Source: USDA, Agricultural Statistics, 1962, p. 679.

Most incomes in the United States now are so high that further increases will cause only small increases in the demand for food. The nonfarm income elasticity of the demand for food in the United States in 1955 (the date of the most recent nation-wide consumer survey) was 0.25 in low-income households, 0.21 in medium-income households, and only 0.15 per cent in high-income households.[3]

USDA DOMESTIC FOOD DISTRIBUTION PROGRAMS

Several USDA programs designed to increase domestic food consumption have been in effect for a number of years.

The quantities and costs of the food distributed under the different programs each year since 1944 are shown in Table

[3] C. R. Rockwell, Jr., "Income and Household Size," Marketing Res. Rept. 340, USDA, June 1961, pp. 1, 6.

12.2. The costs do not include the costs of administration. The different programs are discussed briefly in the next few sections.

School Lunch and School Milk Programs

The school lunch program was started in 1933, at the bottom of the severe depression of the 1930's. It was put on a permanent basis by the National School Lunch Act of 1946.

The program has been continued on a steadily increasing scale ever since, until now it reaches about 14 million children— about a third of all the pupils enrolled in elementary and secondary schools. The total cost of the program from all sources amounts now to nearly a billion dollars a year. The federal government contributes about 25 per cent of this amount. The rest comes from sources within the states—more than half of it, from the school children themselves. In addition, the federal government contributes substantial quantities of surplus foods. But 85 per cent of the food used is purchased in local markets.

Paralleling this, a special School Milk Program was authorized in the Agricultural Act of 1954. Its principal purpose was to increase the consumption of milk by school children. The federal government reimburses the schools participating in the program up to 4 cents per half pint of additional milk consumed, and up to 3 cents per half pint for those not in the school program.

During the 1959–60 school year, over 12.8 million children were served 2,100,000,000 lunches—100 million more than in the previous year. Nearly 1,500 more schools took part in the program, with the final tally being well over 62,000.

Funds for school lunches come from many sources. In 1961, participating children themselves contributed nearly $550 million. State and local governments contributed another $100 million and other local contributors added about $120 million more.

Federal support for the program included USDA apportionment of $93.8 million in cash, $70 million in surplus commodities and an addtional $58.5 million to purchase and distribute highly nutritious foods to help schools meet standards of the program.

The Agricultural Marketing Service comments:[4]

The school lunch program represents a tremendous market for our farm commodities. During the last school year, local purchases of food amounted to $535 million. These purchases from local pro-

---

[4] USDA, *Agricultural Marketing,* Sept. 1960, last page.

ducers and suppliers were in addition to the surplus foods and the foods purchased by USDA with school lunch funds. The total value of food consumed in participating schools amounted to over $664 million—a significant contribution to our farm economy.

George Abschier gives a more conservative appraisal:[5]

The School Lunch Program and the School Milk Program have shown significant growth. During 1957 about 10.5 million of the 38.2 million children enrolled in schools were included in the School Lunch Program. The schools were using 1,816 million pounds of food valued at $562 million. It has been estimated that about 20 per cent of this food represents increased consumption. So the actual increase in consumption would amount to 363 million pounds of food valued at $112 million, or roughly 2/10 of 1 per cent of the retail value of all foods and services.

INCREASING DOMESTIC DEMAND BY INCREASING LOW INCOMES

Another proposal would seek to increase the domestic consumption of food by increasing the incomes of low-income families.

This proposal assumes that low income is the chief reason for low food consumption, so increasing the incomes would increase the consumption.

Table 12.3 shows the proportion of families at different income levels, where the quantity of food brought into the home for family consumption during a week in April–June 1955 did not equal recommended dietary allowances. Vernon Sorensen[6] explains:

"The fact that food intake does not measure up to these standards does not prove that families are poorly fed or suffering from malnutrition. The recommended allowances are subject to a considerable margin of error when applied to individuals and also provide a substantial margin of safety over the minimum needs of an "average" person. What the figures in Table 12.3 do show is that when measured by nutritional standards the problem of food consumption cannot be easily dealt with by assuming that poor nutrition occurs only where income levels do not permit adequate food purchases. This does not mean that there are

---

[5] George S. Abschier, "Expansion of Domestic Demand?" Leaflet No. 2 in "The Farm Problem . . . What are the Choices?" (Sponsored by the Farm Foundation and the Center for Agricultural and Economic Development), 1961.

[6] Vernon Sorensen, "Food Consumption Subsidies for Low-income Families," *Policy for Commercial Agriculture—Its Relation to Economic Growth and Stability.* Joint Economic Committee, 85th Congress, 1st Session, US GPO, Nov. 22, 1957, p. 540.

TABLE 12.3

Percentage of Households Using Food at Home in a Week During April–June 1955, That Did Not Furnish Recommended Amounts of Eight nutrients, House-keeping Households of One or More Persons, by Income, All Consumers.*

(Percentages are computed on a nutrition unit basis thereby allowing for differences in family composition.)

Income Class	Pro-tein	Cal-cium	Iron	Vita-min A	Thia-mine	Ribo-flavin	Nia-cin	Ascor-bic Acid
$0 to $999............	23	37	15	36	17	32	17	51
$1,000 to $1,999.......	15	41	16	30	19	30	13	41
$2,000 to $2,999.......	10	34	10	18	16	25	9	30
$3,000 to $3,999.......	6	31	9	18	16	17	6	26
$4,000 to $4,999.......	3	25	7	12	13	15	4	21
$5,000 to $5,999.......	3	23	6	11	16	12	4	19
$6,000 to $7,999.......	4	23	9	11	17	14	5	16
$8,000 to $9,999.......	4	26	7	10	18	15	3	13
$10,000 and over.......	1	17	6	5	14	12	2	8

* Source: "Dietary Levels of Households in United States," Household Food Consumption Survey Rept. No. 6, Table 12.

no families or individuals eating nutritiously poor diets because their income is too low to buy better food, but only that nutrition by itself is an inadequate basis for developing a subsidy program. Subsidies will not improve the diets of those people where poor nutrition is due to preference, ignorance, custom, or some other reason.

"A recent USDA estimate indicates the possible magnitude of a subsidy program which combines poor nutrition and income as a guide in establishing eligibility for participation. If a program is restricted to persons and families who now receive some form of Federal, State, or local welfare assistance it is estimated that 6 million persons could be included. The total potential cost of direct food supplements to these persons through a food stamp plan would approximate $600 million. This is an expenditure equal to no more than two-thirds of 1 per cent of present retail food sales.

"Since it is only in this very low income group that insufficient buying power prevents the purchase of 'adequate' diets, one conclusion seems to stand out clearly. Compared with the 1930's, the potential for increasing food consumption through a program designed to relieve nutritional inadequancies caused by income restrictions is limited. A broad-scale Federal program with this objective could be effective in moving substantial quantities of food into consumption only if a large number of people were unemployed and could not purchase adequate diets. This implies a period of general economic depression, a condition which very few forecasters foresee at the present time. Under present circumstances a nutrition program for the poor will not move many surplus commodities."

A comprehensive study estimated that under present conditions, increased food consumption resulting from income subsidies to low income families would not utilize more than a quarter of the surplus at reasonable levels of operations.[7] This might involve, for example, raising consumption for all families with less than $500 per person to consumption levels enjoyed by families with $500–$750 per person.

Retail price declines for all food would be equally unsuccessful in solving the surplus problems. Even a 20 per cent retail price decline in all foods, which translates into a 40–50 per cent decline at the farm level, could increase food consumption only 4.5 per cent. A conservative estimate of the annual domestic food consumption increase needed to completely remove surpluses would be about 8 per cent.

Because the United States is already a very well-fed society, with overeating at least as great a problem as nutritional shortages, policies designed to achieve adequate nutrition for everyone could lead to only very slight increases. Overconsumption leading to overweight is a bigger problem in this country than underconsumption. Adequate nutrition for everyone might actually result in a decrease in total food consumption.

The study concluded that demand expansion via the income, price, and nutrition will not provide the answer to the surplus problem.

FOOD STAMP PLAN

During the 1930's a Food Stamp Plan was introduced, under which participants were sold stamps at less than their face value, which were good for the purchase of food. The stamps were of two colors—orange stamps which were good for the purchase of any foods, and blue stamps which were good for the purchase only of surplus foods. The plan reached a peak annual expenditure of about $200 million in 1943, and then was discontinued.

---

[7] John M. Wetmore, Martin E. Abel, Elmer W. Learn, and Willard W. Cochrane, "Policies for Expanding the Demand for Farm Food Products in the United States, History and Potentials," Minn. Agr. Exp. Sta. Tech. Bul. 231, April 1959.

The plan was revived on an experimental basis in 1961 in eight depressed areas in the United States, with a more complicated schedule of reduced prices according to income, size of family, etc. This plan used only one kind of stamp. A study of the results of this experiment reported as follows:[8]

Dollar sales of retail stores in the pilot Food Stamp Program were up 8 per cent, after adjustment for seasonal variation, from sales reported prior to initiation of the Program, according to data from a representative sample of stores in areas of Detroit, Michigan, and selected counties in Illinois, Kentucky, Minnesota, Montana, New Mexico, Pennsylvania, and West Virginia. Sample stores from which sales information was obtained accounted for from 50 per cent to nearly all of estimated total retail food store sales in all areas except Detroit where the test sample stores were drawn to represent only low-income sections of the city.

Combined sales data from all test areas indicated that after the introduction of food coupons, both meat and produce sales increased in about the same proportion as total sales. Sales of products classified as groceries and all other items were 9 per cent higher in September–October 1961, than in April–May 1961, before coupons were introduced. Dairy products, eggs, and in some instances frozen foods, were among the items included in this group.

ADVERTISING AND "ANIMAL AGRICULTURE"

A current argument for promotion and advertising in changing consumer preference, while at the same time helping relieve the surplus situation, includes the promotion of increased consumption of animal products. Since livestock condense 5 to 7 pounds of dry matter in the form of grain and other feed into about one pound of dry matter in the form of meat, milk, and eggs, more agricultural resources would be needed to provide an animal diet than a grain or cereal diet.

But the whole trend of economic progress in the United States has been toward producing, most efficiently and with the *fewest* resources, what consumers demand. A heavy onus of proof would rest on proposals to go against this trend and produce food with the use of more resources.

PROMOTION AND ADVERTISING

Could the demand for food be increased by advertising and other promotional means?

---

[8] USDA, "Effect of the Pilot Food Stamp Program on Retail Food Store Sales," Marketing Economics Div., ERS, Agr. Econ. Rept. No. 8, April 1962, p. iii.

TABLE 12.4

Estimated Funds Expended and Number of Agricultural Groups,
United States, 1958*

Type of Organization	Organizations Promoting	Expenditures
	(number)	(1,000 dollars)
Voluntary producer-processor groups............	345	25,508
Farmer marketing cooperatives.................	574	25,149
Commissions, councils, boards, institutes, etc., established under enabling legislation..........	120	13,961
State departments of agriculture................	20	1,385
Others and unidentified.......................	73	594
Total.......................................	1,132	66,597

* Source: Robert E. Frye and Villet Davis Grubbs, *Promotion of Farm Products by Agricultural Groups,* USDA, Marketing Res. Rept. No. 380, p. 13.

One misconception concerning this question needs to be cleared up at the outset: Many people discuss this question as if nothing, or very little, was being done to advertise farm products at present. This is far from the truth. Over 1,100 groups in the United States were engaged in the promotion of agricultural products in 1958 and 1959. They spent about $67 million during 1958, as shown in Table 12.4.

In addition to the money spent by these groups, it is estimated that roughly 20 per cent of the total of $10 billion spent on advertising of all kinds in the United States was directed to the promotion of food and food products.

Data for the period from 1950 to 1961 given in Table 12.5 show that total advertising expenditures by food manufacturing and wholesaling corporations followed a continued upward trend. The proportions accounted for by manufacturing and wholesaling varied. Manufacturers' expenditures for advertising fell from a high of 78 per cent of the total in 1950 to 73 in 1957, then rose to 76 in 1959. They declined to about 75 per cent in 1960 and 1961. The wholesaling sector accounted for 8 per cent of the total in 1959, compared with 12 per cent in 1951, and dropped to about 7 per cent in 1960 and 1961.[9]

In contrast, expenditures by retailing corporations increased steadily, rising from 11 per cent of total advertising expenditures

[9] Toledo Chumley, "Advertising Expenditures by Food Marketing Corporations, 1950, 1951, and 1953–61," *Marketing and Transportation Situation,* Aug. 1962, USDA, ERS, p. 39.

TABLE 12.5

Expenditures for Advertising Food and Kindred Products by Manufacturing, Wholesaling, and Retailing Corporations, 1950–51 and 1953–61*

Year	Type of Firm				Percentage of Total Expenditures			
	Manufac-turing (million dollars)	Whole-saling (million dollars)	Retailing (million dollars)	Total (million dollars)	Manufac-turing (per cent)	Whole-saling (per cent)	Retailing (per cent)	Total (per cent)
1950	435.1	64.8	60.2	560.1	78	11	11	100
1951	470.1	70.3	69.1	609.5	77	12	11	100
a								
1953	558.4	78.5	91.7	728.6	77	11	12	100
1954	610.9	78.8	106.4	796.1	77	10	13	100
1955	688.3	75.3	135.7	899.3	77	8	15	100
1956	724.0	84.8	167.4	976.2	74	9	17	100
1957	758.9	95.4	183.4	1,037.7	73	9	18	100
1958	782.5	95.4	184.6	1,062.6	74	9	17	100
1959	917.5	88.9	194.7	1,201.1	76	8	16	100
1960b	907.2	85.0	221.8	1,214.0	75	7	18	100
1961b	1,088.2	101.9	266.7	1,456.8	75	7	18	100

* Source: Same as Table 12.4.
a Data for 1952 are not available.
b Figures for 1960 and 1961 are preliminary estimates.

by food marketing corporations in 1950 to an estimated 18 per cent in 1961. Changes in food advertising expenditures at retail reflect simultaneous changes in the numbers and sizes of corporations retailing food. The actual number of corporations retailing food increased by about 6,000 from 1950 to 1959.[10] In 1948, corporations accounted for about 40 per cent of the total retail food sales, and by 1958 they accounted for 54 per cent.[11] These figures also reflect an increased emphasis of advertising at the retail level. There is evidence that this upward trend will continue. If the number of these stores in suburban areas increases substantially relative to density of population, more extensive retail advertising may be anticipated.

Table 12.6 shows that most food manufacturing industries more than doubled their expenditures for advertising between 1950 and 1959. Of particular note are increases by the bakery products, canned fruits, vegetables, and seafoods, and dairy products industries. In each of these industries, there has been an increasing adoption of advertising, especially in metropolitan areas.

There is little likelihood that total food advertising expenditures will lessen. Data available do not enable any estimate of the extent of effectiveness of these expenditures in accomplishing objectives.

The effectiveness of promotional and advertising programs for farm commodities is the subject of much debate. Considering the stability of total food consumption, it appears probable that an increase in the consumption of one product occurs at the expense of another product or products. Thus, advertising by one segment of the industry might result in competitive advertising by other segments. The net result may be that no change takes place in consumption, but all the groups have less income after advertising costs are deducted.

Although no precise appraisal of a particular advertising program for farm products can be made here, this much can be said: The answer to the question whether the program will expand the demand for a product sufficiently for the increase in returns to more than cover the advertising costs requires that certain criteria be met:

---

[10] Internal Revenue Service.
[11] U.S. Bureau of the Census, *Census of Business.*

TABLE 12.6

ADVERTISING EXPENDITURES BY CORPORATIONS MANUFACTURING FOOD AND KINDRED
PRODUCTS, BY INDUSTRY GROUP, 1950, 1955, AND 1958–59*

Industry Group	1950	1955	1958	1959
	(million dollars)	(million dollars)	(million dollars)	(million dollars)
Bakery products....................	56.9	92.2	111.4	121.3
Canning—fruits, vegetables, and seafoods.....................	57.1	106.9	128.9	145.4
Confectionery.....................	34.2	46.7	60.7	67.8
Dairy products....................	54.3	87.0	124.3	136.0
Cereal preparations[a].................	25.3	22.0	....	....
Grain mill products[b]................	23.3	39.9	77.8	134.5
Meat products.....................	51.5	75.3	72.1	80.3
Sugar............................	2.5	3.5	5.1	5.0
Food and kindred products not allocable.	69.2	102.6	119.9	128.9
Other food and kindred products.......	60.8	112.2	82.4	98.3
Total.........................	435.1	688.3	782.6	917.5

* Source: Same as Table 12.4.
[a] Cereal preparations included in grain mill products in 1958 and 1959. Cereal preparations represented about 25 per cent of the total before the adjustment for animal feed.
[b] Excludes animal feed.

1. The advertising product must be identifiable.
2. The product must be such that advertising can convince persons that a difference in quality exists between advertised and unadvertised supplies.
3. Advertising must be backed up by a coordinated program of distribution and favorable display in all stores.
4. Advertising must be concentrated sufficiently to make an impression on consumers.

Giving considerations to the above criteria, it appears that most state and regional advertising of a portion of the total output of unprocessed commodities would likely have little effect on the total demand for those commodities and on the total demand for food.

As Karl Fox suggests:[12]

After considering all the factors related to increasing demand for food we might wish our geneticists would develop an "eat-type consumer" with larger stomach capacity, a voracious appetite and expensive tastes. But practically we cannot eat our way out of the surplus. We must think our way out.

[12] Karl Fox, in *Better Farming Methods,* Sept. 1962, pp. 22–24.

NEW USES FOR FARM PRODUCTS [13]

Adding corn alcohol to gasoline is a popular and frequently suggested solution for the corn surplus problem. The use of gasoline-alcohol blends has been studied extensively and was tried successfully in this country during World War II. There is no mystery about the process of making ethyl alcohol from corn, and alcohol is now being used in blends with gasoline in certain foreign countries.

If we were to blend 10 per cent corn alcohol with the gasoline used in the United States, it would use about 2 billion bushels of corn per year. Score two points: (1) Corn alcohol-gasoline blends can be used successfully for motor fuel, and (2) we could use up a lot of surplus corn. Why is it not done? Why is it not a feasible method of solving the problem of surplus corn?

Too Expensive

The answer is that ethyl alcohol—made from corn or any other known source—is too expensive to be used in motor fuel in the United States at current motor fuel and alcohol prices. The cost of producing alcohol is the sum of the cost of the raw materials and the cost of processing them into alcohol. At present, both of these costs are lower for synthetic than for grain alcohol.

A bushel of corn will produce about 2½ gallons of 95 per cent alcohol. If we add the cost of malt, making an allowance for the alcohol produced from it, the raw material cost when using corn at $1 per bushel is about 46 cents per gallon of corn alcohol.

Estimates of processing costs vary, but 25 cents per gallon probably is a realistic figure. This, added to the raw material cost, gives a total of 71 cents per gallon. The value of any by-products can be subtracted from this cost. Distillers' grains (used as a high-protein feed) and fusel oil are the by-products normally marketed. Carbon dioxide and corn oil are other possibilities which normally are not recovered. A credit of 1 cent for the fusel oil and 13 cents for the distillers' grains can be allowed, for a total credit of 14 cents per gallon.

With this allowance, and with corn at $1 per bushel, the cost

---

[13] Adapted from an article by Lionel K. Arnold, in *Iowa Farm Science*, Iowa State University, Feb. 1960, pp. 15–16.

is 57 cents per gallon of corn alcohol. (With corn at $1.25, the cost would be 68–69 cents a gallon.) But converting the 95 per cent alcohol to anhydrous alcohol, suitable for blending with gasoline, adds another 7 cents to the cost.

These costs explain why alcohol from corn is not added to gasoline in the United States—with the current price of 91 octane gasoline at the refinery at about 12 cents a gallon. Except for medicinal and beverage use, in fact, grain alcohol cannot compete on a cost basis with synthetic alcohol. This is currently quoted on a tax-free basis at 52 cents per gallon for 95 per cent alcohol and at 59 cents for the anhydrous grade.

Increase Gasoline Cost

The addition of 10 per cent alcohol from $1 corn would raise the price of gasoline slightly more than 5 cents a gallon. From $1.25 corn, the cost would increase another cent. These costs do not include any transportation or mixing costs and are based on the price of corn as *delivered* at the alcohol distillery.

At one time, the antiknock properties of alcohol appeared to give it a premium value for use in gasoline. This probably is no longer true with today's improved gasolines. The addition of ethyl alcohol to modern high-octane gasoline would probably do no more than replace part of the cheap butane normally present.

It is a fact—one frequently pointed out—that blends of gasoline and alcohol are used, despite the cost of alcohol, in some foreign countries. But the explanation is that the cost of gasoline in these countries is much higher in relation to alcohol than in the United States.

Looking Further

It probably would not be necessary or desirable to convert all of the corn surplus now stored into alcohol over a period of a few years. It might be more desirable to convert only the annual surplus production each year. Otherwise, some corn might simply come out of storage for alcohol production while new surplus corn was going into storage. The amount of corn placed under support during the past 3 years has averaged about 400 million bushels each year. This would produce enough alcohol for about a 2 per cent blend with gasoline at an increased material cost of about a cent per gallon of gasoline.

This kind of program might be attractive and feasible—*if* it were possible to use a 2 per cent blend. But, at present, the use of less than a 10 per cent blend is considered impractical. Blends containing less than 10 per cent alcohol take up enough moisture from the air to make the alcohol and gasoline separate. We might look forward, however, to the possibility of developing a blending agent that would allow the blending of alcohol containing some water.

Oil Stocks Depleting?

Suggestions have also been made that alcohol can be used to supplement inadequate supplies of petroleum in the near future. But there is no immediate shortage of petroleum. American petroleum producers—to prevent flooding the market—actually are restricted on the amount of crude oil they can remove from their wells at the present time.

When the supply of crude oil becomes inadequate, we can expect production of oil from vast deposits of oil shale. And another possibility is the production of synthetic gasoline from coal—at a higher cost than from crude oil, but from which low-cost alcohol would be a by-product.

Nongasoline Use?

From a cost standpoint, it would seem more feasible to substitute corn alcohol for 52-cent synthetic alcohol than for 12-cent gasoline. The production of synthetic alcohol plants in 1956 was 181 million gallons—about 75 per cent of their estimated capacity. At the same time, the estimated capacity of *idle* fermentation-alcohol plants was 217 million gallons. The lower production costs of the synthetic plants account for their dominance in the industrial alcohol market.

It is not probable that synthetic alcohol costs will go up materially in the near future. And the price of delivered corn would have to be *substantially lower* than either the $1 or $1.25 figures used earlier for industry to even *consider* reactivating the fermentation-alcohol plants. Even the synthetic plants are not operating at capacity, and the production costs for these are less than for the idle fermentation plants.

It is possible that the cost of producing corn alcohol can be reduced somewhat. Experimental work indicates that the substitution of fungal amylase for malt can reduce the material cost perhaps 5 cents per gallon. It has also been suggested that the removal and use of the corn protein for human food before the starch of the corn is fermented could result in lower alcohol costs. This would require considerable research.

But a fact to face is that, even if *all* of the synthetic alcohol now produced could be replaced by corn alcohol, this would require only about 18 per cent of the current annual corn carry-over.

Still another suggestion is to use corn alcohol in the manufacture of butadiene for synthetic alcohol production. This was done during World War II. At present, butadiene is made from butane or butylene originating from petroleum. To be competitive, it is estimated that the alcohol, however, would have to be available at 20–25 cents a gallon.

Ethylene, used in polyethylene plastic, can be made from ethyl alcohol. But here again, the cost would be too high to compete with the product from petroleum.

In summary, ethyl alcohol and its derivatives have large present and potential uses. But, because of the present cost of alcohol produced from corn, it is being used only to a limited extent.

13
Prospects for Increasing Foreign Demand For Farm Products

We have seen that the prospects for increasing the domestic demand for food in the United States are not good. What are the prospects for increasing the foreign demand?

The foreign trade of the United States in farm products has been increasing since World War II, making the United States the world's largest exporter of farm products. Exports are becoming an important component of the total demand for United States farm products. Table 13.1 shows that exports of farm food commodities have risen from 8.4 per cent of net utilization just after World War II to nearly 14 per cent in recent years; United States imports of farm food commodities meanwhile have remained practically constant at about 12 per cent. So the United States has changed from a slight net farm food import position to a slight net export position.

Total United States exports of farm products, including non-foods such as cotton, for example, as well as foods, amounted in the calendar year 1962 to about $5 billion. This was equivalent to about 15 per cent of all cash received by farmers for their products. The make-up of these exports in recent years is shown in Figure 13.1.

Some United States farm products depend heavily on the export market. The percentage of exports of soybeans in 1962 was about 25 per cent of the crop; of wheat and flour, about 55 per cent; and of cotton, about 27 per cent.

TABLE 13.1

Index of Net Supply-Utilization of Farm Commodities, 1947–49 and 1957–59
Averages, and 1960–62*

(Percentage of net utilization in each year)

Year	Net Produc- tion[a]	Net Im- ports[b]	Stock Change[c]	Domestic Use		Net non- food[e]	Exports and Ship- ments
				Food			
				Civil- ian	Mili- tary[d]		
1947–49......	91.4	11.5	−2.9	75.1	3.3	13.2	8.4
1957–59......	90.2	11.6	−1.8	76.0	1.4	10.9	11.7
1950..........	87.3	12.4	.3	75.2	1.7	14.2	8.9
1951..........	85.4	11.6	3.0	72.7	3.4	13.3	10.6
1952..........	91.6	11.6	−3.2	75.8	2.5	12.5	9.2
1953..........	92.9	12.0	−4.9	77.0	2.3	12.7	8.0
1954..........	93.5	10.6	−4.1	77.5	2.0	11.6	8.9
1955..........	93.0	11.0	−4.0	77.1	1.7	11.9	9.3
1956..........	90.1	10.8	−.9	75.3	1.6	11.5	11.6
1957..........	88.4	10.7	.9	75.0	1.4	10.7	12.9
1958..........	93.2	11.4	−4.6	76.6	1.5	10.8	11.1
1959..........	89.4	12.7	−2.1	76.1	1.4	11.3	11.2
1960..........	90.5	11.6	−2.1	74.4	1.2	10.6	13.8
1961..........	87.8	12.1	.1	74.5	1.4	10.5	13.6
1962..........	88.1	12.9	−1.0	74.7	1.4	10.7	13.2
1963[f].	87.1	12.5	.4	74.7	1.3	10.5	13.5

* Source: USDA, *National Food Situation*, Aug. 1963, p. 2.

The term "net" in this table means that commodities used for feed and seed are excluded to avoid double counting. Developed from quantitative data on supply and use of processed and unprocessed farm products, valued in terms of farm prices (1947–49 prices prior to 1955; 1957–59 prices thereafter). For description of basic procedure see Agriculture Handbook No. 91, *Measuring the Supply and Utilization of Farm Commodities*.

[a] Excludes feed and seed used from domestic production.

[b] Excludes imports for seed and feed use.

[c] Includes farm and commercial stocks and holdings under government programs. Negatives indicate increases in stocks from beginning to end of year; positives signify withdrawals from stocks.

[d] Includes civilian feeding in areas occupied by our Armed Forces.

[e] Excludes feed and seed; includes some waste and loss at farm level.

[f] Preliminary.

INCOMES IN MOST OTHER COUNTRIES ARE LOW

It is not easy to expand United States exports of farm products. One of the reasons for this is that incomes in most other countries are low, so they do not have much purchasing power to buy food from the United States.

Figure 13.2 shows per capita incomes in the United States and in a number of other countries, in terms of 1959 United States dollars. The figure shows that there is no significant rela-

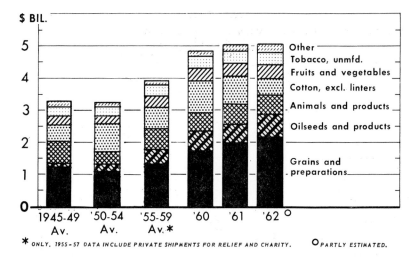

U. S. DEPARTMENT OF AGRICULTURE   NEG. ERS 1779-63 (2) ECONOMIC RESEARCH SERVICE

Fig. 13.1. United States agricultural exports by commodity group, 1945–62.

tion between income and acres of arable land per person. Evidently it is not overcrowding on available land that makes per capita incomes low.

In an attempt to overcome the depressing effect on United States food exports of low incomes in other countries, gigantic export subsidy programs were put into effect after World War II.

EXTENT OF GOVERNMENT ASSISTANCE

Figure 13.3 shows that commercial sales for dollars were a record in fiscal 1962—69 per cent of the United States total. Of the total, $3.5 billion were commercial sales for dollars. An additional $1.6 billion moved as foreign currency sales, donations, barter, and long-term supply and dollar credit sales under Public Law 480 and the Act for International Development, making the total in excess of $5 billion.

To compete in world markets for some major products such as wheat, rice, cotton, and certain feed grains, CCC made export payments in cash or in kind or sold stocks at less than domestic market prices. An estimated $2 billion moved in this way, equally divided between the specified government-financed programs and dollar sales. Dollar sales also benefited from short- and medium-term credits from CCC and the Export-Import Bank. Exports under credits rose to $90 million in 1961–62 from $33 million in 1960–61.

INCOME PER PERSON*

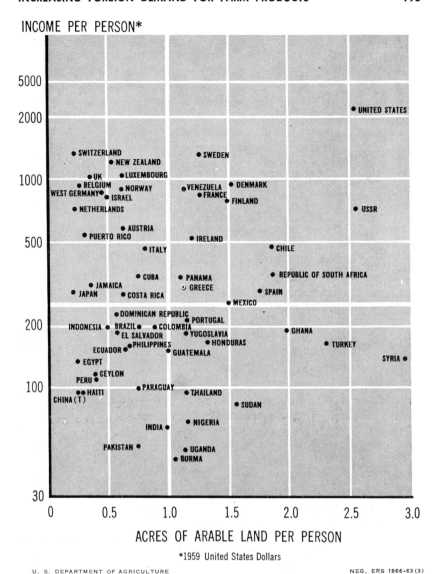

ACRES OF ARABLE LAND PER PERSON

*1959 United States Dollars

U. S. DEPARTMENT OF AGRICULTURE   NEG. ERS 1866-63(3)

Fig. 13.2. Income and acres of arable land per person, in terms of 1959 United States dollars.

THE EUROPEAN "COMMON MARKET"

Canada, Japan, and the United Kingdom each take about 10 per cent of our total farm exports. Our biggest customer, how-

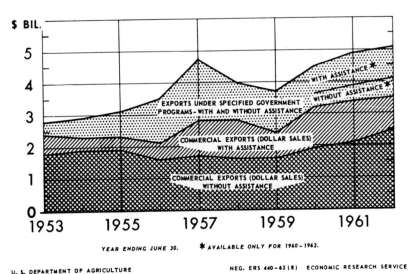

U. S. DEPARTMENT OF AGRICULTURE   NEG. ERS 440-62 (8)   ECONOMIC RESEARCH SERVICE

Fig. 13.3. Total United States farm exports, 1953–62. Dollar sales account for 69 per cent 1961–62 total.

ever, is the block of 6 countries (Belgium-Luxembourg, France, Italy, West Germany, and the Netherlands) which make up the European Economic Community (EEC), usually referred to as the Common Market.

Figure 13.4 shows that this Common Market took 22 per cent of United States $5 billion farm exports in 1961. Entrance of the United Kingdom and other applicants for admission to the Common Market would create a controlled trade area that would account for two-fifths of United States farm exports.

But it is an open question whether this percentage will rise in the future, or decline. The Common Market countries aim to end trade barriers among their members and erect common barriers against imports from nonmembers.

These barriers include variable import levies designed to raise the prices of imported products to the common levels established in the area.

A variable levy is simply a device for assuring that imports enter the domestic market at prices somewhat higher than the predetermined level of domestic support prices. If EEC domestic support prices for wheat, for example, are at $3 a bushel, and imports are offered at the frontier for $2 a bushel, then a levy of at least $1 would be collected on imports. If import prices dropped to $1.75 a bushel, the variable levy would increase by

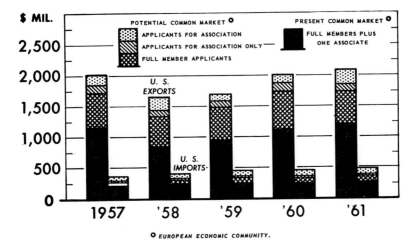

Fig. 13.4. United States agricultural trade with present and potential members of EEC (Common Market).

25 cents. The EEC seems likely to set its domestic price levels high. If it does, this will encourage increased agricultural production in the area and thus reduce imports into the area.

France now supports wheat at about $2.15 a bushel; Germany supports it at more than $3 a bushel, and these prices are for a quality of wheat that brings 30 or 40 cents a bushel less, on world markets, than our hard red winter wheat. If the common agricultural policy of the EEC should set a price for wheat close to the German level, French farmers would probably put 6 million additional acres into wheat. They could then supply nearly all Common Market needs, and even create a surplus that would press toward "dumping" in world markets.

"The EEC is moving to apply variable levies on grains, poultry and other commodities to effectively prevent any imports coming in at less than domestic support prices. If these target prices should be established at unreasonably high levels the result will be a substitution of uneconomic production within the EEC for imports. It is thus critically important to us that these prices should be set at moderate levels, if the United States and other agricultural exporting nations are to have continued access to EEC markets." [1]

---

[1] Orville L. Freeman, "An Agricultural Policy for Today's World." National Agricultural Policy Forum, Dec. 11–12, 1962, *Proceedings*, pp. 128–29.

That is to say: The United States wants to set its own domestic farm prices high(it raised the price support for corn for example 14 cents a bushel in 1961, and 5 cents more in 1963) but it does not want other countries to do the same.

"We are disturbed by the level of agricultural protectionism likely to prevail within the European Economic Community but resort to a wide variety of devices to shield our own farm sector from movements in world-market prices." [2]

UNITED STATES AGRICULTURAL EXPORT PROGRAMS

In an attempt to resolve the paradoxical coexistence of surpluses of farm products in some countries and deficits in other countries of the world, the United States Congress passed in 1954 the Agricultural Trade Development and Assistance Act, commonly referred to as PL 480. The objective of the Act was to dispose of United States farm surpluses and assist economic development in the recipient countries. Farm surpluses then were accumulating in CCC hands at the rate of nearly $3 billion per year. It seemed logical to try to dispose of some of them abroad where they might do some good.

Title I of the Act authorized the sale of United States farm surpluses for local currencies in countries which have need for the commodities, but lack the dollars to pay for them. Title II authorized the use of commodities held in stock by CCC to help friendly foreign people to meet famine or other urgent relief requirements. Title III authorized donations of surplus foods for domestic and foreign distribution and barter sales of surplus commodities for strategic and other commodities.

Up to June 30, 1962, over $11.6 billion of surplus farm products valued at CCC cost ($8 billion at export market value) were moved under this Act. Nearly $6 billion valued at export market value moved under Title I. The data by commodities are given in Table 13.2; the quantities, by recipient countries, are given in Table 13.3.

Nearly one-third of United States agricultural exports in 1961–62 were financed under PL 480 and other government programs.

---

[2] Boris C. Swerling, "Problems of International Commodity Stabilization." *Amer. Econ. Rev.*, Vol. 53, No. 2, p. 65, May 1963.

TABLE 13.2

COMMODITY COMPOSITION OF ALL TITLE I AGREEMENTS SIGNED THROUGH JUNE 30, 1962*

Commodity	Unit	Approximate Quantity	Export Market Value	Estimated CCC Cost
		(million units)	(million dollars)	(million dollars)
Wheat and wheat flour...	Bushel	2,470a	4,058.7	6,724.2
Feed grains............	Bushel	378b	445.6	555.2
Rice.................	Hundredweight	78	447.6	740.4
Cotton...............	Bale	7c	1,049.6	1,463.8
Cotton linters..........	Bale	.007	.3	.3
Meat products.........	Pound	113	38.1	38.1
Tobacco..............	Pound	352	256.9	256.9
Dairy products........	Pound	366	58.9	91.4
Fats and oils..........	Pound	6,060	834.8	841.8
Poultry..............	Pound	20	6.2	6.2
Dry edible beans and peas	Hundredweight	1	4.7	4.7
Fruits and vegetables.....	Pound	196	18.0	18.0
Seeds................	Hundredweight	.01	.4	.4
Total commodities..........................			7,219.8	10,741.4
Ocean transportation to be financed by CCC........			895.8	895.8
Total, including ocean transportation.............			8,115.6	11,637.2

* Source: "Sixteenth Semiannual Report of Activities Carried on Under Public Law 480." House Doc. No. 526, 87th Congress, 2nd Session, p. 6.
a Wheat and wheat equivalent of flour.
b Includes the following feed grains: (1,000 bushels)

Corn..............................	176,955
Oats..............................	6,807
Barley............................	137,463
Grain sorghums.....................	52,544
Rye...............................	4,737
Total...........................	378,506

c Includes 72,800 bales extra-long-staple cotton.

These shipments under the Act helped, in the short run, to reduce or slow down the increases in the size of CCC stocks. Their longer run effects are more difficult to assess.

The shipments relieved the pressure on United States markets, but this may have retarded the basic adjustments that needed to be made in order to adapt United States agriculture to the new technology. It tended to permit United States farmers to go right ahead increasing production beyond market needs; the government took the surplus off their hands.

TABLE 13.3

Status of Foreign Currencies Under Title I, Public Law 480*

(In million dollar equivalents)

Country	Agreement Amounts Through Dec. 31, 1961	Allocations Through Dec. 31, 1961[ab]		Collections Through Dec. 31, 1961[b]		Disbursements by Agencies Through Dec. 31, 1961[d]
		Sales proceeds	Other proceeds[e]	Sales proceeds	Other proceeds[e]	
Argentina ..	64.1	33.5	...	30.5	....	17.5
Autsria.....	42.9	40.1	0.9	40.1	....	36.6
Bolivia.....	3.7	.2	...	.2	....	...
Brazil......	284.4	251.4	2.6	257.8	0.8	137.4
Burma.....	40.7	37.8	3.5	37.7	4.2	11.7
Ceylon.....	26.1	21.0	...	21.9	....	9.6
Chile......	71.9	59.8	...	61.6	....	38.4
China (Taiwan)...	95.8	62.1	...	65.6	....	35.0
Colombia...	70.9	59.0	...	55.2	1.3	36.6
Congo.....	7.5	....	...	....	....	....
Ecuador....	13.2	10.2	.5	10.5	....	7.4
Finland....	46.5	42.0	...	41.9	.2	29.3
France.....	35.8	34.4	...	34.6	....	23.5

Effects on Recipient Countries [3]

The shipments abroad had, by and large, beneficial short-run effects on per capita consumption in a number of underdeveloped countries. The effects on economic development in the recipient countries are more difficult to identify and assess.

The simultaneous existence of food deficits and of food surpluses in the world has given rise to several misconceptions:

1. The notion that there are millions of starving people in the world who could use our food if we would only release it.

There have been no reports of widespread starvation anywhere in the world in recent years, although there sometimes are isolated pockets of famine in Asia and elsewhere. What does exist on a big scale, especially in the less-developed areas, is "undernutrition." Diets are not down to the starvation level, but they are so substandard as to mean chronic undernourishment for millions of people. These diets need upgrading. That is one aim of the Food for Peace program.

---

[3] Most of this section is adapted from Max Myers, "The International Age in Agriculture," an address presented to the USDA Graduate School, May 1960, pp. 37–39.

TABLE 13.3 (*continued*)

STATUS OF FOREIGN CURRENCIES UNDER TITLE I, PUBLIC LAW 480*
(In million dollar equivalents)

Country	Agreement Amounts Through Dec. 31, 1961	Allocations Through Dec. 31, 1961[ab]		Collections Through Dec. 31, 1961[b]		Disbursements by Agencies Through Dec. 31, 1961[d]
		Sales proceeds	Other proceeds[c]	Sales proceeds	Other proceeds[c]	
Germany...	1.2	1.2	...	1.2	....	1.8[e]
Greece.....	97.2	85.3	...	86.7	.9	76.3
Iceland....	12.2	10.3	...	10.5	....	8.7
India......	2,337.3	1,716.3	...	1,211.8	6.0	319.9
Indonesia...	186.8	162.6	...	161.1	.2	53.7
Iran.......	34.3	26.5	...	23.0	....	19.5
Israel......	194.4	185.9	1.2	183.9	.6	118.6
Italy.......	152.9	144.2	...	144.2	....	115.3
Japan......	150.8	143.1	...	146.3	....	139.0
Korea.....	217.0	214.1	...	197.6	....	180.2
Mexico.....	28.2	25.2	...	25.2	....	21.0
Netherlands.	.3	.3	...	.3	....	.9
Pakistan....	1,065.9	373.6	...	412.2	4.5	264.3
Paraguay...	9.9	2.9	...	2.9	....	2.5
Peru.......	37.3	28.5	...	27.4	.5	21.6
Phillippines.	36.2	14.1	...	13.8	....	12.4
Poland.....	409.9	51.6	...	352.5	....	1.9
Portugal....	7.1	7.1	...	7.1	....	6.8
Spain......	505.6	449.7	...	463.9	....	260.5
Sudan.....	4.6	....	...	....	....	....
Syrian Arab Republic.	37.0	21.9	...	23.6	....	4.1
Thailand...	4.6	4.3	...	4.3	....	4.4[e]
Tunisia....	15.3	4.1	...	4.1	....	.2
Turkey.....	328.9	263.9	...	270.1	2.3	163.3
United Arab Republic.	311.9	213.3	...	224.4	1.3	111.4
United Kingdom.	48.2	43.9	...	48.5	....	29.8
Uruguay...	46.4	34.3	...	34.7	.5	15.0
Vietnam....	49.2	20.4	...	21.7	....	7.4
Yugoslavia..	517.5	400.2	...	455.9	....	266.2
Total....	7,651.6[f]	5,300.3	8.7	5,216.5	23.3	2,609.7

* Source: Same as Table 13.2, p. 11.
ᵃ Allocations by Executive order or by the Bureau of the Budget. Includes amounts specified in the agreements, to be used for grants and loans under Sections 104 (e) and (g), not subject to allocation.
ᵇ Calculated using the collection rates of exchange.
ᶜ Public Law 480 Sections 104 (e) and (g) loan interest and repayment of principal and proceeds from sale of Section 104 (d) commodities.
ᵈ Prior to July 1, 1961, disbursements under Sections 104 (c), (d), and (e), grants were calculated at collection rates; Section 104 (f) sales at current Treasury selling rates; Section 104 (g) loans at loan agreement rates; Sections 104 (a), (b), (e) loans (h) through (r) at the weighted average rates at the end of the months in which transfers are made to agency accounts for the balances remaining in such accounts. Subsequent to June 30, 1961, disbursements under Sections 104 (a) through (r) are calculated at the end of the quarter market rates.
ᵉ Disbursements exceed collection because of conversions from other currencies.
ᶠ Differs from Table 13.2 which reflects purchase authorization transactions.

2. We can export all our surpluses.

It is easy to become enthusiastic about exports as a solution to our marketing problems. There are even those who say, "If a $4 billion export program is good, an $8 billion operation is twice as good. Let's hold a bargain sale and export all the stuff we don't need here at home."

There are strong forces working against an expansion of trade in farm products. These forces affect world as well as United States trade.

Most of the countries of the world have erected protective devices of one kind or another—tariffs, quotas, embargoes, bilateral arrangements, and the like. Despite much effort, and some success, in getting liberalization, many of these barriers still exist—both in underdeveloped and economically developed countries, even though additional quantities of reasonably priced food and fiber are urgently needed in some countries and would greatly improve standards of living in others.

Trade restraints are erected for many reasons. A heavily populated country, whose agricultural resources are inadequate to meet all the needs of the people, may still impose quotas on certain food imports to protect domestic farm prices. Another country may limit imports so as to conserve scarce foreign exchange. Even the United States, under Section 22 of the Agricultural Adjustment Act of 1933, controls imports of agricultural commodities that interfere with USDA programs such as price supports, marketing agreements, and the like.

Every exporting country tries to persuade other countries to lower their trade barriers. This is called trade liberalization. The United States also works continuously for liberalization. This is done through diplomatic channels; periodic meetings under the General Agreement on Tariffs and Trade (GATT); and activities of other international organizations, including the International Monetary Fund. It is a rather slow process, yet it is an activity which permits no resting on the oars.

An important factor, as we consider possibilities of expanding our own agricultural exports, is the continued increase in farm production outside the United States. Everywhere farmers are learning how to step up production. Some countries have been able to reduce their food imports; those that do import can shop around because there are other sources of supply.

There is still another restraining force: The United States policy of slowing down our exports if they might disturb world prices or interfere with normal commercial marketings—either our own or of friendly foreign countries. International application of the Golden Rule is involved in this self-imposed "code." We are opposed to operations by foreign countries that would disrupt markets; by the same rule, we are determined to act responsibly in our own operations.

There are some other factors in this situation. United States agriculture does a big cash business in the world market. Obviously, then, any United States action tending to lower world market prices would only hurt our own cash receipts. Furthermore, there is a wish in the United States to see the community of free nations remain strong—economically as well as militarily.

Those who suggest the easy export route might well consider whether we can "out-export" the productive capacity of United States farmers, who continue to take advantage of mechanical, chemical, and biological advances; thus it seems likely that for many years to come they will be able to produce beyond our normal capacity to consume domestically and to export. For that reason, moving all our exports to foreign shores in one fell swoop—assuming that this could be done—still would not solve the problem. If the United States suddenly found itself free of heavy commodity surpluses, we probably would soon be right back where we started.

3.   If we cannot sell our food, let us give it away.

Substantial quantities of food already are being donated through the people-to-people approach of the voluntary foreign relief organizations and the country-to-country operations of ICA. Since 1954, for example, foreign food donations of the United States under Titles II and III, PL 480, have had a cost value of $1.8 billion. In most countries, current donations represent just about all that existing charitable facilities can handle.

In many less-developed areas, it actually is easier to sell food than to give it away. The reason for this seeming contradiction is that in every country of the free world it is the commercial distribution system through which food flows to the people, but most less-developed countries lack distributive facilities and organizations through which additional large quantities of donated food can be channeled to the needy.

Transportation is another problem. Railroads may link the larger cities and towns, but there are few good roads in rural sections. All too often villages are connected by nothing better than foot trails.

Lack of voluntary organizations of people is probably the most serious handicap in distributing donated foods. In one Asian country, United States voluntary agencies had to suspend operations for many months when they found themselves unable to obtain any local assistance in distributing the donated commodities. The most effective distribution outlets in the Far East have been schools, hospitals, health centers, and other institutions.

The Situation in India [4]

In India, for example, it is physically impossible, because of the lack of transportation and distribution facilities, to meet the country's food needs by importing more food. Even if enough food were available free or at greatly reduced prices from the United States, India's ports would become too congested to handle it all, and her railroads and roads could not move it into the areas where it is needed. If food production in India increases no faster than it is increasing at present, the gap between supplies and target will be 28 million tons (of food grain) by 1965–66. This will be about 25 per cent shortfall in terms of need. *No conceivable program of imports or rationing could meet a crisis of this magnitude . . .* that is impending. The bulk of India's increasing need for food will have to be met by India increasing her own food production.

USING SURPLUS FARM COMMODITIES
TO FOSTER ECONOMIC DEVELOPMENT [5]

In the following pages, 205 into 209, a competent observer shows how PL 480 can be used to foster economic development as well as simply to provide food.

----

[4] From the Agricultural Production Team, "Report on India's Food Crisis and Steps To Meet It," sponsored by the Ford Foundation, and Issued by the Government of India, April 1959, pp. 3–4.

[5] This section is an excerpt from a paper delivered at Ames, Iowa, in 1962 by Dr. S. R. Sen, Joint Secretary of the Planning Commission, India.

The effects PL 480 and other subsidized exports have on the recipient nations, on the competing nations, and on the sending nation are well discussed in E. L. Menzie, *et al.*, "Policy for United States Agricultural Export Surplus Disposal." College of Agr., Agr. Exp. Sta. Tech. Bul. 150, Univ. of Ariz., Tucson, Aug. 1962. For a more complete discussion, see *Food—One Tool in International Economic Development* (Center for Agricultural and Economic Development, sponsors), Iowa State Univ. Press, 1962.

While PL 480 supplies have generally helped to improve the consumption standard as well as the economic position of all recipient countries, the benefits seem to have been derived relatively more by those countries which utilized this assistance primarily for economic development rather than for other purposes. On the other hand, countries which became too much "addicted" to commodity assistance and used counterpart funds mainly for nondevelopmental purposes became more and more dependent on such assistance. There can be little doubt that it will now be better for them to have a program of gradually phasing out of dependence upon PL 480 assistance for nondevelopmental purposes and to concentrate such assistance on developmental purposes as far as practicable.

No one, surely, could take exception to commodity assistance for meeting emergencies like famine, but in all other cases it is desirable that commodity assistance should be utilized primarily for economic development. Welfare projects, however desirable, should not be of such a proportion that they cannot be ultimately financed from the income generated by the economic development projects included in the over-all national program for development.

These are substantial points on the credit side of the surplus disposal policy adopted by the United States. There is no doubt that if United States surpluses had been thrown on the international market and prices allowed to crash, most other exporting countries would have suffered serious loss. On the other hand, if PL 480 supplies had not been available, the programs for economic development in a number of underdeveloped countries would have been more modest, or their people would have had to face much more stringent control over consumption than they have to do at present.

There is general appreciation in these countries that the PL 480 supplies have been of great help to their economic and social development. The use that has been made of the counterpart funds in building up the infrastructure of the economy, in constructing irrigation and power facilities, improving transport and communications, and promoting research and extension is certainly noteworthy. But no less important is the indirect influence of these development projects in creating an urge among the people, preparing them for change, and thus creating favorable material as well as psychological conditions for further progress.

I cannot emphasize too strongly the point that while commodity assistance is helpful, much of its value is lost if it is not backed by an adequate supply of foreign exchange, especially under the conditions which obtain today in most of the under-developed countries. If the commodity assistance that the under-developed countries are receiving is not supplemented by enough foreign exchange aid and if their economic development is retarded thereby, the commodity supplies which they have contracted for may prove to be a drag on their economy. On the other hand, if enough foreign exchange assistance is available, their economic development will be accelerated, and they will be able not only to absorb the supplies which they have contracted for but even to import more in the future, and also to advance the date when they will be able to pay for their imports in dollars.

It should be appreciated that, other things remaining the same, any large-scale import of agricultural products over and above normal imports is likely to impair agricultural development in a recipient country. It is only if the latter has a balanced program for industrial and agricultural development, which is designed to create additional employment and purchasing power, that the effect of surplus disposal will become truly beneficial.

My second point relates to the counterpart funds which are rapidly accumulating in all the recipient countries. So long as the use of these counterpart funds is fitted into the plans for economic development of these countries in a general way, there may not be much difficulty. But if the impression gets around that these funds may be available for projects outside these plans, serious difficulties are likely to follow. It will not be easy to convince the interested parties that these funds do not represent any additional real resources. Pressure will develop both in the recipient and donor countries for spending these counterpart funds on various types of new projects, and to the extent that these pressures may prove successful, there will be a diversion of material resources from the projects included in the balanced programs of economic development already prepared by the countries concerned.

On the monetary side, that would lead to inflation. On the material side, it would lead to maldistribution of scarce resources. And on the operational side, it would lead to serious political and economic difficulties, to the extent that the decisions about spending the counterpart funds at the first stage when they are lent to the recipient governments, and especially at the second stage after they have been repaid by these governments, differ from the investment programs and policies of the authorities of these countries themselves. The latter, in particular, is likely to become a serious source of friction in the future unless some satisfactory solution is found right now. It may also be a fertile field for bureaucratic interference and conflicts.

What has just been mentioned about difficulties arising out of the diversion of resources applies with equal force to funds retained for United States uses, including those to be disbursed under the Cooley Amendment, especially if these happen to be large. In addition, the disbursement of Cooley funds may in certain recipient countries, involve the donor country, unless it is very careful, in local political controversies which may undo much of the good will that the commodity assistance is otherwise expected to create. It is, therefore, important that an early solution should be found for this problem of growing accumulation of inconvertible local currencies.

My third point follows from the second. The growing anxiety in donor countries to show that specific projects have been financed from the commodity sales funds is understandable. But economically as well as operationally the project approach is always much less satisfactory than the program approach. If a country has a comprehensive program for economic development it is, in my judgment, a retrograde step to insist on a project approach. On the other hand, if a country does not have such a program and the project approach is found to be indispensable, the over-all economic situation and policies should be carefully examined before a project involving a large-scale investment is considered for commodity assistance.

It is true that if the projects are merely picked out of the country's national plan—where such a plan exists—not much harm may be done. But even in such cases, the insistence on a project approach may give a slant to the aid program which may not be conducive to economic progress if there is a tendency to select projects which are more spectacular and less productive, in preference to others which may be more productive but are less spectacular. Whether an underdeveloped country has an economic plan or not, it is essential that there should be a proper balance between projects of economic development and social welfare in its development program, so that when foreign assistance ceases, the welfare projects can be continued with the income generated by the economic development projects.

I would suggest that the American authorities concerned should give careful consideration to this point. The fact that they are assisting the general program for economic development of the underdeveloped countries will be always gratefully acknowledged. There is no further point in pressing for the project approach, especially in those countries which have a comprehensive plan for economic development. The only result that will follow will be either distortion of the balanced program which the country has adopted, or irritation among interested parties in the donor as well as the recipient countries that the projects sponsored by them could not be accommodated because they did not fit in with the general program or policy for economic development.

The time has now come when, on these and other related points, the donor and the recipient countries should take a long-term rather than a short-term view. For present indications are that the problem of surplus disposal is going to remain with us for several years to come. It will be helpful if new markets can be found for the surplus products, in order to avoid at least direct restriction of production, which has several undesirable features. And as I have mentioned earlier, that can be best done by promoting the economic development of countries which are underdeveloped and are, therefore, also underfed. Since many of these countries are in the Tropics, their agriculture is complementary to the Temperate Zone agriculture of a country like the United States. If the agriculture of the former can be developed and trade with the latter stimulated, some outlet could be found for the surplus of the latter.

It is, however, mainly through the industrialization of these underdeveloped countries that a really large-scale expansion of markets can become possible. After all, even today the best customers of America's industries are other industrialized countries and not countries which have yet to industrialize. To the extent that surplus commodities can be used for the development of the agriculture as well as the industry of the underdeveloped countries, it would help not only recipients but also donors.

But here I would like to stress once again that commodity assistance is necessary but, by itself, it is not adequate. Surplus commodities cannot be used effectively unless they are matched adequately by free foreign exchange resources.

The keynote of this program should be "phasing out"—for the United States, out of the burdensome surplus; and for the underdeveloped countries, out of the vicious circle of shortage. But such a program can be practicable only if both the parties are prepared to sacrifice to some extent their present consumption for future investment. For the underdeveloped countries it would mean a special effort for saving a larger proportion of their meager income for investment in a program for economic development. For the United States it would mean a diversion of a small share of its evergrowing prosperity in the form of direct foreign exchange assistance to the underdeveloped countries—an assistance which is essential for making the optimum use of the commodity surplus that is threatening to become such a burden on its economy.

PROSPECTS FOR THE FUTURE [6]

The prospects for sharply increased commercial exports of farm products by the United States are not good.

With hunger and malnutrition widespread in the less-developed areas of the world, opportunities for expanding Public Law 480 exports might appear almost unlimited. However, without collateral development programs in these countries, this is not the case. Transportation and distribution systems are inadequate to handle greatly increased quantities of food. Governments also are reluctant to accept substantial special imports of food for a few years without assurance with respect to future supplies.

In the longer run, it is probable that most of the increased food in the less-developed areas must come from increased domestic production. These countries must fit food imports acquired under Public Law 480 programs into development plans which assure adequate future food supplies from home production and commercial imports. Expanded imports under Public Law 480 programs might, under some circumstances, delay and weaken increased home production programs. Responsible governments in underdeveloped countries are unwilling to assume the risks involved in becoming heavily dependent on noncommercial food exports from the United States.

This is not to prejudge the extent to which abundant food supplies in industrialized countries can be utilized effectively to wipe out hunger and malnutrition in underdeveloped areas. Nor does it deny the possibility of increased utilization of abundant foods in speeding economic development in the free world. But there is a definite limit to the quantities that can be used in an orderly manner even in countries where hunger and malnutrition are widespread.

---

[6] "Economic Policies for Agriculture in the 1960's." USDA, GPO, Washington, 1960, pp. 12–13.

14
Different Approach Needed

The analysis in the preceding chapters can be summarized and appraised at this point.

It is clear that the existing price-support programs are in no sense a cure or solution for the farm problem. They are at most only an expensive palliative which temporarily alleviates the symptoms, but leaves the disease to run unchecked. In this case indeed the palliative—the price-support program—makes worse the twin diseases of overproduction of farm products and over-supply of farmers. The stability and higher levels of prices initially resulting from the program reduce consumption and in-duce further overproduction—just the opposte of what is needed. And the price and income-raising effects of the impounding of surpluses in CCC stocks are only temporary; they will be re-versed when the stocks are returned to the market.

Price supports are designed to raise prices for the existing supply of farm products and increase incomes for the existing supply of farmers, right where they sit, when what is needed is to adjust the production of farm products to the demand for farm products, and adjust the supply of farmers to the demand for farmers. Prices and incomes then would rise to remunerative levels of themselves.

What is needed is to act, not on the symptoms (low prices and incomes) but on the twin diseases that cause the symptoms. These are (1) overproduction of farm products, and (2) oversupply of farmers. These diseases are both evidences of maladjustment of agricultural supply to agricultural demand.

OVERPRODUCTION OF FARM PRODUCTS

The appropriate way to solve the problem of the oversupply of farm products is to reduce the supply, or increase the demand for farm products, or reduce the price—or all three. These alternatives have been discussed in earlier chapters.

But however successful land retirement programs or lower price programs may be in reducing agricultural production, they alone will not be able to solve the farm problem. For the most basic farm problem is not a price problem resulting from a chronic oversupply of *farm products;* it is an income-per-farmer problem resulting from a chronic oversupply of *farmers.* Production control alone can solve only part of the problem. It can raise *total United States* farm income, but it cannot deal effectively with the other part of the problem that results from the excessive supply of farmers and keeps income *per farmer* low. This excessive supply of farmers continues to depress the return of farmers—their per capita net income—just as an excess supply of farm products depresses the prices of those products. Dealing with this part of the low-farm-income problem calls for measures to reduce the number of farmers.

The situation again can be illustrated by an analogy. When General Motors controls its production of automobiles, that benefits the stockholders, the owners of the business. But it may not benefit the employees at all; if they remain as numerous as ever, their wages may not rise at all. They might in fact fall, since there would be fewer jobs to go around. Similarly, in agriculture, reducing the input of land will raise the price of land, as in fact it has, but increases the incomes of farm operators as such only temporarily and to a small extent, if their numbers continue excessive.

The farm population in the United States has declined from a peak of more than 32 million in 1933 to about 13 million in 1964. But the decline has not been rapid enough to keep up with the decline in demand for farmers. The problem no longer is, "How're you going to keep 'em down on the farm?" but, "How're you going to help them get off?"

The kind of supply control program that *would* benefit farmers rather than acres would be one that would be achieved by reducing the number of farmers rather than reducing the number of acres.

OVERSUPPLY OF THE HUMAN FACTOR IN AGRICULTURE

Programs for controlling the input of land in agriculture, even if they were completely successful in bringing production in line with consumption, could not solve the farm income problem; for they would leave the supply of farmers as great as ever, and this large supply would continue to depress per capita farm income.

The large supply of farm operators relative to the demand for them results from two things: (1) the high farm birth rate and difficulties that impede movement off farms—this keeps the supply of farm operators high; and (2) the decline in the demand for farm labor, largely as a result of rapid technological advance and mechanization—this reduces the demand for farm operators and farm labor.

Farm births exceed farm deaths by about 400,000 per year, a rate high enough to result in a continuous increase in the number of farmers if all boys and girls born on farms stay in farming.

The high birth rate on farms can be measured in another way. "Replacement indexes" show the number of young children present in a population group in relation to the number needed to replace the female population of childbearing age. An index of 100 (termed "unity") would signify exact replacement and a population potentially stationary in numbers.[1] In 1950, the United States replacement index figure for "all farm-operator households" was 168.[2] (The figure for commercial farms was 171.) That is to say: the number of farm children was at least 68 per cent higher than the number needed to maintain a stationary farm population.

The demand for numbers of farmers is declining, and farm practices have become more laborsaving. Increased mechanization and machinery size have increased the size of farm that a family can handle. The average size of farm in the United States increased from 174 acres in 1940 to 215 acres in 1950 to 302 acres in 1959. From 1947–49 to 1955–57, the number of com-

---

[1] Farm Population—Characteristics of Farm-Operator Households by Number of Young Children, USDA, AMS-118, June 1956, p. 9.

[2] *Ibid.,* p. 25.

mercial farms dropped 21 per cent; and in 1961, the most efficient size of farm in Iowa was about 350 acres.[3]

For every 100 farm operators between the ages of 20–64 in the United States, there were 168 boys living on farms who reached the age of 20 in the decade 1950–60. For every 100 farm operators between the ages 25–69, 135 farm boys reached age 25 during this decade.[4]

And this does not take into account the continual decrease in the number of farms. Since 1955, this decrease has been at the rate of 89,000 farms per year, or about two farms per township.

According to a recent estimate, if present trends continue, only 10 to 15 per cent of the farm boys reaching 20 between the years 1954–63 are likely to find good farming opportunities on farms which can net them more than $2,500 per year.[5]

What is needed to increase income per farmer on more than a temporary basis is a program to speed up the movement of the continuing excess of farmers into urban jobs where there is a continuous relative deficit of workers.

Obviously, this does not call for a program to "move farmers off farms." It calls for a program to help those farmers who *want* to move off farms but need help to overcome the serious obstacles that impede their movement. It is these *obstacles* that need removing, not farmers who need removing. If the obstacles are removed, the farmers will move off themselves.

Farmers, in this context, refers to *potential* as well as actual farmers. That is, it refers to the farm boys and girls who are growing up on farms, who find it easy to go into farming because of their farm background and experience, as well as to actual farmers who are already established in farming.

Obstacles To Mobility

The obstacles to the mobility of these potential and actual farmers are well known, especially to those who are familiar with the farm situation at first hand. They are: (1) insufficient general education, (2) insufficient training for urban jobs, and (3) lack of clarity and unanimity of means for attaining objectives among the different programs.

---

[3] Earl O. Heady, and Ronald D. Krenz, "How Big Will Our Farms Get?" *Iowa Farm Science*, Vol. 16, No. 5, pp. 3–5, Nov. 1961.

[4] U.S. Bureau of the Census, "Farm Population." Series Census-AMS, P-27, No. 22, 1956.

[5] Karl Shoemaker, "Opportunities and Limitations for Employment of Farm People, Within and Outside Farming." USDA, AEP 89, June 1958.

TABLE 14.1

EDUCATION BASED ON FATHER'S OCCUPATION*

Father's Occupation	Percentage of High School Graduates Who Enter College	Percentage of High School Graduates Who Also Graduate From College	Percentage of College Entrants Who Graduate From College
Professional and semi-professional	67	40	60
Managerial....................	50	28	55
White collar-clerical, sales, service....................	48	27	57
Factory, craftsmen, unskilled, etc..	26	15	58
Farmer......................	24	11	44

* Source: Dael Wolfle, *America's Resources of Specialized Talent*. Harpers, 1954, p. 160.

1. *Insufficient general education.*[6] Are the youth leaving the farms well enough trained to compete with urban youth for town and city jobs? The answer for most of them is "No." Farm-reared adults living in nonfarm places in the United States have more than their proportional share of low status and low-income occupations.

Relative to the rest of the population, very few farm children who graduate from high school go on to college; and a relatively high percentage of those who do start to college drop out and do not graduate.

Table 14.1, based on census data, shows the educational handicap of farmers' children in the United States.

Our society is missing an opportunity to provide college training for many bright young rural people. Few if any of us would argue that there is an inherent difference in the mental capacity of rural and urban children.

Many farm youths are handicapped by a lack of high school education. Farm-reared young men and women have less high school as well as less college education than those living off farms.

Table 14.2 shows that farm-reared adults working in factories, offices, and shops include more than twice their proportionate share of persons with no more than a grade school education.

---

[6] This Section 1 is adapted from "Vocational Training for Rural Youth." NPA Agr. Comm., Spec. Rept. No. 58, Sept. 1960, pp. 6–7.

TABLE 14.2

LEVEL OF LAST COMPLETED YEAR OF EDUCATION OF FARM-REARED AND
NONFARM-REARED ADULTS*
(In per cent)

	Grade School	High School	College	Total
Farm-reared...................	60	31	9	100
Nonfarm-reared...............	27	54	19	100

* Source: Freedman and Freedman: "Farm-reared Elements in the Nonfarm Population of the U.S.A." *Rural Soc..* Vol. 21, March 1956, pp. 50–61.

TABLE 14.3

FAMILY INCOME OF ADULT NONFARM POPULATION IN 1952*
(In per cent)

	Less than $2,000	$2,000–$4,000	$4,000–$5,000	$5,000–$7,500	$7,500–$10,000	$10,000 or more	Total
Farm-reared......	30	40	12	14	3	1	100
Nonfarm-reared....	11	39	17	21	7	5	100

* Source: Freedman and Freedman: *Ibid.*

The lack of education shows up in the earning power of farm-reared people living in towns and cities. They have more than their proportionate share of low-status and low-income occupations, as shown in Table 14.3.

Detailed examination of the records of students at Iowa State University made by USDA over a 4-year period shows that students who came from rural high schools were often accepted for college despite deficiencies in high school credits. Many had to enter on probation.

In fact, the proportion of rural students who were deficient in required high school courses was twice as high as the proportion of city students with deficiencies.

Lack of a complete round of high school preparatory courses was one reason the rural students usually fell well below the marks set by city students on college entrance examinations.

Once in college, however, farm-area students generally held their own with city scholars. Their grade levels were about the same and just about as many graduated with honors.

The specific situation in a typical state, Minnesota, illustrates the above adaptation and is pinpointed in the following quotation:[7]

There is evidence to support the frequently cited statistic that no more than one of every five Minnesota farm boys who graduate from high school will be able to remain in farming. Of all senior farm boys in 12 southern and central Minnesota counties in 1953, 4 of every 10 were gone from the farm within 6 months after graduation. Six years later only 24.5 per cent were engaged in full time farming, with further shrinkage likely. Over half (53.3 per cent) were in nonfarm employment, the rest in military service or in some educational program.

A careful followup of those employed off the farm revealed 28 and 19 per cent engaged in semiskilled and unskilled labor positions, respectively, as compared to 11.8 per cent in professional and 5.7 per cent in semiprofessional employment. The level of post high school education secured was positively related to level of employment. The limited numbers in more rewarding positions appeared definitely to be a function of the limited numbers who sought further educational experiences beyond the high school. While 23.7 per cent of those studied were enrolled in a school the first year after graduation, only 11.8 per cent had completed 4 or more years of post high school study within 6 years of high school graduation.

T. M. Nelson's study, pointing to the limited interest of farm boys in post high school educational programs, is reinforced by an analysis of post high school plans of 44,756 high school seniors in 1960–61.

R. Berdie and A. B. Hood report that although 45 per cent of all senior boys indicated plans for college, farm boys, with 28 per cent, lagged well behind nonfarm, 48 per cent, and metropolitan boys, 54 per cent. When a substantial sample was followed up after graduation in 1961 to compare plans to actual performance, 28 per cent of farm boys were enrolled in college, and twice as many, or 56 per cent, of metropolitan boys.

Of farm girls, 26 per cent were in college, as compared to 45 per cent of metropolitan girls.

Implications of these findings are clear. In a period of employment stress, with increasing competition for available positions, those best qualified hold an advantage. And educational qualifications play a crucial role in placement.

Some comfort may be drawn from the Berdie and Hood study. A high proportion of top level senior farm boys anticipated college. The proportion increased from 61 per cent in 1950 to 82 per cent in 1961. This good showing of farm boys from the top of the senior classes on aptitude measurements does not carry down into the upper middle and middle ranges of high school graduating classes, where markedly fewer farm boys and girls look forward to college programs.

Many explanations can be offered for the limited participation of rural youth in post high school educational programs. But the fact

---

[7] Keith N. McFarland, "Do Farm Youth Go on to College?" *Minnesota Farm and Home Science,* Vol. 20, No. 2, Winter 1963, p. 24.

remains: facing a decline in work outlets for the unskilled or those without special training, farm boys and girls are not taking advantage of the state's schools and colleges to the extent that others are. And, since the majority of farm youth will have to compete for off-farm jobs with their better educated urban friends, many will do so at an extreme disadvantage.

2. *Insufficient training for urban jobs.* As shown above, there are good opportunities in farming for only about 15 per cent of the boys growing up on farms; the other 85 per cent need to move into better paying urban jobs, and they need proper training for those jobs.

Yet at present the greatest emphasis is still placed on "voc-ag" training for the 15 per cent who can remain in farming. What is needed is greatly expanded "voc-ind" training facilities for the 85 per cent who will go into agricultural-related or industrial urban jobs.

Excluding home economics, 45 per cent of total urban and rural vocational education funds was devoted to training for agriculture. In some agricultural states, the proportion spent for vocational agriculture exceeds the two-thirds. This represents a highly disproportionate share when compared to sources of income within the states. "This means that in many states where farming is the strongest, vocational education tends to perpetuate the farm problem of too many people in agriculture by holding out extraordinary opportunities to train for farming as a vocation." [8]

"Today only 8.1 per cent of the nation's labor force is engaged in farming, and only 3 per cent of the personal income is derived from farming.

"But 36 per cent of the nation's vocational funds are spent on vocational agriculture!" [9]

This is not a call for less voc-ag training for farm boys; the country needs more college-trained farmers. It is a call for more voc-ind training for farm boys and girls, 5 to 10 times greater in scale than the present voc-ag setup.

Technical high schools, which can provide this kind of training, are located in most of the big cities of the United States. They are not, however, a part of the general educational system of the states; they are set up to serve only a portion of the students in

[8] "An Adaptive Program for Agriculture," Committee for Economic Development, July 1962.
[9] Charles Bailey, "Study Cites High Farm Birth Rate." *The Des Moines Register,* May 14, 1963, pp. 1, 4.

a particular city's school district. Iowa has only one in the whole state, located in Des Moines. Further progress along this line is being made by a few regular high schools, which are beginning to include some vocational industrial classes in their offerings.

Other states have a variety of these and other types of technical schools, but there is need for greatly increased facilities of this type all over the country.[10]

3. *Lack of clarity and unanimity of means for attaining objectives among the different programs.* Even the programs to help excess farmers move off farms are not clear and unanimous in the means that they are working out to attain their objectives.

Three different programs concerned with rural development have been set up:

Rural Development Program	(RDP)
Rural Areas Development Program	(RADP)
Area Redevelopment Program	(ARP)

The first of these, the Rural Development Program, was set up in the latter part of 1955. On January 11, 1954, President Eisenhower had asked Secretary of Agriculture Benson to "give special attention to the problems peculiar to small farmers." The results of this study appeared in an agricultural bulletin, "Development of Agriculture's Human Resources," published in April 1955. It was transmitted to Congress as House Document No. 149. This became the basis of the Rural Development Program.

Its main feature is the emphasis placed on self-help.

With the change from the Eisenhower to the Kennedy Administration in 1960, the Rural Development Program was replaced by the Rural Areas Development Program in which the original plan was broadened and extended.

In 1961, Don Paarlberg, formerly Assistant to the Secretary of Agriculture under the Eisenhower Administration, published an appraisal of the first six years of the rural development programs.[11] In his opinion the main achievement of the RDP was the fact that problems of small farmers which previously had

---

[10] I. W. Arthur, "On Vocational-Technical Education," *Iowa Farm Science*, Vol. 15, Jan. 1961, pp. 7–8.

[11] Don Paarlberg, "Rural Development Achievement and Shortcomings as Seen at the Federal Level." *Jour. Farm Econ.*, Vol. 43, Dec. 1961, pp. 1511–18.

been glossed over were brought into the open so that they could be better understood. He listed four of the most important problems which the program faced:

1. The existence of rural poverty.
2. The poor utilization of human resources in agriculture.
3. The failure of the price support programs to help the small operator.
4. The limited opportunity which now exists in agriculture to operate farms.

His major criticisms of the program were the lack of sufficiently large funds and the tendency to dilute the program's effect over too large an area.

Rural Areas Development is a program of the USDA. It is not to be confused with the Area Redevelopment Program which is a program of the U.S. Department of Commerce. The USDA has certain assigned responsibilities in Area Redevelopment, but these responsibilities are distinct and separate from RAD. Area Redevelopment came into existence with the passing of Public Law 87-27, known as the "depressed areas bill," on May 1, 1961. Four hundred and sixty-eight (468) predominantly rural-farm counties in 38 states were designated as eligible for assistance under ARP.

The divergence of means or methods of helping farmers attain higher incomes is reflected in the foreword to a recently published RAD handbook: [12]

With the complexities and special problems of urban living, with the huge public and social costs of overcoming the problems of large-scale urban population growth, and the implications of nuclear, chemical, and biological war, it would seem sensible to direct National policy toward the maintenance of population in rural areas. In fact, these serious social and economic problems of large urban concentrations would justify renewed emphasis on the stream of thought popularized by Thomas Jefferson that rural America might be a good place sociologically for a sizable share of our population to live and work.

The job of selecting and building new industry to provide productive employment for surplus farm population is complicated and difficult. It involves many talents inside and outside of agriculture.

This statement has some attractive features, but in practice it leads to some difficulties.

---

[12] "Pegs for Rural Progress." USDA, Rural Areas Development Handbook, Agr. Handbook, No. 229, 1962, p. 2.

In many areas, the program proceeds to try to induce industry to move in where the farmers are, rather than help the farmers to move to where the jobs are. This is sensible enough, if the areas have other desirable features for the industry concerned—good location with respect to raw materials and markets, adequate transportation, adequate water supplies, etc. But in many cases, these other features do not exist. An industry may be induced to move in by the offer of a free site, tax privileges, etc., only to languish and fail, leaving the area worse off than before.

It is necessary for a community to recognize some of the hard facts of industrialization. Berg and Fienup have pointed out some of these:[13]

1. *Rural development is not synonomous with rural industrialization.* The facts show that industry is most strongly attracted to larger metropolitan areas. Little industrial growth has occurred in predominantly rural areas. For the United States as a whole, the percentage of manufacturing employment located outside of the standard metropolitan counties declined from 28 per cent in 1947 to 26 per cent in 1958. When industrial growth does occur, it will usually take place in population centers over 5,000. Centers smaller than this usually do not have the labor supply potential or the social overhead investments necessary to attract outside industry. Considerable population growth has occurred in cities of 5,000 to 50,000 population. In the past decade, cities in the 5,000 to 10,000 class grew by 19 per cent, those 10 to 25,000 grew 48 per cent, and cities in the 25 to 50,000 class increased population by 69 per cent. These rates of growth indicate expanding economic opportunities. There is a minimum level of size necessary to provide the specialization and completeness of services demanded by both rural and urban people. Efforts for growth will likely be most successful in population centers over 5,000 people.

2. *The bases for industrialization of farm communities are frequently lacking.* Opportunities for industrialization are dependent on several economic and social considerations, some of which the community can do little to control. Distance of the community from product markets, availability and quality of raw materials, transportation rates, adequacy and training of the labor supply, availability of capital and credit, level of public services and living conditions in the community, and the tax structure are some of the major factors determining industrial location. Some communities are located too far from markets to compete successfully with other areas. Often little can be done to change transportation rates. Through community effort and often additional outside help, some of the other factors affecting industry location can be modified. However, costs of producing and transporting the product to its final market must be comparable to other producing areas. The number of

[13] Sherwood O. Berg and Darrell F. Fienup, "Development Programs for Rural Areas," *National Agricultural Policy Forum,* under the auspices of the Chicago Board of Trade, Dec. 11–12, 1962, pp. 111–13.

communities desiring more employment opportunities far exceeds the number of possibilities.

3. *Rural development is not limited to the poverty problem in rural areas.* Rural development involves the entire rural community in both depressed and commercial farm areas. Actually, rural towns in the more prosperous farm communities may face one of the greatest problems of adjustment and further development. The need for improved public services—school consolidation, vocational training, recreational facilities, and the like—are common to most rural areas. There are indications that today's commercial farming areas, including the small towns facing decline, may be areas of high unemployment and underemployment ten years hence if action is not taken to facilitate the adjustment process in shifting of resources.

This emphasis on bringing industry in rather than helping farmers out frequently leads to an attitude, naturally fostered by local business, that regards a decline in the local population in the area as a disaster, something to be resisted rather than encouraged. Thus, a move to help farmers migrate to better jobs elsewhere, generally favored by economists, is resisted rather than supported. Those who hold these divergent views find themselves working at cross-purposes in the RAD program.

Community conferences to bring out the consequences of the different views help to reconcile these divergent tendencies, and help to bring about convergence toward a common goal. This provides a solid basis for action, worked out by the participants themselves.

Need for Training for Urban Jobs

At the same time that farm incomes are low, urban incomes are increasing. Take engineering, for example; the average engineering graduate at Iowa State University in 1959 had four job offers, at a starting salary of over $500 per month, based on a 40-hour week. There are a large number of good urban jobs for people with training to handle them. But one big reason why farm boys do not take these jobs is that they do not have the training for them. Farm boys, as well as urban boys, can compete for these good jobs if they have the training.

They need to know about these jobs and the training required to qualify for them while they are young—before they have trained themselves as farmers and sunk a good share of their capital and lives into farming. An established farm family finds it most difficult to leave farming. Also the established farm operator cannot expect to get one of the higher paying urban jobs when he does not have the training for it.

So the best way to deal with this problem is to reach farm boys and girls while they are still in high school. They need to be shown what percentage of them can expect to find places in farming and helped to compare farm and nonfarm incomes so that those who want nonfarm jobs can take the necessary training and compete on more nearly equal terms with urban youth.

Karl Shoemaker[14] of the Federal Extension Service, USDA, estimates that 85 per cent of the youngsters on farms today will not be able to find good opportunities as farmers as they grow up. Farms with gross sales of $5,000 or more are not plentiful enough to go around. This 85 per cent will flood the farmer market and keep farmer incomes low just as in the 1950's. This will happen unless they can be informed of their prospects, provided with "vocational-industrial" training, and helped to find urban jobs after they are trained for them.

This would call for a big change in our vocational agriculture training program—with agricultural training concentrated on the smaller number of farm boys who will actually become farmers. A greater number will need training for nonfarm jobs and help in obtaining them.

Several states now have area vocational schools that provide this later type of training. Noncollegiate technical training of this sort was offered at Iowa State University in 1959 for the first time. Much more extensive development of this field will be needed to train and help farm youths who will not remain in farming obtain the relatively better-paid nonfarm jobs and occupations. The National Defense Education Act of 1958 may be one source of funds for this purpose.

Until the excess farm population problem is solved, most of the benefits of technology and production control programs will continue to be capitalized into land values and show up more in the form of higher prices for farms than in higher incomes per farmer. In view of this situation, we should face the possibilities and encourage and help farm boys train themselves for the occupations they will follow, for off-farm jobs as well as for farm jobs.

Program Development

To deal with area problems, what is needed is a group of separate but related income and cost programs, area by area.

---

[14] Karl Shoemaker, *op. cit.*

These programs need to deal separately with the particular net income or return-to-family-labor problems in each area—and to deal with them, not by supporting prices or bolstering income as such, leaving unchanged the underlying causes of low income, but by dealing with the underlying causes in each area.

The programs should be directed, not to supporting prices and creating huge surpluses, nor even toward reducing the supplies of farm products and increasing the demand for farm products, but also to specific action that will benefit farmer incomes.

This involves research to determine in each area whether farm incomes are low there because there are just too many farmers—depressing their incomes as surpluses of farm products depress their prices—or whether incomes are low because farms are not of the size and organization that can benefit most fully from recent technological advances. If the former, then *farmer*-adjustment programs are needed to help surplus farmers off farms into better urban jobs; if the latter, then programs are needed of a *farm*-adjustment sort, focused upon the areas that need it most, and differing from area to area as may be needed to fit the different situations in the different areas.

In areas where the underlying causes are chiefly local, the programs need to deal chiefly with these local causes. In southern Iowa, for example, farm incomes are much lower than in northern Iowa, year after year. This is not just because the soil is less fertile, and it is not just a commodity problem. It arises mostly because the type and organization of the farms are not properly adjusted to the soil, topography, and other characteristics of the area. In cases like these, more local or area research is needed to determine the nature of the maladjustment: why more farmers' sons, if not farmers themselves, do not move to more prosperous areas; the kind of solutions that are required to correct the maladjustments; and the programs that need to be developed by local or area groups in collaboration with state and federal agencies and put into effect to carry the solutions through.

These programs would need to include programs to deal directly with the human factor as well as with the farm products; otherwise they could not by themselves solve low-farm-income problems which result from a continuous oversupply of farmers as well as farm products. The birthrate in agriculture is higher than necessary, and these surplus farmers depress incomes per farmer just as surplus farm products depress prices per unit of product. Excess farm boys and girls need schooling and training for urban jobs, and facilities for this purpose are inadequate in many farm areas. Programs to deal with training excess farm youths and helping them get in touch with urban jobs illustrate what we mean when we call for programs to deal with basic causes rather than with symptoms. Economic and sociological community problems would also need to be considered—the effects on schools, churches, stores, etc.

These programs could supplement the Rural Development programs that were started in 1955 and are now operating in more than 200 of the 1,000 low-income counties in 30 states.

Pointers From Labor

Some of organized labor's present and proposed programs can provide food for thought, for rethinking what needs to be done in farm policy.

Labor's wage raising activities are as well known as agriculture's price raising activities. But in addition, labor has recently been proposing to deal with the problems created by automation, much as agriculture needs to deal with its problems created by the technological revolution on farms.

Labor leaders are advocating specific programs to be supported by government and private company funds, to help workmen who are thrown out of their jobs by automation. This program would be a direct income payment program for laborers, but only to help them retrain for new jobs, not simply to keep them going on the old jobs. The payments would provide tuition to train laid-off men to learn new skills, living expenses while they are learning, and money to move them and their families to new jobs.

A second program would require appropriation of federal funds for communities which are hard hit when a company, in modernizing, abandons its old community factory and moves to a brand new automatic factory in another city or state. The unions are bringing pressure on Congress to provide low-rate loans to businessmen who would take over the old factories and start new businesses to keep labor employed and the community thriving. The money would buy new machinery and equipment.

Federal legislation in the direction of these proposals was passed in 1962. About half a billion dollars was appropriated for retraining workers who were thrown out of work by automation or other forms of technological advance. A considerable share of these funds was allocated to vocational rehabilitation centers located all over the country.

The application of ideas of this sort to agriculture requires more research and program development, in many cases of a different character from previous programs. More research is needed all along the line to help farmers not only to increase production and marketing efficiency, but also to adjust to the results of this efficiency so as to benefit rather than be harmed by it. Some research of this character is already being done to point the way; what is needed is to work out more detailed maps and directions and develop programs to deal with the problems revealed—different programs adapted to the different problems in the different areas.

Programs could be developed with the help of a series of separate conferences in each region. These conferences could include research men from the USDA and the state universities in the region in their role as research scientists; the organized farm groups in the region—Farm Bureau, Grange, Farmers Union, etc.; the commodity groups involved, such as the Milk Producers' Federation and the Great Plains Wheat Market Development Association; farmers and businessmen in the region; and consumers. If the views of these conference members were divergent, the conferences would be a good means for resolving them.

The state universities could well take the initiative in calling these conferences as part of their agricultural adjustment research and extension activities.

The conferences could be expected to develop programs to be coordinated with programs from other regions; or, if more research is needed before such programs could be worked out, the conferences could outline the needed research areas and arrange for getting the research done.

15

A Farmer Adjustment Program

What kind of a "farmer adjustment" program might be devised to help those farmers who want to leave farming and get a more useful job in town to do so? And how much might it cost?

A number of years ago, T. W. Schultz proposed a "Homesteads in Reverse" program in brief general terms, under which farm families would be offered funds to help them move off farms and retrain for urban jobs.[1] R. S. Dougan[2] spelled out in greater detail a similar program:

Farmers who were interested in moving off their farms into urban employment would be offered some special services for moving, retraining, etc., and a grant of money to help them carry their plans through.

An intensive training program should be established which would help prepare the participant for a nonfarm job. This program should be directed toward three major areas: (1) intensive training of each farmer who would be making a complete change in his vocation; (2) training of members of family who are not now farming but who will be available for a job in the near future; and (3) training of the entire family for living in a different environment concerning various social problems which might arise.

---

[1] T. W. Schultz, "Homesteads in Reverse." *Farm Policy Forum,* Summer, 1956, pp. 12–15. Also see his "A Policy To Redistribute Losses From Economic Progress." *Jour. Farm Econ.,* Vol. 18, Aug. 1961, pp. 554–65.

[2] This program outline is adapted from R. S. Dougan, "Resource Adjustment Through a Voluntary Transfer of Human Resources Out of Agriculture." Agr. Ext. Serv. Mimeo, Ohio State Univ., 1961.

The education function could be administered by existing educational agencies in cooperation with employment services and private industries. The nature of the job openings would be different enough to require separate types of training programs. Actually, this phase of the program would vary a great deal according to the family's current situation. Such training aid also could be made available to nonfarmers who are interested in changing jobs. This special training would continue until a period of time after the family became established in the non-farm job.

COST OF PROPOSED PROGRAM

The cost of the program described here, of course, would vary with the size of payment to each family induced to move: Dougan recommends $5,000 as the average value of money and services (the same figure that Schultz suggested). Included in this would be a payment of $3,000 cash divided in diminishing amounts over the 5-year period of the contract.

It would be expected that the cost of services provided to the family for moving, for training, etc., would average about $2,000. This added to the $3,000 paid in cash adds up to the total of $5,000 payment.

If this would cause 250,000 eligible farm families to move per year, the cost would be $1.25 billion per year.

Other costs such as administration, preparation of material on occupational opportunities, training, etc., would amount to a considerable sum. One might estimate an average cost of $1 billion per year for this type of activity, making the total cost of the program $2.25 billion.

A great deal of the cost of supporting farm products would be eliminated with the program described here. Programs primarily for stabilization of farm prices and incomes now cost about $2.5 billion per year. This should be gradually reduced to, say, no more than $0.5 billion in any year after the first 5 years except in cases of emergency. The average for the first 5 years might be $1 billion per year.

It would be expected also that after 5 years of such a program, fewer than 250,000 families would be induced to move each year. At that time one might estimate that no more than $0.5 billion per year (100,000 families) would be spent. This

TABLE 15.1

EMPLOYMENT BY OCCUPATIONAL GROUPS, 1960 AND PROJECTED 1970*

Occupational Group	1960	1970
	(millions)	(millions)
Professional and technical................	7.4	10.4
Proprietors and managers................	7.1	8.8
Clerical and sales.......................	13.9	17.6
Craftsmen (skilled)......................	8.7	10.8
Operatives (semiskilled)..................	12.5	14.8
Laborers, industrial.....................	3.8	3.8
Service occupations.....................	8.1	10.1
Farm occupations.......................	5.9	4.9

* Source: Bureau of Labor Statistics, U.S. Dept. of Labor.

assumes that a few of the families who have left the farm would return to their farms after their 5-year contract has expired.

APPRAISAL OF SCHULTZ'S AND DOUGAN'S PROPOSALS

The program outlined above is directed at the root of the farm adjustment problem. The chief obstacles that lie in its path arise from the huge sums of money and enormous problems of administration that would be involved in translating such a proposal into a program.

The costs of helping families to move from one occupation to another, in terms of money and tribulation, are high, running into billions of dollars. The costs of not helping them also are high, probably higher. Is there any way to get the job done at less cost?

A kind of preventive medicine could be used for this purpose. After a family has become established in farming, a major personal and financial effort is required to help them to move. The job could be done at only a fraction of that cost, however, if the program were focused not on the families that are already established in farming, but on the farm boys and girls as they are growing up—say at about high school age, before they have become established in any occupation. Only a small amount of information and money is required to help a farm boy or girl to decide which fork of the road to take—into farming, or into some other occupation—compared with the size of the job of helping him make a change after he already has chosen the farm road and established himself and his family in it. It is far easier to reduce the inflow of young people into farming than it is to speed up the outflow of older people out of farming.

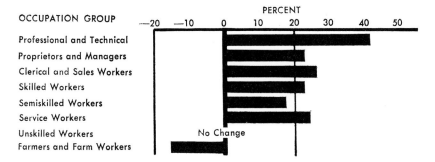

Fig. 15.1. Projected percentage change in employment from 1960 to 1970.

JOB INFORMATION

What is needed is a nationwide expansion of the programs of information concerning alternative job opportunities, salaries, and training required for them, focused upon teen-age farm boys and girls before they have chosen their occupations.

The kind of job information that is needed is shown in Table 15.1 and Figure 15.1. This table and figure show that farming is the only occupation which is expected to require fewer workers in 1970 than in 1960. The prospects are for no change in the number of industrial laborers. For all other groups, for jobs that require considerable education or training, substantial increases are projected.

More detailed and specific information of this sort is needed, area by area and occupation by occupation, current for immediate use and forecasted to provide guidelines for those who need training.

If there are good opportunities on the farm for only 15 per cent of farm boys and girls, they should be informed about this. They also need to be informed what other occupations are in need of more men, and what training is needed for them. If the 85 per cent were helped into better urban jobs, within a few years the excessive numbers of farmers on farms would decrease. Therefore, as the program continued, the total number of farmers would decline to that number which could make as good a living on farms as in other occupations. Those who moved off the farm would be better off. Those who remained would benefit, and the nation as a whole would have a higher level of living and, after a few years, a lower burden of costs for maintaining agriculture as a healthy segment of the national economy.

TRAINING FOR NONFARM JOBS

The job information service could be performed relatively inexpensively by already existing agencies expanded in this direction for this purpose. But along with this service would need to go a substantial program of training for nonfarm jobs, both for the farm boys and girls who were ready to start preparation for their life occupation, and for the farm men and women who were already engaged in farming but wanted to move out.

The basic importance of education and training is emphasized by Varden Fuller of the University of California.[3] He raises the question whether the widely made appeals for accelerated off-farm migration are addressed to the proper problem. In his words:

"It has been commonly recommended that proper therapy for several of the pathologic conditions in agriculture required some people to move somewhere else. Various notions of income disadvantage have been the principal element of the syndrome. For some writers, the prescriptive image has been that people should not persist in agriculture if they can do better elsewhere. For others, the image has been that somebody should get out of agriculture so that *those who remain* can do better. Although the validity of these propositions (especially the latter one) is suspect, I will press on to my own allegation that both fail to address basic pathology, and if the prescription is right, it is by chance.

"The essence of democratic society is not maximum or equal income but equal and unrestrained opportunity to be productive. Identifiable pockets of poverty may be attributable to disabilities in an area economy, or to disabilities in the population, or to a combination of the two. Outmigration from such a pocket may relieve the burden upon an underpar local economy, but it is likely only to transfer elsewhere the disabilities of its migrating populace. Disabilities associated with poor education, poor physical or mental health, or discrimination should presumably be as solvable in place as elsewhere. Such problems are not actually solved by getting them out of sight or through attenuation elsewhere, regardless of whatever asepsis that may occur in the income statistics of the places of evacuation.

---

[3] Varden Fuller, "Factors Influencing Farm Labor Mobility," Chap. 3 in *Labor Mobility and Population in Agriculture.* (Center for Agriculture and Economic Development, sponsors), Iowa State Univ. Press, Ames, 1961, pp. 34–35.
See also, Schultz, *op. cit.*

"Under the circumstances in prospect, it is important that a distinction be recognized between the development of capacity to be productive, and therefore to be mobile, as against the more superficial notion of motivating the movement of disadvantaged people to some place where it is assumed they will be better off. If primary emphasis is placed upon developing capacity, it may be found that preferred solutions can be found for many within the locale of their present domiciles. Proposing better education, of course, is not unusual. Moreover, it is usual to imply that the immediate purpose of better education is to enhance mobility. For example, D. Gale Johnson[4] emphasizes primary and secondary education in farm areas, but he also clearly regards this education as being valuable because it will better prepare people to move somewhere else. What I am attempting to say is let us have the educational, health, and manpower policies that will result in capable, self-dependent people and leave to them the question of where and at what they will work."

NEED FOR EXPANSION OF TRAINING FACILITIES FOR URBAN JOBS [5]

The need and opportunities for technically trained and qualified personnel is growing on both the national and international levels. And vocational-technical education is receiving increased attention in a number of states in the nation.

To meet the growing opportunities and needs for technically trained personnel, attention is being focused on vocational-technical training of less than college grade.

The high schools in a number of Iowa's larger cities and towns in recent years have started or expanded their offerings in technical education and training, in the trade, industrial, business, and service fields. For example, the Des Moines school district maintains Des Moines Technical High School. It grants a high school diploma and also offers training in 31 trade, industrial, vocational, and technical subjects including 4 "area" vocational programs. It also runs 50 adult classes including 13 for apprentices.

---

[4] Fuller's reference to D. Gale Johnson, "Policies To Improve the Labor Transfer Process," *Amer. Econ. Rev.*, Vol. 50, May 1960, pp. 403–12.

[5] This section is adapted from I. W. Arthur, "On Vocational-Technical Education," *Iowa Farm Sci.*, Vol. 15, Jan. 1961, pp. 7–8, and a later unpublished article on "Changing Educational Trends in Iowa." These articles are focused on Iowa, but they are a "case study" representing the situation in the nation as a whole.

At Mason City a vigorous development along these lines is going forward with 5 high school programs in trade and industry subjects, 2 "area" programs, and 22 adult education programs including one for apprentices. Davenport teaches 7 trade and industry programs including one "area" program to serve students from nearby high schools. Davenport also offers 27 adult evening classes including 14 for apprentices. Burlington, Centerville, Clinton, Ottumwa, and Sioux City high schools have growing industrial programs and have been designated as area schools, begun in 1961, to offer training for students from nearby high schools in their area. The 30 Iowa high schools which are offering trade and industrial programs include 11 points which have been designated as "area" schools. Other high schools in several of the bigger towns in Iowa are following the plan recommended by J. B. Conant, former president of Harvard University, who devoted a number of years to the study of public education at the high school level in the United States.

J. B. Conant's Suggestion

Dr. J. B. Conant believes that separate vocational-technical schools should be established only after most careful study and proof of need. He feels that it is better to have comprehensive high schools in the bigger towns. A comprehensive high school is one large enough to offer a broad range of educational services all the way from the rigorous courses in mathematics, science, and foreign languages to training in vocational-technical education and work experience for students while they are in high school. Conant says that usually not more than 15 to 20 per cent of the average high school student body is academically talented and has the ability to study effectively and rewardingly such difficult subjects as advanced mathematics, physics, science, and foreign languages. He believes that these subjects should be on the educational bill-of-fare of every bright student. He also thinks that the 75 or 80 per cent of the student body who are not capable or not interested in doing first-class work in these subjects should elect a consistent program directed toward the development of a specialized talent or vocation.

Recent Developments

Connecticut has spent $40 million since 1945 in building vocational schools. Louisiana maintains 26 such schools. North Carolina has 21 and offers to train workers at state expense for new industries coming into that state. Minnesota has 8 vocational technical schools. California, Texas, and New York have established vocational-technical work in junior colleges as well as in the high schools. Many other states have emphasized vocational work in their comprehensive high schools.

The first class of students to graduate from the Technical Institute Program, a 2-year technicians school at Iowa State University at Ames, completed their work in May 1962. All were placed immediately upon graduation and there was an average of more than four job opportunities available per graduate. The starting salaries for these workers ranged from $400 to $500 per month with an average of $447. They were trained as electrical, mechanical, and structural engineering technicians. Requests are now being received for chemical technicians.

It is necessary in operating vocational-technical schools to maintain good relations with labor unions. Other states have found by experience that it takes outstanding skill in supervision to coordinate the work of vocational-technical schools with the requirements of unions and of the apprentice training system. Where the relationship is good the unions will give apprentices credit for work done in the vocational-technical schools. Where relationships are not good the unions may not allow such credit to apply on apprentice requirements and may not readily accept vocational school trainees as apprentices. School superintendents and principals are usually good at academic subjects but are seldom skilled in negotiating with craftsmen and labor unions.

Disproportionate Share for Vocational Agriculture

For the period 1955–59 almost half of the vocational education funds spent in Iowa were allotted to vocational agriculture; only about 18 per cent to trade, industrial, and distributive education. These latter areas need to be expanded because far more of Iowa's young people will enter these areas than will enter farming. Vocational agriculture departments in many high schools are beginning to devote a part of their efforts to orienting some of their students into the trades and agencies marketing farm products and distributing farm supplies. More could be done on a basis similar to the work experience programs now available in 16 of the larger high schools in Iowa.

Should Farm and Nonfarm Money Incomes Be Equal?

The job information and training programs outlined above would help to bring farm incomes toward equality with nonfarm incomes. Could they bring farm incomes into full equality with nonfarm incomes? Should they be expected to do this?

One observer, D. Gale Johnson,[6] says no. He made adjustments for differences in the purchasing power of farm and nonfarm income, in the burden of income taxes, and other things. He concluded:

"While one major farm organization believes that per capita incomes should be as high for the farm as for the nonfarm population, I know of no economist who holds this view. However, we must admit that we know far too little about the relative income levels that would be consistent with an efficient allocation of labor between agriculture and the rest of the economy."

His calculations lead him to conclude that, ". . . if per capita farm incomes are 68 per cent of per capita nonfarm incomes, labor of equivalent earning ability would be receiving the same real returns in the two sectors of the economy. Because of the crudeness of the data and the estimating procedure, it might be safer to argue that the equivalent level is somewhere in the range of 65 to 70 per cent."

Comparisons of farm and nonfarm incomes generally carry the implication that the incomes "should be" equal. This belief may be based on general considerations of fairness and equity— that it is unfair for one man to be getting less than another man of similar ability; or it may be based on more objective economic considerations—that production is maximized when the factors of production are applied out to the point where their marginal returns are equal.

According to usual economic criteria, farmers should receive the same incomes as other workers, however, only if the other workers are *comparable* workers. It is fair for one man to get the same income as another only if they are comparable or equivalent in some earning sense. Very few farmers or other citizens of the United States would argue that everyone should receive the same income regardless of his ability.

The same thing is true on economic grounds. Production is maximized only when *comparable* or *equivalent* factors of production receive equal marginal returns.

---

[6] D. Gale Johnson, "Labor Mobility and Agricultural Adjustment," Chap. 10 in *Agricultural Adjustment Problems in a Growing Economy.* (North Central Farm Management Research Committee, sponsors), Iowa State Univ. Press, 1956, p. 164.

The same thing is true for different groups. Farmers as a group should receive the same incomes only as other *comparable* groups. And this raises a difficult question: What is a comparable group?

It would be only an accident if nonfarm workers as a group were comparable with farm workers as a group. Nonfarm workers include a tremendous range, from business tycoons, those who have inherited large fortunes, and movie stars at the top, to itinerant, unskilled laborers at the bottom. The average income of this highly diverse group does not mean much, because of the wide diversity behind the average. And there is no logical reason why the incomes of the two groups should be the same, just as there is no reason why the incomes of barbers should be the same as those of nonbarbers, or the incomes of bank presidents should be the same as those of nonbank presidents.

MONETARY INCOME IS ONLY PART OF TOTAL INCOME

The implication that farm incomes should be equal to nonfarm incomes in any case needs an important qualification. Usually, when farm and nonfarm incomes are compared, it is only the monetary incomes that are taken into account; both incomes are only money incomes. Large nonmonetary components of total income thus are ignored.

What moves a man to leave one occupation and take another is the difference not only in money income but also in nonmoney income. Bellerby[7] compiled the farm and nonfarm statistics for a number of countries of the world, and found that what he calls the "incentive ratio" (the ratio between farm and nonfarm incomes that provides sufficient incentive for farmers to continue to farm) ranged from under 35 per cent in some countries up to "probably over 75 per cent" in others, but nowhere does it come close to 100.

Everett Hagen,[8] unaware of Bellerby's work, did the same sort of thing a few years later, drawing on data chiefly from Simon Kuznets. The data showed that money income per person engaged in manufacturing since 1900 substantially exceeded the income in agriculture in all but one country (New Zealand) out of 11 countries; the ratio for five countries was higher than two.

---

[7] J. R. Bellerby, *Agriculture and Industry Relative Income*, St. Martins Press, 1956, p. 270.

[8] Everett E. Hagen, "An Economic Justification of Protectionism." *Quart. Jour. Econ.*, Nov. 1958, p. 501.

Does this low ratio of farm to nonfarm money incomes reflect the obstacles which hinder the migration of surplus farmers off farms, or the nonmonetary values of farm life, or both?

Brewster[9] has set his question in bi-polar terms.

Monetary income is lower in agriculture than in other occupations, he says, for one of two reasons:

1. Farm money incomes may be low because farmers' values are not typical. Perhaps, farmers prefer to live in the country, in the uncongested open air, where each can be his own boss, can hunt, fish, or loaf as and when he pleases, so much that he is willing to take substantially lower money incomes than his city cousin. If this is the case, there really may be no farm income problem; farm incomes plus the nonmonetary values of country life may be equal to urban incomes. Brewster calls this the "endodermal" theory of the farm problem.

2. Alternatively, farm money incomes may be low because of high birth rates on farms, which create a continual surplus of farmers; the impediments or obstacles to migration of these surplus farmers off farms keep the supply of farmers continually excessive, and this excessive supply depresses farm incomes. This may be called the "environmental" or "exodermal" theory.

A recent study by Kaldor et al.[10] at Iowa State University indicates that both reasons are at work. Their relative importance is not uniform for all farmers; it differs from one individual to another. Table 15.2, compiled in 1959, shows that if farm incomes were equal to nonfarm incomes, 55 per cent of a sample of 860 Iowa high school senior farm boys would prefer to farm. The table also shows that 34 per cent of these boys would still prefer to farm even if farm incomes were only 80 per cent as high as nonfarm incomes.

The table shows further that farm boys are quite responsive to changes in relative farm and nonfarm incomes.

This has important implications for farm policy. It means that farm programs that raise farm incomes without restricting

[9] John M. Brewster, "Society Values and Goals in Respect to Agriculture," Chap. 6 in Goals and Values in Agricultural Policy. (Center for Agricultural and Economic Development, sponsors), Iowa State Univ. Press, 1961, pp. 114–36.

[10] Donald R. Kaldor, Eber Eldridge, Lee G. Burchinal, and I. W. Arthur, "Nonincome Values Important in Farm Boy's Career Plans." Iowa Farm Sci., Iowa State University, Ames, Vol. 17, Oct. 1962, pp. 284–86.

TABLE 15.2

Apparent Relationship Between Occupational Preferences and Relative Income in Farming, of 860 Iowa High School Senior Farm Boys, 1959*

Relative Income in Farming[a]	Job Preference			
	Farming		Nonfarm job	
	(number)	(per cent)	(number)	(per cent)
1.62 and over................	793	92	67	8
1.50........................	770	90	90	10
1.37........................	696	81	164	19
1.25........................	624	73	236	27
1.12........................	550	64	310	36
1.00 (equal income)..........	480	55	380	45
0.89........................	406	47	454	53
0.80........................	292	34	568	66
0.73........................	191	22	669	78
0.67........................	98	11	762	89
0.62 and less................	69	8	791	92

* Source: Kaldor et al., "Nonincome Values Important in Farm Boy's Career Plans." *Iowa Farm Science*, Vol. 17, Oct. 1962, pp. 284–86.
[a] Income in farming divided by income in nonfarm employment.

entry or facilitating egress are likely to increase the number of farm boys seeking entry into agriculture. This in turn means that programs that raised farm incomes would be self-defeating over the long run; they would cause an increase in the number of persons entering agriculture, and this would reduce agricultural income per person.

Other studies have shown that there are good farm opportunities for only about 15 per cent of the farm boys growing up on farms. Table 15.2 indicates that about this percentage of boys would be willing to farm even if farm incomes were only about two-thirds as high as nonfarm incomes, because they strongly like the nonmoney characteristics of farming.

Kaldor et al. continue: "If people who enter farming do attach a positive net value to the nonincome characteristics of farming in this way, this would help to explain the long-run disparity between earning opportunities in farming and those in other employments. There also are other factors that influence the long-run level of relative income in farming, and some operate to prevent attainment of a perfect state of economic adjustment in farming. But there could be a disparity in earning opportunities even in this perfect state of adjustment—because of the value that people who enter farming attach to the nonincome characteristics of farming. The evidence from our study strongly points in this direction.

"A person attaching a positive net value to the nonincome features of farming could sacrifice some income in farming and still feel better off than in some other occupation. So, up to a point, a negative disparity of income in farming would not prompt him to change a decision to enter farming, or to shift out of farming if he already was a farm operator. Thus, if many or all farm operators react in this way, a limited negative disparity of incomes in farming could exist without bringing about the adjustments that might bring incomes in farming back into line with the incomes of other occupations.

"This would mean that incomes in farming could remain below those of other lines of activity indefinitely. The size of the disparity would depend mainly on the willingness of farmers to sacrifice income to have the nonincome advantages which they associate with farming."

Kaldor's study indicates that a considerable percentage of farm boys value the nonmoney characteristics of farm life highly; as many as one-third of them would prefer to farm even at money income 20 per cent lower than they could earn in town. To their minds, the total psychic income—money plus such nonmoney characteristics as freedom, uncongested housing, etc.—would be equal to what they would have in town.

A QUESTION OF VALUES

This comes down ultimately to a question of values, which usually are considered sacrosanct. If large numbers of farm boys prefer to farm, earning 20 per cent less than they could earn in town, that is usually considered to be a kind of value-judgment to be accepted as given.

An agronomist now on the staff at Iowa State University is impressed by the "endodermal" theory. He refers to personal interviews that he has had with numbers of farmers back in the hills in southeastern United States, who profess to be quite content with their incomes of less than $1,000 a year. They work when they want to, go squirrel hunting when they feel like it, and do a little fishing when the spirit moves them. Many a harassed businessman—or professor—luxuriates in this kind of living on vacation and plans to do it all year round when he retires. But these farmers live almost as relaxedly as this all their lives. Who will say they are making a mistake?[11]

If the number of these farmers were large enough, equilibrium would be reached with considerably lower *money* incomes on farms than in town. But part of this disparity would be made up by higher nonmoney incomes—much as professors at some western mountain universities are reputed to take about $1,000 of their salary in mountain scenery and recreation—so that *real* incomes would be nearly equal.

A small disparity would still remain, even then. For there has to be enough difference between farm incomes and nonfarm incomes to induce the continuing excess of farmers to move off the farm and into urban jobs. The obstacles to this movement can be reduced, but it is too much to hope that they can be completely eliminated. Farm income will remain a little below nonfarm income for comparable ability, enough for the difference to overcome the obstacles that still remain after everything possible has been done to remove them. Water will flow only downhill, unless it is under pressure; and in free-enterprise United States, governmental occupational pressure would be out of place.

To this extent, then, equality of farm and nonfarm income in the United States is likely to remain an objective that can be closely approached but not fully attained.

But even if a satisfactory relationship between the two types of income can be established domestically, the broadening involvements in international problems of agricultural production may cause serious fluctuations in the stability of this relationship. The next three chapters deal with these international problems, which must be given consideration in the formulation of any policies controlling agricultural production.

---

[11] I have gone into this subject more fully in three papers: "What Can a Research Man Say About Values?" (reprinted from *Jour. Farm Econ.*, Vol. 38, Feb. 1956); "What Can a Research Man Do in Agricultural Price Policy?" (reprinted from *Jour. Farm Econ.*, Vol. 37, May 1955); and "Discussion" from *Goals and Values in Agricultural Policy.* (Center for Agricultural and Economic Development, sponsors), Iowa State Univ. Press, Ames, 1961, pp. 164–70.

The World Food Problem

Part ■ 3

In this book, chief attention up to this point has been focused on the farm problem in the United States. This country, however, is only one part of the world as a whole, with only about 6 per cent of the total world population. It is necessary now to broaden our horizons and take the whole world into our purview.

When agricultural action programs were first undertaken in the United States in the late 1920's and early 1930's, they were paradoxical. (1) They focused on some of the most international farm products in the United States (those which were exported in large quantities; two of these were cotton and wheat). Yet (2) the programs were set up and operated as domestic programs, without much attention to their international ramifications.

This parodoxical situation was sustained after World War II by massive subsidies to bridge the gap between the supported domestic prices and prices in the other countries of the world.

It is time now, however, to review this situation, in the light of developments such as the Common Market in Europe, the wider powers granted to the President of the United States over matters of international trade, our increasing involvement in world affairs, and the clearer recognition of what the farm problem in the United States really is and how it might be solved.

This is necessary because the United States exports and imports large percentages of some of its farm products, and is therefore directly affected by what goes on in the countries with which it maintains these exchanges. Thus, even from a limited United States point of view, we cannot even define what the United States wheat problem is until we know whether future exports of wheat to other countries are going to be in greater or less demand. If the foreign demand is going to increase, that may take care of the wheat surplus problem, at least within a few years. But if the foreign demand is going to decline, there is more trouble ahead. The answer to this question of wheat export demand depends upon what happens in competing wheat-supplying countries as well as in wheat-consuming (deficit) countries.

In addition, problems of any kind in one country are seen in better perspective if they are viewed in the light of problems in other countries.

BROADER CULTURAL AS WELL AS GEOGRAPHICAL HORIZONS

It is also necessary to see the farm problem in the United States in a broader cultural as well as geographical setting.

Farm policy in any country is developed in a context of cultural environment which determines the kind of policy that will survive. The plantation-slave policy in early United States history became intolerable as the cultural environment changed during the 19th century. The policy of making two blades of grass grow where only one grew before that prevailed until recent years needs to be supplemented now by a policy directed toward letting farmers *benefit* from this policy rather than *suffer* from it.

This sort of change requires a change in the cultural environment and in the goals and values which underlie that environment. This is the subject of the last two chapters of this book.

16
World Food Deficits and Surpluses[1]

The important questions, basic to all farm programs in the United States and other countries, are: What is the food problem in the world, as a whole and in different parts? Is it a problem of impending famine, as population growth continues on its headlong course; or is it impending surpluses, as agricultural technology continues *its* headlong course? Or is it the one problem in one part of the world and the other problem in the other? And if the latter, can the countries in the one category help the countries in the other? Is the problem in any case a problem of calories, or proteins, or some other nutrient?

Answering these questions requires some understanding of the parts that the different nutrients play in meeting the nutritional needs of people, and the values of different foods for meeting these needs. A preliminary statement of this sort follows:

THE ROLE OF DIFFERENT NUTRIENTS

Calories as a Measure

The basic nutritional need is for food energy measured in terms of calories. Calories are derived chiefly from the protein, fat, and carbohydrate in foods. Part of the total requirement is needed to satisfy the minimum calorie need for basal metabo-

---

[1] This chapter is adapted from Esther Phipard and G. Shepherd, "Nutritional Needs by World Regions," Chap. 3 in *Food—One Tool in International Economic Development*. (Center for Agricultural and Economic Development, sponsors), Iowa State Univ. Press, Ames, 1963, pp. 60–71.

lism—calories spent to keep the body functioning. The remainder represents the calories needed for daily activities. The minimum calorie need usually accounts for more than half of the total daily need of a moderately active adult. Calorie needs are related to age, body size and composition, climate (including environmental temperature), and physical activity. Without knowledge of these factors it is difficult to estimate with any degree of accuracy the food energy requirements of a population group.

When calories are deficient for long periods, the body adapts to a lower plane of existence by conserving energy. Growth is slower, the basal metabolic rate declines, weight loss occurs, and physical activity is curtailed. Efficient use of dietary protein is reduced when calories are too low, because protein will have to be burned for food energy.

Protein

Protein is essential as a constituent of all body cells, for the growth of new tissue and for other metabolic functions. Proteins are complex chemical substances composed of varying combinations of simpler components called amino acids. Some 22 are known to be physiologically important. Of these, 8 have been shown to be required ready-made from food sources in the adult diet; the others can be synthesized in sufficient quantity for body needs. The amounts and proportion of amino acids in a dietary protein determine its effectiveness in meeting protein needs. In proteins of good quality the amino acids are in the right proportion for maximum efficiency of utilization by the body. Proteins in animal foods are of best quality. However, in mixed diets it is the amino acid assortment in the entire diet, rather than in each food, that is important.

Protein needs are usually expressed in relation to body weight. Protein allowances for normal adults have been made on the basis of one gram per kilogram of desirable body weight. This level provides a reasonable margin of safety to allow for differences in the protein quality of different foods. It assumes a diet adequate in calories and other essential nutrients.

Protein deficiency in the form of kwashiorkor, hunger edema, and certain other conditions is widespread among young children in some of the developing countries of the world. Evidence of protein deficiency among adults, however, is rarely seen in the nutrition surveys conducted by the ICNND (the United States

Interdepartmental Committee on Nutrition for National Defense).

Fat

Fat is a valuable source of food energy contributing more than twice as many calories per unit of weight as carbohydrate and protein do. Food fats provide essential fatty acids, and are important in the diet as carriers of fat-soluble vitamins. Minimum requirements for fat are not well established; there is even less basis at present for recommending an optimal intake. Fat consumption varies widely among countries and different population groups, providing as little as 10 per cent of the calories in a few countries and as much as 40 per cent or more in the United States and Canada. High levels of fat intake, however, are not presently thought to be compatible with best health.

Carbohydrate

Carbohydrate is the main source of food energy in many areas of the world in which grains are the dietary staple. In some countries carbohydrate accounts for 75 to 80 per cent of the calories; in the United States, for less than half.

Minerals and vitamins, essential to good nutrition, are not discussed to any extent in this chapter.

EXTENT OF WORLD FOOD DEFICITS TODAY [2]

A number of studies have indicated that there are several serious food deficit areas in the world today. They are shown in the form of a world map in Figure 16.1.

According to this map and report,[3] ". . . diets are nutritionally adequate in the 30 industrialized nations in the temperate Northern Area which account for a third of mankind—more than 900 million people." However, "For most of the 70 less-developed countries in the semitropical and tropical Southern Area, diets are nutritionally inadequate, with shortages in proteins, fat, and calories. These countries contain over 1.9 billion people." This indicates that roughly two-thirds of the world's people have poor diets.

[2] See also, E. Eppright, M. Pattison, and H. Barbour, *Teaching Nutrition;* especially Chap. 3, "International Nutrition, A Resource and a Responsibility." Iowa State Univ. Press, Ames, 1963, pp. 238–67.

[3] "The World Food Budget, 1962 and 1966." FAS Rept. 4, ERS, USDA, Oct. 1961.

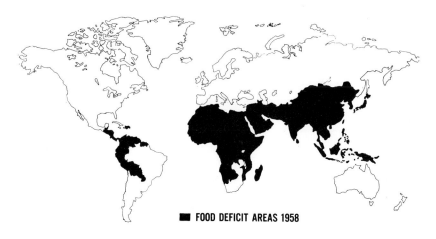

■ FOOD DEFICIT AREAS 1958

U.S. DEPARTMENT OF AGRICULTURE   NEG. ERS 1010-62(4)   ECONOMIC RESEARCH SERVICE

Fig. 16.1. Food deficit areas of the world, 1958. Note that they lie mainly in the tropical and semitropical areas where economic development has been slow.

Such broad statements greatly oversimplify the nutrition problems that are the ultimate objective of this group's activity. A closer look at dietary shortages in some of the major regions and their component countries illustrates this point. By the standards adapted for this study, calories were short in many countries of West Asia, Northern and Eastern Africa, the Far East, and Mainland China, Central America, (excluding Costa Rica), as well as in Bolivia, Peru, Ecuador, Columbia, Venezuela, and Paraguay.

This is not to say that people in all other countries have enough to eat; but that the calorie *average* for the country met the reference standard. Great differences in food consumption occur within most countries, usually between the well-to-do and the poor, or perhaps between urban and rural groups, between those living in low and high places of a country, and even among individuals within family groups.

Protein shortages are often but not always associated with calorie deficits. The kind and amount of grain or starchy roots which serve as the dietary staple can make quite a difference in the total protein content of the diet. To illustrate, 1,500 calories from the foods listed below would provide the different amounts of protein shown (in grams):

Cassava	6.7	White Flour	43
Millet A	28	Millet B	45
Rice	28	Oatmeal	55
Cornmeal	37	Whole Wheat	60

In Africa, total dietary protein was low compared to the reference standard in half of the countries. Diets of eight of the 21 countries were low in animal and pulse protein, but only one of these was also low in calories. In the Far East, animal protein was particularly low in India and Indonesia, although the consumption of pulses helped to improve the average protein quality of the diet. Eight of the 11 countries were below the reference standard in both total protein and in calories.

Most of the Latin American countries had diets that easily exceeded the reference standard (floor) for animal protein. But because of the nature of the rest of the diet, they failed to provide enough "total" protein. In 13 of the 20 countries in this region, the average diets provided less than the reference standard for total protein, especially low figures being estimated for the Dominican Republic, Haiti, and Ecuador. Calories were also exceptionally low in these countries.

AREAS NEEDING MORE RESEACH

The World Food Budget is an excellent introduction to the subject of food deficits. Helen Farnsworth has expressed some cautious reservations whether FAO and other reports of this kind overstate the extent of actual malnutrition existing in the world.[4] Further evidence is needed to deal with their reservations. Much more research work needs to be done to define the problem more specifically. This research falls into three groups, as outlined below:

1. More accurate pinpointing of nutritional needs

The nutritional needs of a population group are usually expressed in terms of per capita averages. Ideally these are based on the requirements of (or allowances for) individuals of different age and sex for calories and the major nutrients—such as

---

[4] Helen C. Farnsworth, "Defects, Uses, and Abuses of National Food Supply and Consumption Data." Reprinted from *Food Research Institute Studies*, Vol. 2, No. 3, Stanford Univ., Stanford, Calif.

protein, fat, and calcium—weighted by the proportion of each such category of individuals in the population. For these calculations, data on population distributed by age and sex are needed. It would be desirable to have such estimates of nutritional needs developed separately for each country, taking into account factors influencing calorie requirements—climate, body size of the people, and activity, as well as available knowledge of the nutritional status of the people. Few countries have at hand all the information needed for developing such estimates of nutritional need, and for pinpointing the area, age, or income groups where the need is greatest. The number of trained professional persons—nutritionists, physicians, and other health workers—who could give help with these estimates is increasing steadily in many countries, making available even more information.

ESTIMATING FOOD CONSUMPTION

The most comprehensive information on the food supplies of various countries is provided by the "Food Balances" prepared in ERS, USDA. Similar data are developed by FAO for their periodic reports on the state of food and agriculture. These data are invaluable in studying the world's food resources and needs, and for trade and marketing programs. They also provide rough estimates of consumption, country by country.

As a basis for nutritional evaluation, however, balance sheets can be misleading. There may be incomplete reporting of food consumption, especially of locally produced foods that do not enter into foreign trade. Also, in many countries population figures for deriving per capita averages may be unsatisfactory. Then there is the usual problem in dealing with averages, which mask the inequitable distribution of food supplies within the country. A case in point is Brazil, which appears on the basis of calorie and protein estimates per capita to have reasonably adequate food supplies; yet in certain areas of Brazil dietary levels are extremely low.

In appraising food supply data, there is a chance for a discrepancy in calculating the calories and nutrients provided, depending on the food composition values used for calculations. For example, the energy value of beef carcass can vary from less than 800 to more than 1,600 calories per pound, depending on the degree of fatness. A pound of wheat provides about 1,600 calories, but if milled to white flour will yield only about 1,200 calories, assuming the branny layers are not eaten by humans.

Also there are many indigenous foods consumed in some countries for which nutritive values are not found in food composition tables.

Estimates by USDA of the calorie value of per capita food supplies may vary by 10 to 15 per cent from those published by FAO in the "State of Food and Agriculture, 1961." Some of this discrepancy may be accounted for by the use of different food composition values, but more important probably were differences in per capita consumption estimates.

NUTRITION REFERENCE STANDARDS

Some reference standard is needed against which consumption can be measured to determine deficits. At best this can only be a very gross indication of the extent to which the food needs of the people are being met. Such standards are useful, however, for depicting with broad strokes the poorly fed areas of the world and for making time-to-time comparisons of food consumption levels.

For practical use, nutrition reference standards are stated as fixed figures. This suggests a precision in our knowledge of per capita nutritional needs that does not exist. For example, in the World Food Budget study the reference standard for fat, stated as the amount to provide 15 per cent of the calories, was based on judgment as to what might be a reasonable nutritional floor. The level might have been 12 per cent or perhaps 20 per cent. There is no research basis at present to support a precise percentage. Yet the difference between 12 and 20 per cent is highly significant in terms of tons of vegetable oil needed to meet the reference standard.

The foregoing discussion is presented as background for interpreting reports on food supplies and nutritional deficits of individual countries and areas. As an overview of the magnitude of the world food problem such studies are extremely useful, pointing the way to the food planning needed to assure adequate food supplies for ever-increasing populations.

For a more realistic appraisal of a country's food consumption and dietary adequacy, food balance sheets need to be supplemented by dietary studies among representative samples of the population, and by nutritional status surveys. It is only in this way that the nature and extent of exising malnutrition can really be determined.

A considerable amount of such information is available. The nutrition program of FAO includes assistance to countries in making studies of the diets and food habits of their people. Results provide a basis for recommending modifications in food selection or preparation, or perhaps in home food production that will improve diets. Since the early 1950's such assistance has been given in nearly all the countries of Latin America, many in the Far East, and in two or three countries in Africa.

Also, more information on the food consumption and dietary levels of population groups within countries will become available if the FAO succeeds in its promotion of sample surveys.

The Interdepartmental Committee on Nutrition for National Defense was established in 1955, for the purpose of providing assistance on nutrition problems of technical, military, and economic importance in foreign countries. At the request of the countries, survey teams of United States specialists representing many disciplines (physicians, biochemists, laboratory technicians, nutritionists, dentists, food technologists, and agricultural economists) have, as of July 1961, conducted nutrition surveys, in 16 countries—five in the Far East, four in the Near East, four in South America, two in Africa, and one in Europe. The United States nutrition teams work side by side with their counterparts in the host countries and suggest many ways of making more effective use of the country's food resources. These surveys are continuing. The survey reports provide detailed information on the diets and the nutritional status of the military forces and, in many of the countries, of civilian groups as well, constituting an important resource for pinpointing special nutrition problems.

2. Meeting the needs with the most economical, acceptable foods

In order for a population to be well fed, enough food of the right kinds must be on hand; people must be able to produce or buy it, or it must be made available through special feeding programs; and to be acceptable, the foods should be compatible with the customs and habits of the groups. This is a simple statement, but it embodies complex problems of agricultural science, nutrition, public health, economics, logistics, sociology, and other fields. For these reasons the problems of poor nutrition need to be attacked on a broad front, with the combined efforts of many countries or groups supplementing what each country can do for itself.

THE PROTEIN PROBLEM

One of the important questions in maximizing food resources is this: *Does some part of the protein deficiency need to be satisfied by animal protein, or can all the protein deficiency be satisfied by much cheaper and more locally available vegetable protein?*

The answer to this question is crucial, for animal proteins are several times more expensive and difficult to obtain than vegetable proteins.

The USDA "World Food Budget, 1962 and 1966," is not clear on this point. It refers to "deficiencies in animal protein" in terms of nonfat dry milk. But if these deficiences could be remedied much less expensively by proper vegetable diets, the problem would be much easier to solve.

The USDA explains that ". . . the deficiencies could be satisfied by many other commodities which, in some instances, can be more easily produced in diet-deficit countries than the commodities used in describing the deficiencies."

But later, the same report goes on to say *"Animal Protein. . . .* The reference standard for animal protein is seven grams per day per person or about 12 per cent of the total protein. This is a minimum. Where a deficiency occurs it may be critical for it affects lower income persons, and most adversely preschool children and pregnant and lactating mothers—those most in need of this food nutrient."

So is this a problem of supplying expensive animal protein, or can the need be satisfied by proper mixtures of cheap vegetable protein?

In most food-deficient countries, the limited quantity and poor quality of dietary protein is a major nutritional problem. Particularly affected are young children whose postweaning diet is not adequate to support growth nor health. Milk, eggs, or other desirable sources of good quality protein which would prevent or alleviate protein malnutrition are not likely to be available in these countries in sufficient quantity to solve this problem. For immediate relief, of course, imports of dry skim milk distributed through special feeding programs of UNICEF, Care, and other agencies are helpful as far as they go. For the long run, however, the chief reliance must be placed on locally available sources of protein.

Vegetable Protein

Considerable progress is being made around the world in finding ways of meeting the need for protein from vegetable proteins. In many countries nutrition scientists familiar with food resources as well as the customs and food habits of their people have been working on this problem with assistance from FAO and WHO, (World Health Organization). Their efforts have been greatly extended and augumented by a world-wide research program on food sources of protein which was begun in 1956 under the supervision of a Committee on Protein Malnutrition established by the Food and Nutrition Board, NAS-NRC.

As stated in a report of this committee, the program is " . . . aimed at increasing the supply of safe and nutritionally adequate protein foods for the most vulnerable groups, nursing and expectant mothers and young children." Research plans and programs were developed in close association with the staff of FAO, WHO, and UNICEF who had a background of experience with this problem, and with financial support from several sources.

Results of these studies have shown clearly that suitable mixtures of vegetable protein foods can be prepared that will prevent and cure protein malnutrition in young children; that such mixtures can be prepared from a variety of different foods locally available and at a relatively low cost compared to animal sources of protein.

High-protein vegetable mixtures usually have included concentrates from: oilseeds—cottonseed, sesame, peanut, or others; legumes—soy or other beans, peas, etc.; one or more grain products; and other minor components. One such mixture, whose use is believed to make animal protein unnecessary so far as nutritional needs are concerned, was developed at the Institute of Nutrition of Central America and Panama (INCAP) in Guatemala and therefore called "Incaparina." This mixture contains:

> Whole ground corn . . . . 29 per cent
> Whole ground sorghum . . . . 29 per cent
> Cottonseed flour . . . . 38 per cent
> Torula yeast . . . . 3 per cent
> Calcium carbonate . . . . 1 per cent
> Vitamin A . . . . 4500 IU per 100 grams

Feeding tests with animals and with children have demonstrated the high nutritional value of this mixture. When mixed with water and suitable flavoring, it is well accepted by children and adults.

In India, a multipurpose food (MPF) has been developed which is a blend of low-fat peanut flour and Bengal gram flour (a legume) fortified with vitamins and calcium. This product is an effective supplement to diets based mainly on cereals and low in protein.

Several other combinations of foods and specially processed products are being investigated in India as potential sources of dietary protein. In some countries products of the soybean—so-called soybean milk, fermented soybeans, and soy flour—are proving valuable supplements to a basically cereal diet. In Indonesia a product called Saridele has been developed from a dried extract of soybean, supplemented with minerals, vitamins, and sugar. The product, which resembles dry milk powder, has proved so acceptable that factory production had to be expanded to meet the demand. Because protein sources must be low in cost as well as nutritionally effective, the use of by-products of various industries such as the pressed cakes from oil seeds—is a promising resource hitherto not fully explored.

Fish flour offers another potential source of concentrated protein of good quality, which could be produced at low cost from species not now used for food or from resources now wasted. FAO has been very much interested in this resource for improving diets. Pilot processing plants have been set up in several countries and feeding trials are being made. Although certain technical production problems can certainly be overcome, there are other difficulties to be reckoned with in getting fish flour into the diets of people who need it most. Special planning will be needed for teaching people how to use it, or perhaps for incorporating it into other foods (i.e. bread) at the producer level.

Chemically Produced Amino Acids

Another possibility for improving the protein quality of diets is the addition of chemically produced amino acids to basic cereal foods in which one or more of the essential amino acids is low in relation to need. For example, the nutritive quality of wheat protein is improved by the addition of lysine. However, effective fortification of other grains used in many areas of the world would require the addition of two or more different amino acids some of which are not now available in quantity and are prohibitive in cost. Even if they were available and cheap, the practical problems of distribution and incorporation of amino acids into foods in the food deficit areas would be enormous.

In most diets there is no reason to depend on a single food to supply all the amino acids in favorable proportions. Foods complement each other in providing the assortment and quantities of amino acids needed by the body just as they do in providing minerals and vitamins. In other words there is great nutritional advantage in mixed diets even though the major components are of vegetable origin. This is why the combination of different food sources of protein—grains, oilseeds, legumes, and vegetables—is being encouraged. The development of protein concentrates from such foods as cottonseed meal, soybeans, and green leaves offers further opportunities for supplementing diets.

Although many of the products being developed show great promise for improving protein nutrition, the laboratory tests and feeding trials are just beginning. It is important to remember that mixtures of vegetable proteins such as in Incarparina must be combined in rather exact proportions to be most effective. Hence, the preparation and packaging of such foods need careful development and supervision. Also special plans are needed for distributing them to the people who need them most and for educational programs to assure acceptance and actual use of the new foods. A great deal of food management will be required.

3. Producing the needed foods most economically

In some cases the foods required can be imported at lower cost than produced domestically. But in the great majority of cases they will have to be produced domestically. There are several reasons for this; most food deficit nations suffer from a shortage of foreign exchange; local machinery for distribution is not at hand; and transportation facilities are inadequate. These things make it physically impossible to import and distribute more than a small fraction of the quantities needed. The bulk of the food must come from indigenous production.

The problem of increasing indigenous production lies in the area of farm management. Agricultural economists feel at home with this problem. It is dealt with extensively in books on farm management, so that it does not need to be explored here.

OVER-ALL PERSPECTIVE

The broad concept we are dealing with can be illustrated in concrete form by the Common Market in Western Europe. Our objective is to develop the research basis for a *world* common market—a common market for food for the world as a whole.

The Common Market countries in Europe have shown that this is not an idle dream, but a practical, workable program that is already producing impressive results in Europe. It is time to lay plans for research and development work that is needed to underlie the world common market for food and help to establish it on a solid factual basis.

Most reports of world food deficits are based on averages by countries. Three types of additional information are needed before the nature, extent, and incidence of malnutrition in the world can be accurately set down. These are indicated by the following questions:

1. Beyond the information offered by country averages, which groups in which countries suffer malnutrition? What kinds? How much? There is need for more accurate pinpointing of nutritional requirements than national averages can provide.

2. What are the most economical foods for satisfying the nutritional needs identified under the preceding point? Can vegetable proteins fill the bill? The answers will differ from country to country and by areas within large countries.

3. How can these needed foods be produced most economically? In some cases the foods required can be imported at lower cost than they can be produced domestically. But in the vast majority of cases they will have to be produced domestically for reasons of foreign exchange, local conditions, and the sheer physical impossibility of importing and distributing any more than a small fraction of the quantities needed.

17

World Food Prospects for the Future

The preceding chapter indicates that the food shortage problem for the world as a whole needs to be solved chiefly by increasing indigenous production in the deficit areas.

Table 17.1 indicates that something has been accomplished along these lines over the past few years. The upper part of the table shows that agricultural production has increased substantially in the deficit areas.

The lower half of the table, however, shows that much of the gain in agricultural production has been offset by a gain in population. The increase in agricultural production *per capita* shown in the lower four rows is only a third or less of the increase in agricultural production *per country* or area shown in the upper half. In Western Asia, indeed, the increase *per capita*

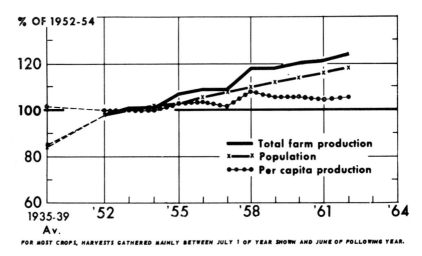

FOR MOST CROPS, HARVESTS GATHERED MAINLY BETWEEN JULY 1 OF YEAR SHOWN AND JUNE OF FOLLOWING YEAR.

U. S. DEPARTMENT OF AGRICULTURE   NEG. ERS 665-62 (11)   ECONOMIC RESEARCH SERVICE

Fig. 17.1. Total world output of farm products shows rising trend while per capita output shows slower growth.

TABLE 17.1

INDICES OF WORLD AGRICULTURAL PRODUCTION, TOTAL AND PER CAPITA BY REGIONS,
AVERAGE 1935–39 AND ANNUAL 1959-60 TO 1962-63[*a]
(Average 1952-53 to 1954-55 = 100)

Region	Total				
	Average 1935–39	1959-60	1960-61	Preliminary 1961-62	Estimates 1962-63
Canada.........	68	98	105	86	114
United States.....	69	111	114	115	115
Latin America....	72	126	126	130	129
Western Europe...	81	112	119	117	121
Eastern Europe...	106	128	127	128	128
Soviet Union...	100	129	126	129	130
Other Eastern Europe......	119	127	129	126	122
Far East[b]........	88	122	127	131	133
Western Asia.....	69	121	121	124	129
Africa...........	80	120	125	120	128
Oceania[c]........	78	121	125	127	132
World[d]........	85	118	120	120	124

Region	Per Capita				
	Average 1935–39	1959-60	1960-61	Preliminary 1961-62	Estimates 1962-63
Canada.........	92	83	87	70	91
United States.....	85	100	101	100	99
Latin America....	103	107	104	104	101
Western Europe...	92	107	112	110	113
Eastern Europe...	107	118	115	115	113
Soviet Union...	101	117	112	113	112
Other Eastern Europe......	120	120	121	118	113
Far East[b]........	110	108	110	111	111
Western Asia.....	97	103	100	99	101
Africa...........	107	105	107	101	105
Oceania[c]........	103	105	107	107	109
World[d]........	102	105	105	104	105

* Source: "The 1963 World Agricultural Situation." USDA, FAS, ERS, Jan. 3, 1963, p. 4.
[a] Value of production at constant prices. Crops included in the index are harvested mainly between July 1 of the first year shown and June of the following year. For a few crops and most livestock production, estimates are for the calendar year of the first year shown.
[b] Excluding Communist Asia.
[c] Australia and New Zealand.
[d] Including estimates for Communist Asia.

is practically nil. Figure 17.1 shows that even for the world as a whole, agricultural production per capita has been rising only slowly and irregularly. Malthus would feel almost as alarmed over the situation today as he was 150 years ago.

What are the prospects for the future—say over the next 15 or 20 years?

PROSPECTS FOR THE NEXT FEW DECADES[1]

The world food problem results chiefly from the recent acceleration in the rate of population growth. Throughout much of man's history, a high birth rate offset the high death rate and insured the continuation of the human race. But with the reduction in death rates, resulting from widespread application of medical technology, population is now growing rapidly, as shown in Figure 17.2.

From the time of Christ until the end of the 16th century, world population grew at an average rate of 2 to 5 per cent per *century*. But since about 1960, population has been growing 2 per cent per *year*. This population growth is concentrated in the less-developed regions—the regions least able to afford these population increases.

Figure 17.3 shows that an estimated 3 billion people—about as many as the present world population—are to be added to

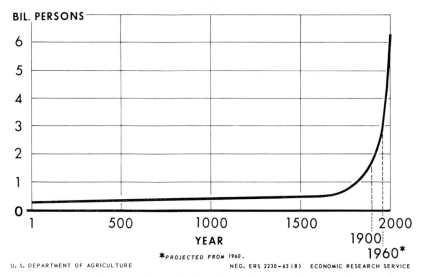

U. S. DEPARTMENT OF AGRICULTURE   NEG. ERS 2230-63 (8)   ECONOMIC RESEARCH SERVICE

Fig. 17.2. Twenty centuries of world population growth.

[1] The rest of this chapter is based upon Q. M. West and L. R. Brown, "Looking Ahead at the World Food Problem," USDA mimeograph, undated, and L. R. Brown, "Man, Land and Food," USDA Foreign Agr. Econ. Rept. 11, Nov. 1963; see also, L. R. Brown, "Increasing World Food Output," Foreign Agr. Econ. Rept. 25, USDA, April 1965.

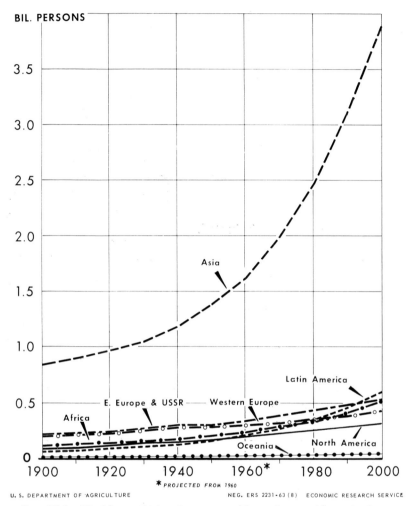

BIL. PERSONS

Fig. 17.3. World population by geographic regions, with projections.

the present population of the less-developed regions over the 4-decade span between now and the year 2000. Thus the less-developed regions must expand their food output by an amount equivalent to the output of the entire world today.

Food output can be increased by expanding the area under cultivation, or by raising yields. Throughout much of man's history, the area under cultivation expanded at about the same rate as population; additional food output resulted from expanding the cultivated area. Shortly after World War II, about 1950, the source of additional food output changed from expanding the cultivated area to increasing the yields. This occurred mostly in the developed regions.

It is not difficult to increase yields in the developed regions. Capital for investment in agriculture and the technical know-how required are more than adequate. But yields have not been rising appreciably in the less-developed regions of Asia, Africa, and Latin America.

Increasing the output of food to keep pace with the growth of population is only part of the problem. At present, most of the people in Asia, Africa, and Latin America have diets which are nutritionally inadequate. A substantial expansion in output, higher than the rate of population growth, must occur if nutritional deficits are to be eliminated.

Per capita grain output, an indication of food output, has actually declined over the past quarter century in the less-developed regions. The per capita production of grain, averaging 224 kilograms per year just prior to World War II, was only 215 kilograms per year during the 1957–60 period.

The less-developed regions, faced with this decline in per capita output, sacrificed their net grain export position to become net grain importers. During the late 1930's the less-developed regions of Asia, Africa, and Latin America had a net grain surplus of 11 million tons annually. This net surplus flowed from the less-developed to the developed regions. But between prewar and the 1957–60 period, the net flow was reversed as the less-developed regions developed a net deficit of 15 million tons.

Why were the less-developed regions not able to raise per capita output over the past 25 years, when a technological revolution was taking place in the developed regions?

There was no one reason, no one obstacle. Rather, there were many.

One very serious problem was the primitive state of tropical agricultural technology. In Northwestern Europe, the technological revolution in agriculture began at about the same time and in the same place as the industrial revolution. Emigrants leaving Northwestern Europe and settling in temperate regions such as North America, Australia, and New Zealand were able to apply their knowledge of advanced agricultural techniques with only minor modifications.

But most of the less-developed countries are in tropical and subtropical regions, and for them the direct borrowing of agricultural technology was not possible. In these countries, individual farmers lack the technical and financial resources required to do effective research. Collective action is required, and in developing countries, only the government can provide this.

The governments of the less-developed countries, however, put only moderate emphasis on agriculture. There are several reasons for this.

One reason is the strong competition in any underdeveloped economy for the limited resources available. Another is the view that progress means expanding the industrial sector while neglecting agriculture. There seems to be little appreciation of the need for a viable, progressive agriculture in a progressive economy. The importance of this need is indicated by the fact that virtually every advanced country in the world today first had an improving agriculture as a precondition. Also, agriculture lacks status in most underdeveloped countries, and most of the young people who are fortunate enough to attain a higher education do not elect to work in agriculture.

As population grows faster than the agricultural land area and it becomes necessary to get more and more food from the same amount of land, the cost per unit of food produced rises. It is surprising that so little attention is given to the long-term implications of this trend. Japan, one of the most densely populated countries in the world, supports rice prices at a level 2 to 4 times the world price level. What will happen when other countries, less able to pay such high food prices, find themselves with similar man-land ratios?

Grains as a Common Denominator

In looking ahead at future world food needs and agricultural resource requirements, we can rely heavily on statistics of all grains considered aggregately. Grains account for 70 per cent of the harvested crop area in any given year; they are thus an indicator of agricultural land area. Grains provide 52 per cent of all calories when consumed directly and a large part of the remainder when consumed indirectly in the form of meat, milk, and eggs. In terms of food energy, grains completely dominate world trade in food. Data on all grains considered aggregately thus provide a convenient common denominator for combining data on production, trade, and consumption.

The developed regions of North America, Western Europe, Eastern Europe, the Soviet Union, and Oceania do not now have, and are not likely to have in the foreseeable future, any serious nutritional problems. The developed regions are involved in these projections primarily because they are a source of food for the less-developed regions.

Figure 17.4 shows that the net flow of grain from the developed regions to the less-developed regions in 1957–60 amounted to 15 million metric tons per year, accounting for 3 per cent of the total grain supply in the less-developed regions. By the end of this century, the net grain flow into the less-developed regions is expected to account for 5 per cent of the grain requirements. But because the populations of these regions will be more than double their present size, the net grain flow will be nearly 70 million metric tons per year instead of the current 15 million metric tons. These projections are based on the United Nations "medium" level projections—projections now considered too low by many demographers and economists.

On the basis of these projected net imports into the less-developed regions, it is a relatively simple matter to project pro-

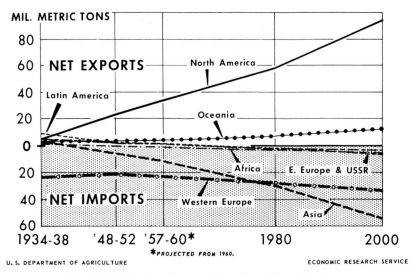

Fig. 17.4. Regional net grain trade, with projections.

duction requirements. The difference between the 230 kilograms of grain available per person in Asia and the 880 kilograms in North America is the difference between an economy in which nearly all grain is needed for direct human consumption and one which can afford to convert large quantities of grain into meat, milk, and eggs.

Let us then make some modest assumptions concerning the per capita level of grain availability in the less-developed regions. We will not assume that per capita grain availability will reach that of North America or even half that of North America. Let us assume simply that it will increase 10 per cent above the current level of 222 kilograms, or to 244 kilograms, by 1980, and an additional 10 per cent, or to 266 kilograms, by the end of the century.

What will this mean in terms of production requirements? Figure 17.5 shows that grain production in the less-developed regions (Asia, Latin America, Africa, and Oceania) must increase from the present 433 million metric tons to 732 million by 1980 and to 1,250 million by the end of the century. That is, output will have to nearly triple over the next 4 decades. The additional output required in this part of the world will be nearly equal to the entire output of the world today.

Very little new land can readily be brought under cultivation;

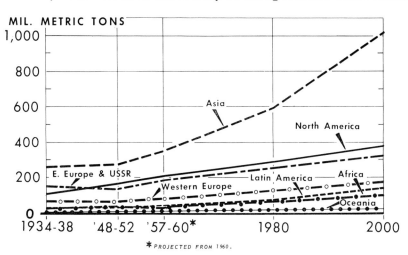

U. S. DEPARTMENT OF AGRICULTURE   NEG. ERS 2253-63 (8)   ECONOMIC RESEARCH SERVICE

Fig. 17.5. Regional grain production, with projections.

most of the additional output must come from increasing yields. These will come partly from improved varieties, but mostly from the use of more fertilizer.

A standard rule of thumb for estimating grain-fertilizer response ratios is 10 to 1. That is, under most conditions, a ton of fertilizer plant nutrients will increase the yield of grain about 10 tons. Thus Asia, using 3 million metric tons of fertilizer (measured in terms of plant nutrients) a year in 1960, would need 27 million tons by 1980, as shown in Figure 17.6. This would closely approach current world fertilizer consumption. By the end of the century Asia would need 68 million tons. In Africa fertilizer consumption would need to go from the current 1 million tons to 3 million by 1980 and 7 million by the year 2000. For Latin America, currently using 1 million tons, fertilizer requirements would rise to 4 and 10 million tons, respectively, in 1980 and 2000. These summary figures concerning production requirements and fertilizer needs show the magnitude of the world food problem in concrete terms.

The conclusions concerning the world food problem in the future, therefore, are as follows:

1. Contrary to popular opinion that all countries pass through similar demographic stages, the currently developed world

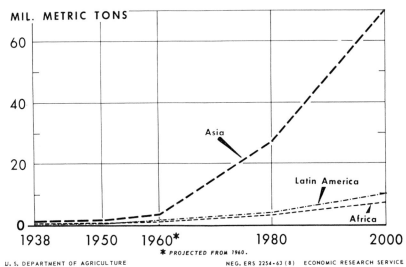

U. S. DEPARTMENT OF AGRICULTURE   NEG. ERS 2254-63 (8)   ECONOMIC RESEARCH SERVICE

Fig. 17.6. Projected fertilizer requirements of less-developed regions.

has never experienced a rate of natural increase comparable to that which now faces the less-developed world. The highest decade rate of growth during this century by the developed world was 12.8 per cent, while the decade rate for the underdeveloped world is now 22.4 per cent and still rising.

2. The effort required to feed adequately the numbers of people projected for the less-developed regions over the remaining 4 decades of this century will severely tax man's ingenuity and the earth's resources. The problem will be most severe in Asia.

3. The role of United States agriculture, as a source of food and technical assistance for the rest of the world, is growing steadily and promises to achieve an unprecedented importance in the future.

4. The solution to the food problem of the less-developed countries must come from improving the agriculture within these countries. Food shipments from the developed countries can help but they cannot account for more than a very small fraction of projected increases in food needs over the next several years.

18
Value Problems in Food Deficit Countries

The analyses and prescriptions in the first two parts of this book are based chiefly on the situation in the United States. The principles involved, however, are applicable to the situations in other countries—in other technically advanced countries like the United States, and in technically underdeveloped countries like Africa, India, and South America.

Bellerby and Hagen, working independently, showed that average farm incomes run considerably below nonfarm incomes in most countries of the world, much as they do in the United States (their work is reported in Chapter 15). The reservations concerning the United States farm income data which they expressed apply also to the other countries, so that the actual farm incomes do not run so much below the nonfarm incomes as the raw data indicate; but other evidence (chiefly on farm outmigration) supports the view that farm incomes run lower than nonfarm incomes in nearly all countries.

Over the past 30 years or more, most of the countries of the world have attempted to raise their farm incomes by enacting agricultural price-support programs of the same general nature as those in the United States.[1] Most of these programs have turned out to be about as unsatisfactory as those in the United States. The agricultural policies being hammered out in the European Common Market in recent years represent an attempt to break away from these unsatisfactory programs. We can ob-

---

[1] Organization for European Economic Cooperation, "Fourth Report on the Agricultural Policies in Europe and North America." See also, FAO Commodity Policy Studies, No. 6 and No. 11.

TABLE 18.1

VENEZUELAN EGG IMPORTS, 1950–61 *

Years	Imports
	(1,000 kilograms)
1950	10,122
1951	8,660
1952	11,309
1953	11,072
1954	13,009
1955	15,652
1956	17,288
1957	24,247
1958	25,398
1959	24,910
1960	19,974
1961	8,976

* Source: Geoffrey Shepherd, Walter Gudel, and Cesar Jimenez, "Report and Recommendations Concerning Food Marketing in Venezuela," Consejo de Bienestar Rural, Caracas, Venezuela, April 1962, p. 116.

serve this struggle with sympathetic interest, since it is similar in many ways to our own.

Changes in these programs are being induced in several other countries by the emergence of surplus problems in what were previously deficit situations, under the impact of technological revolution that has been under way in the United States. Abundance is creating problems in these other countries much as it has been doing in our own. Great Britain is already self-sufficient in milk, and approaches self-sufficiency in pork. France already has become a net exporter of feed grains. Western Europe as a whole has a net export surplus of dairy products, averaging 600,000 tons in terms of whole milk from 1955 to 1957, which is expected to grow to 4 to 6 million tons by 1965. France and Italy are expected to export half a million tons of sugar by 1965. The Common Market is expected to cease importing wheat and become self-sufficient in that commodity by 1965.

How rapidly a country can change from deficit problems to surplus problems is clearly shown by the recent experience of Venezuela with eggs. All during the 1950's, eggs, bulky and perishable though they be, were the chief agricultural import into Venezuela, as shown in Table 18.1. Then in the early 1960's

the Venezuelan government started an intensive drive to increase egg production in Venezuela. The drive was so successful that domestic egg production tripled between 1958 and 1961.
Almost overnight, in 1962, Venezuela changed from a deficit to
a surplus situation for eggs, plunging at one jump out of the
deficit frying pan into the surplus fire. It was not nearly as
prepared to deal with this egg surplus situation as it was with
the preceding deficit situation, and conditions in the egg industry
in Venezuela suddenly became chaotic.

Most of the prescriptions outlined in this book for the United
States apply to other food surplus countries as well as to ours—
the need to reduce price supports; the need to develop long-run
farm *income* "outlook" work to show what the prospective farm
income situation is; the need for information about urban job
opportunities and the kind of training required for them; and
the need for the removal of other impediments to the migration of surplus farmers out from agriculture and into urban
jobs. In those countries, as in the United States, attention is
turning from programs for farm products to programs for
farmer incomes.

PROBLEMS IN TECHNOLOGICALLY UNDERDEVELOPED COUNTRIES

In technologically underdeveloped countries, most of the
problems that appear in the technologically advanced countries
are only potential, not actual. The actual farm income problems result mostly from insufficient production, not from excessive production; they result from low productivity per farmer,
not from high productivity.

These problems cannot well be solved by massive imports
of food from the United States. In India, for example, it would
be physically impossible to do this with existing facilities, even
if it were economically possible, for if food production increases
no faster than present rates, by 1965–66 the production of food
grains will be about 25 per cent short of needs. The only possible solution is a rapid increase in food production in India.

Production problems of this sort are the kinds of problems
which the United States faced 50 and 100 years ago. The same
techniques which the United States used can be adapted, with
proper modification according to the different circumstances, in
the underdeveloped countries today. What they accomplished
in the United States is shown earlier in this book; what they

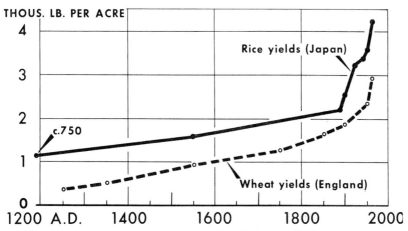

SOURCE: H. L. RICHARDSON "INCREASING WORLD FOOD SUPPLIES THROUGH GREATER CROP PRODUCTION" IN OUTLOOK ON AGRICULTURE VOL. III NO. 1, 1960.

U. S- DEPARTMENT OF AGRICULTURE NEG. ERS 888-62(2) ECONOMIC RESEARCH SERVICE

Fig. 18.1. Long-run trends in rice and wheat yields, A.D. 750—1960.

accomplished in some other countries is illustrated in Figure 18.1.

More productive seeds, better tillage instruments, even of the simplest kind—plows, cultivators, seed drills, harvesters, etc.—and better cultural practices, including fertilization, crop rotation, insecticides, herbicides, etc.—the list is long and familiar.[2] Extension organization to get word of these new instruments and practices out to farmers, and research in land tenure, farm management, and marketing to explore further applications of economic science in those fields, are other features of farm productivity programs which have demonstrated their usefulness.

But the greatest need underlying all of these potentials is widespread education of the whole population. An educated citizenry will seek out and apply new technology, even over great obstacles, if it is given a chance. An uneducated one will not do this even when the tools are placed in their hands.

---

[2] See, *Food—One Tool in International Economic Development.* (Center for Agricultural and Economic Development, sponsors), Iowa State Univ. Press, Ames, 1963. See especially, Sherman E. Johnson, "Food and Population Pressures: A 25-Year Look Ahead," pp. 112–24; John W. Mellor, "Increasing Agricultural Production in Early Stages of Economic Development," pp. 219–43; and Mordecai Ezekiel, "Research Work by FAO," pp. 278–301.

Hampering Influence of Irrational Attitudes and Values

Still more basic than education in physical science is education in social science. Visiting teams of technological experts in India, for example, have been told by the Indians that their technological advice would be welcomed on almost all points, except on sacred cows; recommendations to slaughter these half-starved animals, to relieve the populace of the heavy burden of supporting them, fall on deaf ears—not for any reasons that seem rational to a Westerner, but purely for religious ones. Western economic advisers in Burma, for another example, report that the greatest obstacles to progress in that country are not physical matters but matters of lack of enterprise, hampering traditions, and seemingly irrational attitudes and values.

Everett Hagen analyzes the situation as follows:[3]

"In Burma, as in other technologically nonprogressive countries, if economic development is to proceed, basic changes must occur in many attitudes. . . . There are perhaps three main emotional interests or attitudes which are still dominant in many persons in Burma, and which to some extent must be replaced.

"One is the lack of respect in the village culture for the person and property of strangers. Many villagers who would not themselves rob or kill outsiders are passive when others do so. Until civil order is enforced, not by physical force and legal penalty alone, but by the sanction of public attitude, economic development will at best limp ahead.

"Another is the deep-seated attitude that the most satisfying occupations and positions in life are land owning, religious learning, military achievement, and civil position in the service of the king and hence, by transfer, of the government. It should be noted that it is the holding of government position, not any given achievement in it, which is satisfying. Business activity has a low place in this system of values. Interest is largely absent in science—that is, in the logic of nature—which is the basis of interest in techniques and in control of nature to the end of improving man's life.

"And the third is the ethic that a junior or subordinate should not express—much less act upon—his judgment in opposition to, or even independently of, an elder or superior."

---

[3] Everett E. Hagen, "The Problem of Economic Growth," *The Economic Development of Burma,* Planning Pamphlet No. 96, Nat. Plan. Assn., Washington, D.C., July 1956, pp. 61–62. For a more recent and extended discussion, see L. J. Walinsky, *Economic Development in Burma,* Twentieth Century Fund, 1962.

The Spanish cultural background inhibits economic development in South America. The dictatorial and autocratic rather than democratic tradition flowers in the form of large haciendas owned by an elite ("40 families own Peru") and manned by peons who work under some such arrangement as three days of the week for the landowner and the rest of the week for themselves. This is bad enough in itself, but in addition the owners typically pay very little in the way of taxes, and have no tradition of investing their large incomes in productive investment in the country; rather, they like to live in high style in Paris, Madrid, and other European resorts. This is true of many wealthy businessmen as well as land owners. It occasionally seems anomalous that United States citizens tax themselves to support AID programs for South Americans who do not tax themselves for this purpose, nor invest their own funds in their own countries.

A broader general example is the divergence between Eastern and Western cultural backgrounds. This is well illustrated in Tagore's appraisal.[4]

I remember how in my youth the feeling of intense delight and wonder once followed me in my railway journey across Europe from Brindisi to Calais, when I realized the vast beauty of this continent everywhere blossoming in a glow of health and richness under the age-long attention of her chivalrous lover, Western humanity. He had gained her, made her his own, unlocked the inexhaustible generosity of her heart. And I had intently wished that the introspective vision of the universal soul, which an Eastern devotee realizes in the solitude of his mind, could be united with this spirit of outward expression in service, the exercise of will in unfolding the wealth of beauty and well-being from its shy obscurity to the light.
I remember the morning when a beggar woman in a Bengal village gathered in the loose end of her sari the stale flowers that were about to be thrown away from the vase on my table: and with an ecstatic expression of tenderness she buried her face in them, exclaiming "Ah, Beloved of my Heart!" Her eyes could easily pierce the veil of the outward form and reach the realm of the infinite in these flowers where she found the intimate touch of her Beloved. But in spite of it all she lacked that energy of worship, the Western form of direct divine service which helps the earth to bring out her flowers and to spread the reign of beauty on the desolate dust. I refuse to think that the twin spirits of the East and the West, the Mary and Martha, can never meet to make perfect the realization of truth. In spite of our material poverty and the antagonism of time I wait patiently for this meeting.

In the West, at least since Calvin, work has been regarded as a calling on the same high level as a religious calling; the accu-

---

[4] *Rabindranath Tagore, Pioneer in Education*, Essays and Exchanges Between Rabindranath Tagore and L. K. Elmhirst. Distributed by John Murray, 50 Albemarle Street, London W. 1, England, 1961, p. 56.

mulation of wealth by one's own efforts is a high ideal and a worthy objective of man's effort. In the East the opposite view is held:[5]

". . . maximizing happiness and minimizing discomforts lies in limiting work to the amount required to support one's customary mode of living so as to be able to spend the greatest amount of time and energy in noneconomic employments.

". . . the dominant striving of people in all cultures is the aspiration to earn an increasingly favorable image (valuation) of themselves in their own eyes and the eyes of others. Whether or not this striving works as an inhibitor or a generator of economic growth turns on beliefs concerning ways of living and of making a living that are taken as prima facie evidence that one possesses capacities which entitle him to the increasingly higher standing which each covets. This status aspiration functions as a powerful inhibitor of economic growth if it is guided by the belief that dependence on economic employments is indisputable evidence that one lacks the capacities of mind and character that entitle him to the higher positions. But the same aspiration becomes a generator of unlimited economic growth if it is guided by the belief that proficiency in economic as well as noneconomic employments is the appropriate way of earning an even higher valuation of himself in his own eyes and in the eyes of others.

"The key step in the rise of our own economically dynamic Western society was a revolutionary shift from the first to the second of these beliefs—the belief that no amount of riches can ever exempt one from the responsibility to be as proficient as possible in any employment which he believes best expresses his productive potential. Once this shift in beliefs was accomplished, economic incentives became effective inducements to increasingly productive effort over and above the limits imposed by any conceivable level of customary wants. May not the same principle apply to the vast areas of the globe that still share the same traditionalist beliefs and values with respect to the economic employments and master-servant types of institutions which Western society shared prior to the 16th Century? If so, the central question is: How may this revolutionary change in traditionalist beliefs and values be facilitated?"

This question is the subject of the next chapter.

---

[5] John Brewster, "Beliefs, Values, and Economic Development," *Jour. Farm Econ.*, Vol. 43, Nov. 1961, pp. 779–96.

Goals and Values Determine
Farm Policy

Part ■ *4*

The farm programs that were adopted in the United States and other countries in the past were those which were supported by the predominant values held by the majority of the farm and non-farm population.

Many of these values conflicted at different points. In these cases some of the values were overridden by others, or both were adjusted to each other by some form of compromise. Farmers held tenaciously to the high value they placed on freedom, for example, and chafed under acreage restrictions, which they accepted only because they helped attain other values, such as equality of incomes with those of other groups—their version of labor's slogan "equal pay for equal work."

The need for birth control in underdeveloped countries is obvious if they are to attain the rising standard of living which they value highly, but this need conflicts with the dogmatic position of the religious creeds which are powerful in many of these areas.

What farm programs and birth control programs will be accepted and put to use in the future will depend not only on the characteristics of the programs themselves, but also upon the values most highly prized by farmers and by other groups whose support will be needed to get legislation through. These values will not necessarily be those that are most highly prized today; values change with time under the impact of world events. It is desirable to look back and see how they have changed in the past to attain the status they have at the present time, in order to see most clearly how the present hierarchy of values was attained and in what directions it may change in the future.

19
The Development of Values

The 18th century Protestant Reformation in Europe produced cataclysmic upheavals in men's value systems. These upheavals had profound economic effects which reverberate to this day. In addition, these economic effects—high productivity, rapid technological change, democracy, etc.—are themselves producing further drastic changes in men's value systems which will create further economic, social, and political changes. This upward spiral appears likely to continue at an accelerating tempo in the future.

What happened as the Protestant Reformation got under way is well told in John Brewster's rich prose:[1]

The feudal system segregated the managerial and labor functions, lodging the one in the lords and the other in the serfs. The lord of the manor did not work; he only managed the work of his serfs, and dispensed his ideas of justice in his realm.

The value systems of those times, prior to the Reformation, held work in low esteem. All classes shared a deep aversion to doing more work than was required to support customary modes of life. The one exception to this was in the monasteries where men viewed themselves as exemplary doers of God's work, organizing the entire 24-hour day into a series of work routines that were known as the Holy Callings. Mechanical clocks were first invented to facilitate their orderly performance.

---

[1] The rest of this section draws heavily, with some condensation and adaptation, on different sections of John Brewster, "Value Judgments as Principles of Social Organization." Farm Economics Research Div., ARS, USDA, mimeo., March 27–28, 1960. Mr. Brewster generously gives his approval.

Then came the Protestant Reformation. Zeal for infusing all human activities with a God-seeking spirit led the Protestant founders to believe that all occupations are equivalent opportunities for unremitting expression of gratitude for God's goodness and gift of eternal life. As this happened, vast energies that hitherto had found release in building great cathedrals now found new expressions of their heavenward urge in sailing the seven seas, turning deserts into gardens, conquering pests and disease, breeding scrub stock into fine herds, and transforming hovels into firesides of good cheer. These were the new songs of salvation. In this way, unlimited productive effort ceased to be inhibited as an expression of avarice and became prized as the proper way of meriting ever greater approbation in one's own eyes and the eyes of others. Thus, production without limit became the handmaiden of the insatiable aspiration for status.

Early in the history of the United States, the philosophical heritage of the Protestant Reformation unfolded into specific value judgments that functioned as the chief guides to social organization without significant change until the 1930's. These value judgments fall into four groups:

The Work Ethic. This includes the Work Imperative, a value judgment that idleness is sin, and that it is incumbent upon each and every one to work to the best of his ability for the good of his family, his country, and his world.

Along with this goes the value judgment that society owes to each: (1) the equivalent of his contributions, and (2) equal opportunity to develop his abilities (by education, etc.) to the fullest extent. The self-made man is the ideal, and human capacities are sufficient to improve without limit the lot of the common man.

The Democratic Creed. This included two central value judgments: (1) all men are of equal worth and dignity, and (2) none should have dictatorial power over any other.

The Enterprise Creed. The third group of organizing principles consists of three judgments comprising the traditional creed of enterprise: (1) Proprietors, or the legal representatives, deserve the exclusive right (power) to prescribe the working rules of their production units. (2) The individual (or family) is and ought to be wholly responsible for his own economic security throughout life. (3) Prime functions of government are, therefore (a) to prevent anyone, including government itself, from invading the unfettered freedom of proprietors, or their legal agents, from running business as they please, and also (b) to prevent the imprudent from pressuring either government or business into shouldering responsibility for their security.

The Ethic of Self-Integrity. As different groups are always in more or less conflict with each other, with respect to what is wrong with the social order, so the individual is always in more or less conflict with himself in respect to the behavior he feels he should follow for the sake of his own respect and esteem, and the conduct he feels he must pursue to gain the approbation and esteem of others. At any early date, America committed herself to this fourth group as the ideally proper approach to this conflict.

In this ethic, the key judgment is that both the individual and his group (or groups) are responsible for seeking a new mode of thought and practice that will unify the hitherto conflicting views of each. In line with this judgment: (1) the community prizes its dissenting members as its agents for achieving new knowledge and practices that will enrich the life of all, and (2) the dissenter in turn feels a strong obligation to identify himself with his own exceptional sentiments and views. In this spirit, both the individual and his group (or groups) take each other's role in order to find a way of composing their differences.

DISRUPTING EFFECT OF THE MACHINE AGE IN INDUSTRY

The next force that changed men's values was the coming of the machine age.

The machine age had one retrogressive effect. It pitched the enterprise and democratic creeds into sharp opposition. When the management and labor roles were separated into bargaining classes, it became self-evident to laboring classes that the enterprise creed was now incompatible with the democratic creed; that it should be ousted in favor of the judgment that the power to prescribe the rules which all in industry must observe is, and ought to be, a joint power of all those involved in firms; and hence that a prime function of government should be to protect each party in the joint exercise of this power under accredited collective bargaining procedures. In contrast, management classes feared that the world would fall apart if the democratic creed were made the organizing principle of the industrial as well as the political sphere of national life.

In recent years, sharp opposition between the older work ethic concepts has tended to dissolve into a common concern to achieve greater security as well as profits through expanding gross national output as rapidly as possible. Two events led to this truce. The first was the national abandonment in the 1930's of the older enterprise creed concerning total individual responsibility for one's own security throughout life. The second was the combination of very rapid economic growth with a marked rise in the level of all personal incomes, the narrowing of extreme income inequalities, and the fact that recognition of collective responsibility for individual security was an incentive to and not an inhibitor of greater productive effort.

But this truce does not mean that liberals have so successfully ousted the older enterprise ethic as an organizing principle of modern life that they have worked themselves out of a job. Two events have thrown this creed into opposition with the work ethic ideal of national responsibility: (1) the discovery that the nation's poverty line no longer lies within the area of privately produced and marketed goods but between this sphere of services and publicly rendered services,[2] and, (2) the launching of the Sputniks that so dramatized Soviet economic growth and military power as to cause the nation to ask "Why did we let them get ahead of us?"

The cause of both events is the failure of the market to make an efficient apportionment of national resources between production of private luxury goods and such public goods as defense services, education, health facilities, parks, playgrounds, transportation, a good police force, and the like. The nation tends to seek a proper social balance of resources between production for private wants and for public needs through expansion of government taxing and spending activities to wipe out scarcity of public goods and services. However, the country no sooner tends to move in this direction than it finds its sense of national duty clashing with the older enterprise creed that publicly produced services are essentially sterile—that "Government is powerless to create anything in the sense in which business produces wealth." [3]

---

[2] J. K. Galbraith, *American Capitalism.* Houghton, 1956, pp. 251–53.
[3] J. K. Galbraith, *The Affluent Society.* Houghton, 1958, p. 133.

Most conspicuous of all the value conflicts occasioned by the rise of machine industry, is the one between the democratic, the enterprise and work ethic creeds with respect to the form of social organization needed to provide adequate protection against the fear of arbitrary power. Such power is of two types: Economic power to coerce by withholding from others what they need but do not own, and political power to coerce by physical duress. The first is usually personified as Big Business and the second is Big Government, that is, government big enough to exercise restraints on Big Business.

Students have observed that Americans are obsessed by the fear of power. This could scarcely be otherwise. They are afraid of it because it endangers the enterprise creed that each has a right to be a sovereign over his business. The widespread identity of firms and households of premachine industry stripped men of economic power by so limiting the size of firms that their business was not big enough to raise or lower the price at which anyone bought or sold. Therefore, full protection against the fear of power merely required a popularly controlled government that left the market alone.

But this fortress was smashed by the rise of machine industry which, in shearing off firms from households, left no limit on the extent to which successful corporate firms might acquire oppressive power. This fact in turn divided the nation over which it feared most: Big Business or Big Government. In line with the imperatives of the democratic creed, nonmanagement classes and small business, by and large, sought protection by using government to offset the power of Big Business, either through severe regulation or even by socializing it in some instances. But, in line with the enterprise creed, the management-minded are most frightened of Big Government. They look upon it "as a bridge of socialism into a police State" while the people are "apathetic and complacent—too busy—looking at television, or tending to their business, to protect the freedom and opportunity which have made America what it is."[4]

In these clashing valuations, conservatives have received a greater assist from liberals themselves than is commonly realized. As Galbraith observed, the liberal's fear of Big Business by no means cancels out his fear of Big Government so that in hard-fisted showdowns he becomes irresolute and verbose.[5] Not infre-

---

[4] J. K. Galbraith, *American Capitalism.* Houghton, 1956, pp. 3–4.
[5] *Ibid.,* pp. 54–60.

quently, the twin fears of both are enclosed in the same skin; then they induce acute frustration. For example, Professor Frank Knight observes:[6]

. . . There is an undeniable natural tendency toward increasing inequality and concentration of power under free enterprise, which political action seems the only way of counteracting. . . .
     But it is my conviction that any great extension of political action is incompatible with political liberty; that "control" will call for more control and tend to run into complete regimentation—calling also, before it goes very far, for regimentation of thought or expression— and finally into absolutism, with or without a destructive struggle for power.

One is thus reminded of Aesop's donkey, afflicted with equal degrees of thirst and hunger. Placed midway between a tub of water and a bale of hay, the poor beast finally perished for lack of ability to decide which is wanted most—the hay or the water.
     Finally, the theme of much present-day literature is that the social structure of machine industry is tending to split the older ethic of self-integrity into opposite ethics of total conformity on the one hand, and total nonconformity on the other.

DISRUPTING EFFECT OF MACHINE AGRICULTURE

The shift to machine *agriculture* did not transmute the age-old sequential pattern of operations into an assembly-line, simultaneous pattern, as it did in industry. Therefore, in farming, the machine process remains as compatible with the identity of firms and households as animal power and hand manipulations. Hence the value conflicts occasioned by the shift to machine agriculture stems mainly, not from the separation of the labor and management roles into new bargaining classes, but from the increasingly high productivity of new farm technology.
     The origin and nature of the conflict is substantially this: In the absence of collective restraints, each farmer seeks to adopt the new practices before others do, in order to improve his income position. But when most of them take on the new practices, they glut the market with price-depressing surpluses. This places them in a cost-price squeeze that transfers the benefits of their improved industry to other groups, leaving farmers the lowest paid of any major occupational group. The remedy would appear to lie in a program of collective restraints on individual producers

---

[6] Frank H. Knight, *Risk, Uncertainty and Profit.* Augustus M. Kelley, Publ. p. 1.

that would enable all farmers to achieve an optimum output from the standpoint of themselves and the public alike. In principle, farmers tend to want such a program in order to prevent the market from denying them an equitable share of the benefits of their technological advance. But they also resist it in the belief that it is wrong to deny proprietors the freedom to run businesses as they please. In this way, new technology puts the farmer's conscience in a jam by placing in opposition his love of justice and his love of freedom. It is questionable whether farmers can ever find a program that can resolve their surplus problem until they really face up to this clash.

The overproduction problem in agriculture therefore will not move very rapidly toward solution until this basic conflict of values is resolved in one way or another.

RESOLUTION OF VALUE CONFLICTS NOT A SIMPLE MATTER

Brewster would heartily agree that this resolution will not be a simple matter. The resolution is more difficult now than it would have been 20 years ago, before the farm programs began to embed higher land values into the farm capital structure. It is difficult to get the patient off this habit-forming drug now that he has become addicted to it and dependent upon it. Grether writes of this conflict:[7]

Agricultural Industries. The agricultural industries demonstrate clearly the issues and impasses created by long continued programs of subsidization, direct and indirect, open and hidden. Many believe that we should now follow the logic of accumulative forces to their end by placing major agricultural industries under rigid governmental supply management. Surely no sterner warning need be given as to the accumulative consequences of continuing programs of short-run, piecemeal subsidization. We should soon decide whether to continue agriculture under its own special and overlapping jurisprudence, partially insulated from the market system. . . .

The decisions with respect to agriculture have enormous portents for our entire economic and political system. If agriculture is diverted into a tightly regulated series of industries, then the pattern is set for similar diversions step by step elsewhere in our economy. Inherent in this approach would be the Balkanization of regional and commodity markets in a manner entirely contrary to the trends of modern technologies and our traditional internal free trade.

---

[7] Ewald T. Grether, "Principles of Economic Policy, Consistent and Inconsistent Public Policies With Respect to Private Business. Consistency in Public Economic Policy with Respect to Private Unregulated Industries." *Amer. Econ. Rev.*, Vol. 52, May 1963, pp. 29, 30.

Regardless whether we move toward more government regulation of agricultural production and prices, or away from it toward the open market as the wheat producers' vote in the spring of 1963 indicates, farm incomes per farmer will not improve, and the other, more basic problem in agriculture—the overpopulation problem—will remain unsolved, until another conflict of values is resolved. This is the conflict between:

1. The high value which United States citizens traditionally place upon rural life as the backbone of democracy and the cradle of such virtues as rugged individualism, which leads to the belief that farmers should try to keep their sons down on the farm and the nation should maintain as large a percentage of its population in agriculture as possible.

2. The high value which United States citizens also place on efficiency, high productivity per person, and equity in income distribution, which calls for increased emphasis on farming as a business, rather than as a way of life, and a continued reduction in the numbers of farms and farmers.

Both of these values are tenaciously held, and neither will give up without a long struggle. The high value placed upon agriculture as a bulwark of democracy is traced by Griswold[8] back to:

. . . the ancient tradition according to which agriculture is the most exalted (and as Jefferson projected the tradition, the most democratic) occupation and its corollary, that the size of the farm population is the best measure of a nation's welfare and its democracy. These ideas appealed to Jefferson and his colleagues in a day when the political circumstances of a republican revolution seemed to bear them out.

But the same author also points out the fallacy of this belief today.

If there were democratic magic in agriculture, why is it that men have been farmers for thousands of years, yet democracy as we know it is not two hundred years old and claims a minority of the earth's peoples as its disciples?

---

[8] A. Whitney Griswold, *Farming and Democracy*, Harcourt, 1948, pp. 175, 177.

The British experience shows us that it is possible to reduce the farm population to an irreducible minimum, and small, owner-operated family-sized farms virtually to extinction, and still have democracy. The French contrast shows us that it is possible to maintain a maximum farm population and carry family farming to its extreme logical conclusion, and all but lose democracy in the bargain.

Farmers continue to write letters to me expressing their belief that it is better to have 5 farmers producing 200 hogs apiece rather than one farmer producing 1,000; yet at the same time they want the 1,000-hog income, not the 200-hog income.

In a progressive democracy like the United States, it is not the economist's responsibility to urge one set of values rather than another.[9] It is his responsibility, however, to point out the consequences of one set of values compared with the consequences of another, so that the citizens of the country can choose which values they want to cling to most or what compromises they want to make among values on the basis of reason and facts more than upon emotion and prejudice.

---

[9] For a more adequate discussion of this point, see Olaf F. Larson, "Basic Goals and Values of Farm People," with discussion by Geoffrey Shepherd, in Goals and Values in Agricultural Policy. (Iowa State University Center for Agricultural and Economic Development, sponsors), Iowa State Univ. Press, Ames, 1961, pp. 164–69.

20

Perspective View

One of the features of a decentralized democracy such as the United States, where technological change and development are proceeding apace, operates to slow down the rate of progress: Legislation that is enacted to cope with the effects of rapid changes tends to be shortsighted and superficial. The changes come fast; people demand that something be done about them, fast; and the fast action that is taken is sometimes not very well thought out or effective.

This is the main reason why the past and present farm programs designed to deal with the effects of rapid technological change in the United States have been so ineffective, in spite of their annual cost of several billions of dollars. The programs have been directed at symptoms rather than at underlying causes. They are designed to support the prices of farm products by loan and storage operations, which are only very short-run palliatives, and by crop acreage-reduction programs which only indirectly, and only for a short time, benefit farm incomes; land values have risen more than farm incomes. "The market value of land has risen almost without interruption despite little real change in total net income of farmers,"[1] and "Realized net farm income in 1963 . . . will approximately equal the $12.8 billion of 1962. Gross income continued to rise, but the increase continues to be offset by rising costs."[2] (It now appears likely that the 1963 net income will be *lower* than in 1962.)

---

[1] "The Changing Market for Farmland," USDA, *The Farm Index*, May 1963, p. 5.

[2] Clark Edwards, "Increasing Gross Farm Income Offset by Rising Costs," *Agricultural Situation*, Vol. 46, No. 12. USDA, Stat. Rept. Serv., Dec. 1962.

The fact that farm land values have risen more than farm incomes makes it more difficult for future farmers to make ends meet.

What is needed is to reconstruct farm policy so that it will deal less with farm products and farm land and more directly with farm people. This needs to be done, not by supporting prices for farm products or increasing incomes to existing farmers—leaving the underlying causes of the problem still at work—but by dealing directly with the supply and demand for *farmers*.

In the present multibillion budget for the United States Department of Agriculture, there are billions for farm products and billions for farm land, but only an infinitesimally small item for farm people. This unequal emphasis on land and people needs to be redressed.

The present price-support programs need to be returned to their original objective of price stabilization about the long-run average instead of being misused to raise that average. The programs can play a useful role in smoothing out the effects of year-to-year variations in yields that result from variations in weather. But when they are used to raise the long-run level of prices, they either incur very large storage costs on huge storage stocks, and even so are only temporarily and partially effective, or involve expensive acreage-reduction programs, or both. And they do not go to the root of the problem, which is surplus farm people, not surplus farm products.

THE ROOT OF THE PROBLEM

The birthrate in agriculture is high and the demand for farmers in the United States is declining. The resulting continuous oversupply of farmers keeps farm income *per farmer* low.

Many farmers try to get out of agriculture into better paying urban jobs, but they haven't been able to do so fast enough. The obstacles are too great. What is needed is a massive program to help those who want to leave.

This program would go to the root of the farm problem—the obstacles to mobility that impede the movement of surplus farmers and potential farmers (farm boys and girls) out of agriculture and into urban jobs.

The program would include information about urban jobs, and the provision of training to qualify for the jobs. The program would need to be supported by adequate funds, not only for the training facilities and personnel, but for the farm people who take the training—for many farm people are too poor and untrained to move off the farm.

In the past, the decline in farm population came about not so much by established farmers moving out of farming, as by young farm boys and girls—potential farmers—refraining from going into farming; they chose other occupations instead. Don Kanel reports on this:[3]

In the decade between the 1950 and the 1959 Censuses of Agriculture, the number of farms in the thirteen North Central states declined by 20.3 per cent. This is the largest decennial decrease in the history of the region. The analysis of census data indicates that few young people entered farming during this period, while withdrawals of older operators from farming were similar to previous decades.

This solution is much easier than going into farming and then trying to get out.

For the future, then, the chief emphasis needs to be put on programs to reduce the inflow of potential young farmers into farming, along with help given established farmers to move out. As farm boys and girls who will not be needed in agriculture are given more information about job opportunities in other occupations and given education and training for those other jobs, they can move into them more easily than older farmers can. This, plus adjustments in farm size by those remaining on farms, will reduce the excessive number of farmers and reduce the disparity between farm and nonfarm incomes.

This program could be and should be a national program, broader than agriculture alone. The problem is more than an agricultural problem, as farmers are not the only ones who have felt the effects of rapid changes in technology. It is part of the stubborn national problem of underemployment and unemployment, which persists at 5 to 6 per cent in spite of strenuous efforts to reduce it. Underemployment is a severe problem in a number of other industries.

In the coal mining industry, for example, the use of new types of machinery and the competition of other sources of power reduced the number of coal miners in the United States from

---

[3] Don Kanel, "Farm Adjustments by Age Groups, North Central States 1950–1959." *Jour. Farm Econ.*, Vol. 45, Feb. 1963, p. 47.

483,000 in 1950 to 190,000 in 1960, a decline of 61 per cent, while coal production declined only about 25 per cent. In the automobile industry, the number of workers producing motor vehicles declined from 677,000 in 1950 to 493,000 in 1961, a reduction of 27 per cent, while production increased. In the railroads, the number of workers declined from 1,247,000 in 1950 to 793,000 in 1960, a decline of 36 per cent, with only a slight decline in revenue ton-miles of freight (though there was a marked decline in passenger traffic).

Yet at the same time, employment in most other occupations was expanding rapidly. Those who knew where the employment opportunities were, and had the training for them, moved into the expanding industries, and total employment rose to an all-time peak of 70 million nonfarm jobs in 1963.

Unemployment was concentrated in the teen-age group that was seeking permanent employment; their unemployment rate in May, 1963, was 18 per cent. The need is great in nonfarm as well as farm occupations for helping the young men and girls to find out where the jobs are and get the training for them.

THE RURAL AREAS DEVELOPMENT PROGRAM

The Rural Areas Development Program (RAD) is one good step towards the solution of the farm problem on a long-run basis.

This 1961 program recognizes that the farm income problem is not a uniform problem covering all areas and types of farming alike. The farm income problem differs in nature, severity, causes and remedies from area to area, type of farm, size of farm, etc. Recognizing this, the program calls for local action adapted to the particular problem in each case, before Federal aid is extended to help with the local problem.

The major criticism of the program is that it has been too small and has not grown properly. For the fiscal year 1961, $2.7 million was appropriated to the USDA for direct administrative, extension, technical, and research services related to the RAD (at that time called the Rural Development Program). This was only $0.7 million larger than the original appropriation in fiscal 1957 when the program was originally set up. The 1961 *total annual* figure of $2.7 million was only about the same figure as the *daily* cost of storing and managing the CCC storage stocks of farm products. The RAD program needs to be greatly expanded if it is to be adequate for the size of the job.

The Area Development Program of 1961 is another program that has important implications for agriculture.

This program recognizes the declining importance of the agricultural labor force relative to other occupations, and the increasing interdependence of agriculture with other economic sectors of the economy. The program is an *area* redevelopment program, not an *agricultural* redevelopment program; it is not even administered in the USDA.

The coordination between these two programs, in Washington and out in the country, leaves something to be desired. Perhaps it can be improved in the future.

THE MANPOWER DEVELOPMENT AND TRAINING ACT OF 1962

The Manpower Development and Training Act of 1962 is a second good step in the direction of a long-run solution of the farm problem. It is designed to provide the kind of training that farm boys and girls need.

It is national in scope, covering all occupations; but it has especially important implications for agriculture, as Bachmura[4] points out:

"Basically, the Act authorizes an adult education program for two classes of people: (1) those whose skills have been rendered obsolete by the advance of technology and by dislocations in the economy, and (2) those new entrants to the labor force who with further education will be able to meet 'shifting employment needs.' Although the word 'education' does not appear in the title of the Act, manpower development and training is conceived in broad terms to include on-the-job and vocational training, as well as formal schooling. The Act specifically cites the need for better trained personnel in the professional, scientific, technical, and 'apprenticeable' fields. Normally, however, the 52-week training allowance limitation will permit only limited upgrading of educational levels of individuals qualifying for benefits under the Act. . . .

"If unemployment were defined in the Act according to the conventional Bureau of Labor Statistics definition, many persons engaged in farming would be ineligible for either the training priorities or the allowances because of their inability to meet the

----

[4] Frank T. Bachmura, "The Manpower Development and Training Act of 1962—Its Significance for Rural Areas," *Jour. Farm Econ.*, Vol. 45, Feb. 1963, pp. 61–63.

unemployment criteria. To a certain extent this problem is obviated by the crucial sentence in the Act, 'Workers in farm families with less than $1,200 annual net family income shall be considered unemployed for purposes of the Act.' Although there is a matter of interpretation as to the farm classification of rural-nonfarm families in the agricultural labor force and a matter of judgment regarding the precise $1,200 dividing line determining eligibility, leaders in rural areas will recognize the importance of this provision both for the welfare of farm people and for the development of rural areas. Such a provision would be of importance to any self-employed person, in or out of farming, but it is of special importance in farming because of the large number of self-employed people in agriculture and because so many of them are at the low end of the income distribution."

DEVELOPMENT AND RETRAINING PROGRAMS ARE NOT DRAMATIC

These are not very glamorous programs, are they?

The existing *commodity* and *land retirement* programs are spectacular and dramatic. They have great popular and political appeal. They concentrate enormous power in the hands of the administrators: more than a billion bushels of wheat in the hands of the CCC, more than a billion bushels of corn—these are big business. The programs have gigantic impact on the grain trade and considerable effects on the economy as a whole. Big deals with Russia and other countries capture headlines when they are discussed; the world is the stage; and the actions of the administrators often provoke tremendous sound effects.

In contrast, RAD and ADP programs require working patiently with many separate community groups on their different local problems. The initiative comes from these groups, not from impressive national directives from Washington. The manpower training program is similarly prosaic; it deals with people as individuals—people with cares and responsibilities, all different, all needing individual attention.

Nobody makes the headlines from this realm; the actors all play inconspicuous parts on a dimly lit stage in a play with little box-office appeal. Rehabilitating and retraining unemployed persons is one of the most fundamental, valuable, and humanitarian activities that a nation can conduct, but it is an inspiration chiefly to dedicated teachers and unemployed people, not to the public at large. Education is a slow and unspectacular process.

EDUCATION AND OCCUPATIONAL MOBILITY

But spectacular or not, education and retraining are the jobs that need to be done. They are basic to the solution of the farm problem. We need to concentrate on farmers rather than on farm products and farm land. And we need to help farmers, not by paying them to stay where they are, but by showing them what the farm problem really is, telling them where the better jobs are, and providing them with the training for those jobs. Then they can solve their problems themselves.

In a flexible and free-enterprise democracy such as the United States, education and occupational mobility are the keys to individual gain and national benefit.

Give our people, nonfarmers as well as farmers, all the information, education, and training that they can use for the jobs that are in demand, and the mobility to go to those jobs, and individual and national well-being will be maximized all around, farm and nonfarm alike.

■
INDEX

The letter n *indicates footnote material.*

Abel, M. E., 182n
Abschier, G. S., 180
Acreage allotments, effects of, 39–41
Advertising agricultural products, 183–89
Agricultural conservation subsidies, 66–69
Agricultural production
  consumption imbalance, 14–15
  future prospects, 14–15
  related to population, 8–9
Aines, R. O., 41n, 45n, 53n, 65n
Area Redevelopment Program, 218–25
Arnold, L. K., 188n
Arthur, I. W., 218n, 231n, 236–38

B

Bachman, K., 34n
Bachmura, F. T., 288
Bailey, C., 217n
Barbour, H., 245n
Barton, G. T., 37n, 176n
Beef cattle, location and production changes, 31
Bellerby, J. R., 235, 266
Benson, E. T., 116
Berg, S. O., 220–21
Blaich, O. P., 130
Bottum, J. C., 45n, 135–36, 150
Brandow, G., 2n, 126
Breimyer, H. F., 37n
Brewster, J. M., 236–38, 272, 275–81
Brown, L. R., 258n
Burchinal, L. G., 236–38

C

CED, 126–27
Census Bureau, definition of farm, 5, 79–82
Christensen, R. P., 41n, 45n, 53n, 65n
Chryst, W. E., 64n
Chumley, T., 184n
Clawson, M., 96n
Cochrane, W. W., 4n, 35n, 126, 129–30, 149–50, 182n
Commodity Credit Corporation, storage operations
  for corn, 18–19, 23
  for cotton, 23
  for wheat, 20–21, 23
Common Market, 196–97, 255, 267
Commodity payments
  direct to farmers, 159–68
  on lightweight hogs, 161–65
Conant, J. B., 232
Conklin, H. E., 41n
Conservation Reserve program
  costs, 47, 54–60
  participation, 44–45
  rental rates, 46–48
Cook, R. C., 92n
Cooley, H. D., 127
Corn
  alcohol, 188–91
  carry-over, 23
  commercial area, 28–29
  loan rates, 18
  location of production, 29–30
  stocks needed, 24–25
Corn-hog price ratio, 168